ALSO BY ANTHONY SHAY
AND FROM MCFARLAND

---

*Balkan Dance: Essays on Characteristics, Performance and Teaching*, edited by Anthony Shay (2008)

*Choreographing Identities: Folk Dance, Ethnicity and Festival in the United States and Canada*, by Anthony Shay (2006)

# Dancing Across Borders

*The American Fascination
with Exotic Dance Forms*

ANTHONY SHAY

McFarland & Company, Inc., Publishers
*Jefferson, North Carolina, and London*

LIBRARY OF CONGRESS CATALOGUING-IN-PUBLICATION DATA

Shay, Anthony, 1936–
    Dancing across borders : the American fascination with exotic
dance forms / Anthony Shay.
        p.    cm.
    Includes bibliographical references and index.

    ISBN 978-0-7864-3784-9
    softcover : 50# alkaline paper ∞

    1. Dance — Social aspects — United States.    2. Dance — United
States — History.    3. Dance — Anthropological aspects.    4. Sex in
dance.    I. Title.
    GV1588.6.S56    2008
    306.4'846 — dc22                                          2008013472

British Library cataloguing data are available

Cover photograph: Loreen Arbus and Alberto Toledano perform a
classic Argentine tango, circa 1993 (photograph by Mike Hishimoto,
courtesy of Loreen Arbus)

Manufactured in the United States of America

*McFarland & Company, Inc., Publishers*
    *Box 611, Jefferson, North Carolina 28640*
    *www.mcfarlandpub.com*

For Barbara Sellers-Young,
generous scholar, generous friend

# Table of Contents

# Preface and Acknowledgments

IN MANY WAYS THIS BOOK IS the fourth in an interrelated quartet of works that began with *Choreophobia: Solo Improvised Dance in the Iranian World* (1999), a study of an Iranian dance tradition, which was one of my first dance experiences; *Choreographic Politics: State Folk Dance Companies, Representation and Power* (2002), a study of state supported national folk dance companies and the political and ethnic implications of their performances that had an impact on my professional life as a choreographer and dancer; and *Choreographing Identities: Folk Dance, Ethnicity, and Festival in the United States and Canada* (2006), a study of how ethnic and immigrant groups in North America shaped their identities through the creation of choreographic images in the context of international folk dance festivals. Participating in the community groups of immigrant communities in the contexts of these festivals were formative experiences. Through these studies and the current work, which describes and analyzes the uniquely American phenomenon of the participation of hundreds of thousands of mainstream Americans in the dance traditions of peoples who are not of their ethnicity, I have attempted to make coherent sense of my own life, in which I have spent over fifty years participating in dances of the Other.

Also, in these studies I introduced the concept of "choreophobia," a notion that analyzes the way in which individuals in certain societies have an absolute fear of dance or regard dance with ambiguity and suspicion, so that, for example, in Iran and Afghanistan, which I have described as choreophobic societies (1999), dance raised such a powerful specter of fear and loathing that it has been banned. This, of course, raises the idea that dance is so politically and socially potent and dangerous that it must be banished from public discourse, and therefore dance in choreophobic contexts provides the researcher with a powerful lens of analysis. This also means that the performance of dance in Iran, which can carry heavy punishment, can be said today to constitute a political act of resistance.

1

I also, in the course of my writing, introduced the concept of "parallel traditions," a notion that many layers of a single dance genre, tradition, or form can exist that are contingent on context, class, gender, ethnicity, and other factors. I created this concept (2002, 2006), in response to purist concerns of authenticity, in order to write about the performance of "ethnic" dance that occurs in contexts other than the original village, region, tribal space, palace or temple in which it was performed by natives without privileging one context over the other. In this way the performances of an amateur folk dance group, an immigrant dance group in an American civic center, an international folk dance festival, the national state-supported ensemble, *Riverdance* or *Cirque de Soleil* theater productions, or a Hollywood film, among other possible venues, can all be described and analyzed without resorting to endless, value-laden discussions of what constitutes "authentic." Each of these performances, all part of a parallel tradition, are potentially fraught with important messages about human behavior and cultural production; each is "authentic" in its own context and is generally regarded as authentic by its participants; and each layer demands the attention of dance scholars and historians. Both of these concepts have been adopted by other dance scholars and entered the literature, and they will be found again in the pages of this study.

When I began my dancing and choreographic career over a half century ago, questions of globalism, transnationalism, appropriation, colonialism, and ethnicity in relation to dance were never raised and the frantic drive for authenticity had not yet begun. Those issues arose along my journey and challenge us all today, both in reality and theoretically. In those early years I was warmly welcomed into a number of different communities who seemed genuinely happy to welcome and embrace a young American who showed an eager interest in their cultural expression.

And so this book addresses those issues, but, more importantly, in this study I seek to find answers about what it was (and is) about American life and culture, or its lack, that inspired massive numbers of Americans to learn the dances of other people, and through those various exotic dance genres to seek new or alternate identities. These Americans did not merely learn the dances, they frequently learned the languages and identified with and adopted aspects of the lifestyles of the peoples whose dances they undertook to learn and perform with an intense passion; ultimately, through learning and performing these dances, they acquired, if only briefly, a new and exotic identity. In many ways this is a micro history, one that occurred under the radar of historians, and even dance historians. I now want to elucidate the meanings of how I and thousands of others like me choreographed the exotic.

In this undertaking over the past decades I have many people that I must acknowledge and thank. First, I must with the deepest gratitude thank my friend and colleague, Barbara Sellers-Young, whose intellectual and personal generosity has been unbounded. She read and commented in great detail on an early draft of the book and saved me from many errors. I also thank Mark Angel, Nancy Dyer Angel, Art Aratin, Loreen Arbus, Pamela Baker, Mona Jean Cedar, Stephanie Cowans, the late Dick Crum, Bonita Edelberg, Cara Gargano, Brandy Maya Healy, David Hillinger, Ann Howe, Trudy Israel, Donald La Course, Robert Leibman, Leonard Pronko, Katina Shields, Victor Sirelson, Alison Snyder, Betty Turtledove, Anne Von Bibra Wharton, Heidi Wohlfahrt, and Linda Yudin for finding the topic so interesting that they gave fascinating accounts of their own encounters with the exotic, or provided me with important insights to the ways in which aspects of American life contributed to their participation.

Over the past twenty years there has been an explosion of dance studies that depart from "dance in the field" and narrow histories of more or less famous individual dancers and choreographers. I am fortunate to be researching and writing this study at a time when many colleagues, just graduating from the expanding doctoral programs in dance history and theory, have chosen to study dance within new contexts seen through critical lens that depart from past studies. I cite frequently recent studies by such individuals as Anne Décoret-Ahiha, Jane C. Desmond, Tomie Hahn, Amy Koritz, Juliet McMains, Sally Ann Ness, Janet O'Shea, Marta Savigliano, and Barbara Sellers-Young, among many others, to whom I owe an intellectual debt.

*Los Angeles Times* dance writer Lewis Segal discussed the idea of investigating the careers of dancers like Ruth St. Denis as an important historical element in this study. He also kindly read the final draft of the book and provided me with many useful comments for its improvement. Colleague Cara Gargano and Larry Rubinstein gave me fine insights on why Americans might want to enter into such an endeavor and why others did not. And, above all, I must always be grateful to my partner, Jamal, who listened to my questions and whose advice helped to shape the book. And, ultimately, his continual support has helped to shape my life. Any errors are entirely my own.

# Introduction

## Choreographing the Exotic

THIS STUDY EXAMINES, describes, and analyzes the phenomenon of millions of mainstream Americans who sought through dance to assume exotic new identities. Sometimes they sought these new, exotic identities momentarily, through stage performances or social dance activities, and sometimes on a long-term basis, through professional immersion in scholarly or performance careers. The high point of this phenomenon occurred in the decades of the late 1950s through the 1980s when, for example, more than one million American women participated in belly dance classes and performances, which was linked to the second wave of the feminist movement (Sellers-Young 1992; Shay and Sellers-Young 2005); and thousands of mainstream, largely white middle class Americans, especially university and college students, pursued Balkan dancing and music with a passion that continues unabated even today.[1] This study searches for the elements in American society that drove so many mainstream individuals to strive to attain new identities through learning and performing exotic dance genres such as belly dance, dances of the various regions of the Balkans, Latin American dances like the tango, and Asian classical dance forms.

In this study I use the word *exotic* frequently, but as Barbara Sellers-Young notes, the term exotic takes on different connotations within each of the genres that this study examines. The term exotic, as opposed to *alien*, tends to connote the positive aspect of an exciting, unknown, and foreign quality of an object, a person, or a dance. There lurks within its meaning an allure and an attraction for something that is strangely beautiful: an exotic flower or a movie star with exotic looks. In this study, I use exotic to mean the beautiful, unknown, the desirable. I also imply the romanticism that is associated with the acquisition of these dances, the performance of which can potentially bestow that exotic quality on the performer.

5

Important differences exist between the mass pursuit of the latest exciting Latin American dance taught and performed in the ballroom and street festival as the latest dance fad, to be replaced in short order by the next dance craze, and the individual who pursues the tango or flamenco as a lifelong study. There also exists a difference between the pursuit of learning and performing belly dance — for over a century an oversaturated icon of the Orient in popular culture media — and the pursuit of classical Asian dances that requires a lifetime of study and devotion. This study will examine those variations.

This book also explores a new territory in dance studies. Until now, most studies in dance ethnography and dance anthropology have concentrated their focus on the dancing that natives do in their own native environments, "dance in the field," in Theresa J. Buckland's terms (1999). My study will look at the phenomenon of hundreds of thousands of mainstream American individuals seeking new identities, attempting to be someone else through dancing the dances and playing and singing the music of the "Exotic Other," if only within the framed moment of a formal professional-level dance performance, an evening in a tango club, or participation in an international folk dance festival. Thus, this group of nonnative performers of exotic dance genres constitutes another layer of the concept of "parallel traditions" of dance activities "parallel" to dance in the field, which I elaborated on earlier (Shay 2002, 2006).

In this study I will also distinguish the activities of those crucial figures who created the imaginative worlds through their choreographies and teaching, such as Dick Crum, Dennis Boxell, Bobby (Ibrahim) Farrah, John Rodi and Dan Gianfala, and Linda Yudin. They, and several other individuals, each founded or directed and choreographed major performing dance companies that were virtual communities, "different villages," in Mirjana Laušević's terms (1998), which formed the center of countless lives for decades.

## An American Passion

I will argue in this study that this mass movement of individuals involved in a wide array of exotic dance traditions was a uniquely American (and perhaps Canadian) phenomenon. As far as I know, nothing like this movement occurred on this massive a scale in any other Western country, or anywhere else, for that matter. Ethnomusicologist Mirjana Laušević from Bosnia, in her study of Americans participating in Balkan music and dance, observes, "But holding the scene up to the light of history, it is its 'Americaness' that most fascinates me..." (2007, 12).

*Los Angeles Times* columnist Gregory Rodriguez suggests that the search for new identities and self-reinvention constitutes uniquely American traits:

> The rhetoric of multiculturalism, which encourages us to maintain our inherited collective identities, may have temporary triumphs, but this is still a hyper-individualist nation in which people are free to reinvent themselves and choose their cultures. This is where the Austrian-born bodybuilder can become governor of California, where Bronx-born Ralph Lipshitz morphs into Ralph Lauren.... At the core of the American dream lies the premise that your past does not predetermine your future. We still tell schoolchildren they can become whoever and whatever they want. But, let's face it, this process of self-reinvention isn't always pretty. Our cult of mobility encourages strivers not only to sell themselves but to pass, to play the part and to pad that resume. In other words, our penchant for reinventing ourselves is intertwined with our heritage of hucksterism [June 4, 2007, A15].

The search for ethnicity through the exotic dances of the Other "reveals aspects of our own shared American culture and ideology — our shared values of individualism and community and the unique ways in which ethnic identities fulfill very American needs" (Waters 1990, xiii). This need for ethnic roots and identity, which seemed to elude many Americans in the 1960s, 1970s and even today, frequently led to the appropriation of the fruits of other people's cultural expression such as their dances and music in order to construct new, more exciting and exotic identities. I will suggest throughout this study that the pursuit of the cultural expressive forms of the Other can have both positive and negative results. When an individual thoughtlessly seizes and appropriates that which belongs to another in a colonialist or frivolous manner, the result can have negative repercussions. One need only remember the Arab-American community's outraged reaction to Disney's animated feature film *Aladdin* (1992), which featured orientalist stereotypes and offensive lyrics, which caused the Disney Company to revise some aspects of the production. As Barbara Sellers-Young observes about belly dancers performing orientalist and stereotypical dances that some Arabs and Arab Americans believe portray Arabs as oversexed and lustful in stereotypical roles of harem girls and sheiks, "Much of the belly dance community was only engaged in this topic when they came up against the political advocacy of Arab Americans" (personal communication, June 4, 2007).

On the other hand, serious, respectful interest in the arts of other societies can be richly rewarding for both parties as I, and countless others, have found throughout our fulfilling and rich artistic and personal lives. This learning through cultural immersion can be productive and create tolerance and esteem for the cultures of other people and a respect for their various forms of cultural expression. "In the beginning it was fascinating to learn of this new music and cultures. I was becoming a little bored with ballet and jazz. This was totally new information, a great education. I was hungry for new experiences and this was given graciously" (Mona Jean Cedar, personal interview, June 16, 2007).

Dance scholar June Adler Vail comments about the Balkan dance group in Maine in which she participated: "I realized that Borovčani could be interpreted as a community of dancers with its own culture, history, structure, and import. Looking back, the group's stage choreographies and social processes seem to illuminate facets of America's fragmented society in the late seventies and early eighties" (1996, 306). In this study I stress the particularly American quality of joining such groups. I agree with Vail that participation in groups and analyzing that participation actually can "illuminate America's fragmented society." However, I suggest that the movement dates from an even earlier period than she suggests, and that it reached the beginning of its peak two decades earlier, in the mid 1950s. The participants in this movement, although they are often unaware, are also subject to historical currents and the roots of the fascination with the exotic. The antecedents for the love affair with exotic dances lie in the past.

## Historical Antecedents

From the period of the late 19th century, with the appearance of large-scale world exhibitions and fairs that were held frequently in the United States, France, and Great Britain that attracted millions of viewers, dancers from exotic lands were one of the greatest attractions on the midway. These fairs and exhibitions were largely designed to establish binaries: civilized-primitive, modern-traditional, metropolitan center-colony, powerful-weak, rich-poor. The second half of each of those binaries was displayed as the (lower) Other in much the manner of a human menagerie. The exhibitions were specifically designed to demonstrate the power and benefits of colonialism and the superiority of white Western civilization (Décoret-Ahiha 2004; Goodall 2002; Karp and Levine 1990; Monty 1986; Ryder 1984; Shay and Sellers-Young 2005; Shay 2006).

The popularity of the various genres of dance, such as Middle Eastern dance, which spawned the "Salomania" movement in Great Britain and the United States, were on display in these venues. The tango craze that was launched in Paris in 1905 — and then spread to New York and London and subsequently to Buenos Aires where the dance tradition became a contested national icon of identity — demonstrates another instance of how dance can circulate internationally, to be consumed like some delicious exotic food. (See Décoret-Ahiha 2006; Savigliano 1995). The popularity of these exotic dance genres demonstrated a new, increased interest in the exotic Other.

The demand for exotic dances became intense on many societal levels. Wealthy women dressed as Salome and held Salome parties, while working class men searched for earthier thrills in "Little Egypt" performing the hootchy-kootchy (Kendall 1979, 82; Bentley 2003, 41–42, Monty 1986, 91–124). Tellingly, surrounding these turn-of-the-century orientalist performances, there existed no discourse of ancient dance practices, the worship of mother goddesses, nor the easing of childbirth, as occurred with the belly dance craze that came more than a half-century later. Women of the earlier period who performed as Little Egypt were not looking for spirituality, they were after money. The hootchy-kootchy dance they performed, a distortion of the original Egyptian dance from the Midway of the Chicago World's Fair, and their appearances in seedy environments like Coney Island and the fact that they performed in public condemned them to be regarded as not respectable at best and prostitutes at worst.

The major attraction of the 1893 Chicago World's Columbia exhibition and subsequent "Little Egypt" performances was the perceived sexiness of uncorseted torso movements for the Victorian and Edwardian male gaze. Most middle-class observers at the turn of the century found the movements crude and lacking in aesthetic value (see especially Koritz 1997; Monty 1986). The attraction for the large audiences in the Cairo exhibit was overwhelmingly a sexual one for male visitors. The perceived sexiness in the performances was shown by the very name for the dance: "belly dance," coined by Sol Bloom, the entrepreneur of the 1893 Chicago Columbia Exhibition, is the name for the choreographic genre, in much altered form, that is still popular today (Shay and Sellers-Young 2005).

While exotic social dance forms such as the tango captured the popular imagination, especially of the upper classes, these early fads were of relatively short duration (Décoret-Ahiha 2004, 110–11). Salomania "lasted only two years" (Kendall 1977, 77). Moreover, most of those mainstream Americans (like their counterparts in France and Great Britain) who viewed the dances from Egypt, Bali, Persia, Morocco, India, Japan, various parts of Africa and other fabled lands during this early period had no desire themselves to perform the "authentic" dances seen on the midways of the world exhibitions. As I will show in chapter 2, the orientalist versions of exotic dances widely performed throughout Europe and the United States by Ruth St. Denis, Maud Allan and others were of far more interest to American (and British) audiences because of both racist and aesthetic issues.

American-born performers at the turn of the century (Ruth St. Denis

(1879–1968), Maud Allan (1873–1956), Isadora Duncan (1878–1927), and later La Meri (1898–1988) for example made their careers through choreographic representations, or perhaps "interpretations" is a more felicitous term, of other times and places — Ancient Greece, India, Egypt, Morocco, all imagined since these dancers had no firsthand knowledge of them — that fed into the popular imagination and inspired these early dancers to create exoticized impressions through their stage performances. All of the early interpretive dancers at some time in their careers took on the role of Salome, except Duncan. After their first forays into the exotic, St. Denis and Duncan read voraciously and visited museums, which influenced their mature dance productions. They were, like those who followed, choreographing the exotic. But these performances of the exotic, while attracting large audiences in New York, London, Paris and elsewhere, did not induce large numbers of people to undertake the study and performance of exotic dances as occurred a half-century later.

Furthermore, these exotic performances provided a source of economic enrichment and a large measure of fame for the daring pioneer dancers which was absent from the mass movement of the second half of the twentieth century. Maud Allan, Loïe Fuller and Isadora Duncan reaped fortunes from their performances, while most belly dancers of the 1950s and beyond barely made a decent living wage and the vast majority of dancers in the Balkan movement largely performed for free. Moreover, the pursuit of performance competency in the Asian classical Japanese, Balinese, and Indian dance traditions, as well as those involved in the Latin American dances of the ballroom industry, can be very costly for the practitioner because they require extensive travel, years of private lessons, and extensive and expensive costume collections, (see Sellers-Young 1992; McMains 2006). The later generations embody the lyrics of "What I Did for Love," the anthem-like song from the Broadway musical *Chorus Line.*

Thus, in many ways the roots of their performances, such as those of oriental dancers, can be discerned in and prefigured by the performances of Ruth St. Denis, Maud Allan, Isadora Duncan, and other turn-of-the century dancers. Although most dance historians think of those figures as the beginnings of modern dance, I suggest that, alternatively, in many ways their performances catered to the cravings for the primitivist exotic that arose in the mid–nineteenth century and prefigured the movement that I focus on in this study. As dance historian Suzanne Shelton notes, "St. Denis herself was not a 'modern dancer.' She was an 'interpretive dancer'" (1981, xv). Thus, I suggest that their performances prefigure the popularity of belly dance and other Middle Eastern forms such as Iranian dance, Japanese and Indian classic dances and other exotic genres in the late twentieth century much more than they presage modern dance as developed by figures like Martha Graham and Doris Humphrey who emerged from St. Denis's school and company. Beginning in the late 1920s, Graham and Humphrey created new styles of modern dance in sharp and negative reaction to their work with Ruth St. Denis and Ted Shawn, with whom they had studied and performed. However, as dance historian and critic Lewis Segal points out, it should be remembered that "Graham's first works, such as "The Flute of Krishna," were 'exotic'" (personal interview, July 23, 2007.

Prior to World War II, we can certainly identify American individuals, like Gertrude Stein, who sought more congenial environments. Stein chose Paris and the French countryside in which to live in relative comfort as a lesbian and a modernist writer far away from uptight and upright Oakland, California, because, to paraphrase her famous words referring to Oakland, "there was no *there*, there." But Stein and others like her would not or could not conform on a number of levels — sexual, intellectual, artistic — to the stifling and moralistic Victorian and Edwardian American environments in which they found themselves. These individuals were frequently extremely wealthy and could afford to lead the life of wealthy expatriates. Stein, as far as I can tell, made no attempt to turn herself into a Frenchwoman, to assume a new identity; she remained an American expatriate.

## A Mass Movement

By contrast to the early twentieth century, the decades of the 1960s and 1970s saw hundreds of thousands of mainstream middle class American individuals attracted to learn new dance forms. Furthermore, this interest constituted the central part of an often lifelong social and private interest, as well as a desire by many of individuals to perform these treasured exotic dance and music genres for the public; performing groups, largely made up of mainstream Americans devoted to exotic dance and music forms, sprang up all over the United States, both on and off college and university campuses. The earlier devotees of Salomania and tango briefly adopted a dress fashion or a dance fad; the mass of individuals, from the late 1950s and later, often adopted a lifestyle and, more importantly, through dance, a new identity.

Dance scholar Cara Gargano noted that this movement contrasted sharply with the previous generation, creating a sea change in the way that many Americans, particularly second generation children, were raised by parents who refused to speak foreign languages or behave in ways that could be construed as "foreign" in the eyes of others. They wanted their children to be true Americans, and hoped to provide their children with the best possible means of

Javanese court dance performed by the Indonesian Performing Arts Association of Minnesota, 2003. Director Joko Sutrisno. Photograph by Pentronella Ytsma. Courtesy of Anne Von Bibra Wharton.

succeeding in American life. They were frequently horrified that their children pursued exotic dance traditions (personal interview, June 24, 2007). But the children were often seeking roots and an ethnic identity that they felt had been denied to them by their families.

During this post 1950s period, literally millions of mainstream Americans, of whom I was one, sought through various exotic dance genres to construct identities different from their own. These new, exotic, and colorful identities were sought across a wide variety of dance genres: Balkan dances of various ethnicities, Latin American dance traditions such as samba, tango, and folklorico, a wide variety of Asian genres such as bharata-natyam, kathak, kabuki, nihon buyo, Chinese Opera, Balinese, Cambodian, and Javanese classical traditions, and Middle Eastern dance genres of various types, but particularly belly dancing, which alone attracted over a million women by the 1980s (Sellers-Young 1992; Shay and Sellers-Young 2005). While this brief list does not begin to exhaust the possibilities of dance genres — for example Mexican folk dance, Scandinavian dances, flamenco, Scottish or Irish dance, and hula, to name a few — it is these forms that I will focus on for analytical purposes because of access to individuals whom I have known throughout the past fifty years and my own participation and active, indeed creative, involvement in several of these micro social and artistic worlds. This book seeks to analyze this phenomenon that has only recently begun to attract serious scholarly attention (Averill 2004; Rasmussen 2004; Evanchuk 2007; Lauševic 1998).

As ethnomusicologist Gage Averill observes of the generations after World War II:

> Extreme versions of musical mimesis are common among those who view Western modernity as a sickness that can be cured by identifying with another culture through the mediumship of music and dance. It is the identity of the performer that is at stake and at issue here. Musical transvestism — performance within another cultural configuration — temporarily displaces aspects of the cultural identity of the performer as though she or he were engaged in a light version of a possession trance [2004, 100].

I suggest that dance as an embodied form of cultural production, the public performance of which requires costumes and other accoutrements, can evoke even more extreme reactions than the playing of exotic music described by Averill above.

Dance historian Iris Garland, in a provocative conference presentation, has argued:

> I contend that the Oriental dance phenomenon in the early twentieth century has parallels to the heightened interest in multicultural dance in our present time. Moreover, burgeoning attention to multicultural dance at the end of the 20th century is not as altruistic as it appears on the surface. I hypothesize that the perceived need for revitalization of Western dance through the incorporation and fusion of non–Western dance forms is comparable to that which occurred at the beginning of the 20th century. The stagnation of Western cultural forms is a significant factor in both eras [2000, 193].

I would suggest that some of the similarities that Garland argues for exist (and I will address them in the following chapters), especially the notion that there are dancers, visual artists and musicians who continue to seek artistic inspiration in foreign music and dance genres and exotic visual forms. However, I argue that the movements, the one at the turn of the twentieth century and the other in the second half of the twentieth century, varied much more significantly than Garland suggests. First, the early exotic dancers in no way attempted to reproduce in any accurate way the "oriental" dances they performed. Even Garland concedes that "The reviewers of the time attributed a standard of authenticity to the European female solo Oriental dancers, although it is unlikely that any Western dancers actually achieved it" (2000, 195).

By contrast I would argue that one of the features of the majority of late twentieth century dancers is a deep-seated concern to exactly reproduce, in the most authentic way possible, the dance and music genres that they perform, as Averill noted above (or at least they claim authenticity in the program notes that accompany their performances). This concern with "authenticity," a concept that is fraught with social and intellectual baggage continues to be of paramount concern among many of the individuals in the later generations of dancers and musicians in most of the genres that I describe and analyze in this study.

The second difference is that the sheer number of dancers seeking to find new identities in the late twentieth century contrasts sharply with the relatively few individuals who sought to perform exotic dances at the turn of the last century, many of whom sought remuneration and fame rather than any deep engagement with other cultures. For the most part, the dancers at the turn of the last century were profoundly ignorant of other societies, reading about them through highly romantic and orientalist accounts written or produced by Western writers and artists.

However, the two movements of those who pursued exotic dances at the turn of the century and those of the latter half of the twentieth century do connect in one important way: the search for spirituality. The point of connection between the later and earlier generations of serious dancers like Ruth St. Denis and Isadora Duncan is the search to find spiritual meaning in their performances. This spiritual content in the dances of St. Denis, Allan, and Duncan constituted a crucial element in the acceptance of these pioneer performers as artists rather than being regarded as prostitutes. These women were among the first stage performers to establish themselves as artists in the eyes of the theater-going general public, and through the spiritual content of their dance creations they acquired an important measure of respectability and recognition of their choreographic creations as art rather than tawdry entertainment that characterized most of the stage presentations of the time.

In the later, post–World War II generations, the expression of a metaphysical spirituality that is frequently associated with New Age lifestyles characterizes many of the participants in all of these genres who not infrequently say, "I must have been a Greek, or a Persian in another life" (Barbara Deutsch, personal interview, December 27, 2006). Many of the informants I interviewed and dancers and musicians with whom I worked conveyed this powerful feeling to me several times throughout my career and during my research for this study.

Another way that this spirituality is expressed is through the shock of recognition that individuals have upon hearing or seeing these dance or musical genres for the first time, which often induces a strong physical reaction: "I almost swooned." A sense of déjà-vu of that "former life" is produced. This is a topic to which I will return in the following chapters.

# Micro Histories

In an important way this study constitutes a type of micro history, a term which I extend to mean a historical phenomenon that took place under the radar of the meta-narratives that characterize the overwhelming amount of scholarly and popular writing of historical events in American history. Those histories constitute meta-narratives that largely limit their grand sweeping focus to wars, economics, politics, inventions, race relations, civil unrest, with a nod to major films, entertainment celebrities, and popular culture.

By contrast, millions of Americans lived, and continue to live, under the radar of history as focused on in historical studies. Frequently the most important aspects of their lives consist of participating in their hobbies, avocations, and leisure-time activities: doll making and collecting, antique collecting (only recently popularized on the PBS hit program *Antiques Road Show*), winemaking and collecting fine wines, showing and breeding prize dogs and cats, gardening, gourmet cooking, making and collecting quilts, mountain climbing, playing chess or bridge, choral singing, and square dancing, to mention just a few activities. All of these — and similar hobbies and activities, sometimes at a professional level of participation, including the involvement with exotic dance genres that I address in this study — involve millions of individuals for whom the events of politics, economics and popular music constitute only a faint, and often irritating, background noise.

Master narrative histories of the United States, such as those written by award-winning writers James T. Patterson (1996; 2005) and David Halberstam (1993), move sweepingly between the major economic, political, and military events and trends, but the hidden histories of the millions of individuals who sought new, exotic identities through dance remain unmentioned, hidden and unanalyzed, even in specialized dance histories.

What was it about American culture that impelled so many people to seek alternative identities? Why dance and music? And, most importantly, why did individuals choose specific forms of foreign dance and music genres that had no connection to the ethnicities of these participants? The answers to these questions are complex, and a phenomenon that involves millions of individuals will inevitably produce many motives and multiple causes and, in fact, multiple and interlocking networks of narrative.

# The Search for the Real

To unpeel the layers of identities, we must look at what constitutes identity, or as I will show, multiple identities, always a complex bundle of multiple roles, intricately woven into a web that intersects with other webs, "webs of signification," as Clifford Geertz suggests (1983), for most individuals living in modern urban societies. To enter into these worlds we must also listen to the many narratives of the individuals who participated in these events.

We must also turn to the history of the second half of the nineteenth century and the first decades of the twentieth century to set the scene and discover the roots for the mass movement to seek alternate identities through exotic dance genres that took place in the second half of the twentieth century. The intellectual, political, and social environment of the late nineteenth and early twentieth centuries was heavily overshadowed and influenced by Charles Darwin and his theory of evolution, in which the grandparents and parents of those who participated in the modern movement that I describe and analyze in this study lived.

The attitudes of the previous generations, and the popular attitudes and morals of that period, deeply affected the young people of the 1960s, many of whom turned their backs on the values of their parents and grandparents. The vast move of millions of middle class Americans to dreary, unending suburbs with rows of affordable look-alike houses, soulless malls, and unbounded consumerism in the post–World War II economic boom appalled large numbers of the generation of the 1960s and 1970s. Suburban life was overwhelmingly white:

> The Federal Housing Administration, which distributed billions of dollars in low-cost mortgage loans in the late 1940s, thereby underwriting much of the suburban expansion of the era, openly screened out applicants according to its assessment of people who were "risks." These were mainly blacks, Jews, or other "unharmonious racial or nationality groups." In doing so it enshrined residential segregation as a public policy of the United States government [Patterson 1996, 27].

As a consequence of government policy and the rampant racism of the time, many mainstream white Americans growing up in the period 1940–1970 and later rarely saw or interacted with anyone who was not like them. I did not realize until late in life that I, along with everyone else, had an ethnicity.

Later, seeking new values of gendered behavior, racial and economic justice, political liberalism mixed with antiwar activism, or just "dropping out," hundreds of thousands of these young Americans embraced the new exotic dance forms they found in college dance and ethnomusicology classes, folk dance clubs, ethnic restaurants, Renaissance Faires, belly dance clubs and coffee houses as one means of giving depth and meaning to their lives. Many set up communes to earn livelihoods from the earth and emulate the imagined lives of rustic people in some remote age in which folk music and dance were integral parts. Folk dance and music were often seen by these young

American men and women as belonging to a past in which simple and deep values were treasured. They regarded the dances and music as primordial; the peasants who danced them appeared real and authentic. "I looked around at the racism, war, and other unpleasant aspects of American life, and I wanted something different. Folk dance gave that to me" (Bonita Edelberg, personal communication, May 14, 2005).

Edelberg was not the only one to feel strongly about these issues. "Many disgruntled Americans in 1974, and later, practiced a form of selective amnesia, which blotted from their consciousness some of the blights that had afflicted the nation in the 1950s — among them constitutionally protected racial segregation, a Red Scare that launched angry assaults on civil liberties, blatant religious intolerance and systematic discrimination against women" (Patterson 2005, 9).

Of course, the vast majority of these Americans, who sensed rootlessness in their lives, came from urban backgrounds and knew nothing of peasants and how they lived. Many of them reacted instead to Anthony Quinn's portrayal of *Zorba the Greek* (1964). His soulful dance appeared to be "earthy" and "real" and "authentic." It also spawned a lucrative business for Greek restaurant and bar owners, both in Greece and in the United States.

Dance scholar Theresa J. Buckland notes: "The songs, dances, poetry, costume, dialect, and so on of the peasantry were collected as relics of antiquity since such expressive forms were believed to be dying out in the advance of modernity. The process and motivation behind this form of cultural rescue archaeology shared similar aims to that of nineteenth-century anthropological activities, and both shared an evolutionist perspective" (2006, 7). The process of collecting folk songs and dances that were perceived of as endangered species of folklore within this evolutionist framework formed a central activity, with many Americans involved in learning and performing folk music and dance. Several of the most serious among them entered the fields of folklore, anthropology, and ethnomusicology. Thus, the evolutionist environment of the previous generations was more or less unconsciously incorporated in to the pursuit of learning and performing exotic dance and music traditions.

## *Identities*

When I was growing up in South Central Los Angeles, our closest neighbors for decades, well back into my mother's childhood, were the Uribes, a Mexican American family who had been my uncle's and mother's closest friends in their childhood and beyond.[2] The middle Uribe son, Robert, courted and ultimately married Estella, a very chic, sophisticated young woman from

Mexico City. My younger sister Kathleen, at age five to six, together with Janet Nelson, the neighbor girl of the same age, loved to dress up in my mother's high heels and one or two other adult clothing items, including a rather rakish Spanish-style hat with a row of cloth balls suspended from the brim. My sister wore it often, in order to become someone grown up, beautiful, and exotic — to become Estella. One day, as the girls were playing and clomping about in their mothers' oversized shoes, my mother was casually listening and she heard Janet inquire, "And who are you?" My sister Kathleen, attempting to imitate Estella's sophisticated demeanor, announced in her grandest five-year-old voice, "*I'm* Estella," to which the neighbor child replied, "Well, *I'm* enchilada."

To what degree do novelty and the desire for the exotic, to dress up and be someone else, play a role in the lives of individuals? We can see that the desire to acquire an interesting and exotic identity, at least in some if not most individuals, as in the case of my sister and her playmate, can begin very early. As we will see, such desires and yearning figured in the careers of Ruth St. Denis (Kendall 1979), La Meri (Ruyter 2005), and Mark Morris (Acocella 1994).

Such yearnings for experiencing the exotic are not merely a product of modern life, though they are sometimes a reaction against modernity. We know that in the Roman period, the exotic, sensual dancers from Gades (Cadiz) were in demand in fashionable social gatherings, but the Romans disdained the idea of dancing themselves. Indeed, the vast majority could not imagine or countenance being or performing any other identity than that of a Roman, even among those few who extravagantly admired the culture of Greece (see Hallet and Skinner 1997). The emperor Nero met his violent death in part because of his most un–Roman desire to perform in public. Roman prejudice, echoed as we will see in nineteenth century America, revealed a "bias against stage performance," which Romans equated with prostitution and unmanliness (Williams 1999, 71). The Iranian king Bahram Gur (V) (r. 420–438 CE) "brought thousands of Indian minstrels into Iran to amuse his subjects" (Klíma 1989, 518). Thus we can see that the thirst for novelty and the exotic has early roots in the history of humankind.

However, in this yearning for the exotic, it is useful to note the difference between the search for the exotic of the ancient world and subsequent historical periods and that of the past century, which has been marked by modern colonialism and racism. It is useful to look at political scientist Marta Savigliano's concept of the commodification of passion and emotion through the circulation of exotic dance genres (1995). Along with the more tangible products of tin, bananas, petroleum, diamonds, coffee and other products mined from the colonial territorial holdings, cultural artifacts such as dance, with its promise of the sexual and forbidden, also became a by-product of the uneven exchange between the metropolitan centers of the powerful West and its more primitive Other. Belly dance, tango, samba, and a host of other dances on display at the world exhibitions were "tamed" for the consumption of white middle-class bodies through the process of "slumming" and the search for the exotic and erotic and became a potent medium of exchange.[3] (See Décoret-Ahiha for a detailed study of the types of dance that circulated as a result of the world fairs held in Paris or as fad dances during the period 1880–1940).

In the past century, continuing to the present, we can observe the annual rush of excitement with which Halloween is greeted by young and old alike who are enabled to assume another identity. Many individuals spend a year planning their next costume for the New Orleans's Mardi Gras; the lives of many individuals in New Orleans revolve around preparing for this annual gala event. This study seeks to address this question of identity and being someone else in the actions of social actors in the twentieth century, especially during the period of 1956 to the present.

## *The Cinematic Effect*

For many Americans, notoriously known to be almost completely ignorant of geography ("geographically challenged," in anthropologist Jeffrey Tobin's terms (1998)), their sources of knowledge of the Other comes from the popular media. Many individuals think that the widespread interest in the exotic may be attributed to the movie industry. Some dance scholars have investigated the ways in which films have influenced the way in which the American public views exotic dances. But for the purposes of this study, the record is mixed, as Allegra Fuller Snyder found: "Admittedly, I began with strong notions about what the Hollywood material would reveal. I had thought I would uncover clear Hollywood biases, misconceptions, and prejudices in dealing with all non–American-based dance forms and cultural expressions. I soon realized, however, that I was at least as biased as I thought Hollywood had been" (1995, 74).

Nevertheless, certain patterns do emerge in the way that Hollywood portrayed certain areas. Snyder notes: "Any film purporting to be located in an Asian country is likely to include visual elements from other areas as well, mixing cultural symbols from China, Japan, Indochina, Indonesia and India" (1995, 84).

However, this finding reveals little information for purposes of this study. The majority of those who pursued, and continue to seek, mastery in classical Asian dance forms in the period after World War II were little influenced by the Hollywood cinema, but rather through exposure to live concerts of authentic performances in ethnomusicology performances, government sponsored concerts like those from Java, Bali, China, Japan and Cambodia that occurred in the 1970s and after, or through appearances by local classical artists in various parts of the United States. I address this topic in chapter 7.

Certainly, cinematic images from the Middle East had an impact in Egypt, as I will discuss later, and these highly orientalist images are featured among the popular images that fueled the belly dance movement. Allegra Snyder cites an example that affected the way many Americans viewed the Middle East:

> Two wonderfully romanticized processionals from *Kismet* (1955), set in Baghdad and, choreographed by Jack Cole, provide a fine example of "oriental" conglomeration. We note all the elements essential to ritual dance dramas throughout Asia — the banners, the umbrellas, the offering of flowers and foodstuffs — but the result is still a hybrid, an imaginative potpourri that is marvelously fantastic and fairy-tale like [1995, 84].

Contributing to the conglomerate effect described by Snyder in *Kismet* is the fact that the director, in true Saidian form, utilized costumes from Persia, Turkey, the Arab world, India, Ballets Russes, *I Dream of Jeannie*, and off-the-rack beggar's rags. The steps and movements are equal parts Broadway jazz studio and hokey Indo-Perso-Arab fantasy. Perhaps more than any other genre, films have affected belly dance, its movements, and costumes. The romanticism these films engender have probably had the greatest impact on the participants of belly dance, which I will address in chapter 6, although serious belly dance participants have been more influenced by the Egyptian cinema and its belly dance stars than by Hollywood. Certainly no one from, or familiar with, the Middle East would have recognized any of the ingredients concocted by the Hollywood movie industry. Stars like Rita Hayworth, who had been a professional dancer prior to her film career, and Hedy Lamarr were incapable of executing the simplest authentic movements from actual contemporary Egyptian belly dance, which in any case would not have been acceptable to middle America and the film censors.

The Latin American ballroom dance scene was certainly influenced by Hollywood. "Quite a different point of view is evident in Hollywood's treatment of South America and its dance forms. By contrast, the attitude toward dance is positive, persuasive, and embracing. The interpretation favored by most directors and choreographers is that rhythm permeates these cultures and that one is drawn into the culture by participating in the dance" (Snyder 1995, 87). I would differ from Snyder's analysis. I think that Hollywood was ambivalent and frequently racist in the way that it depicted Latin America

(Shay 20062, 86). I will show in chapter 8 that many of the participants of Latin American dances, especially in the period of the 1930s and 1940s, have been affected by Hollywood films, which frequently introduced or spiced up popular ballroom dances and placed them in fantasy venues like a nightclub in Rio de Janeiro or a huge ranch in Argentina. The most popular male Latino figure was always a rich playboy.

Interestingly, I cannot think of a single major Hollywood film that shows Balkan dances, outside of *Zorba the Greek.* Therefore, those who sought new identities through Balkan dancing, apart from Zorba's solo, were able to inscribe new identities unhindered by preconceived notions.

## Depth of Meaning

It is important to grasp that, within this phenomenon, the range of involvement and commitment to these new genres, ranging from creative artist and expert to dilettante and hobbyist is crucial to the understanding of the formation of identities, however partial and contingent, within these newly constructed worlds. While some of the individuals involved in these activities became deeply immersed, acquiring linguistic and professional-level musical or dance techniques and artistry many, if not the vast majority, of those involved remained hobbyists whose concerns never went beyond interest in new steps to a particular Bulgarian *horo* or tango figure, unusual embroidery patterns for the next costume, or recipes for new and exotic foods. Gage Averill calls this shallow immersion into ethnic music and dance "musical transvestism" and observes: "To critique an approach akin to donning the musical skin of the 'Other,' I used the term [musical transvestism] to caricature the 'transcendentally homeless' Westerner who finds a spiritual home and belongingness — even a new personality — in a musical tradition not his or her own" (2004, 100).

Yet even those who claimed these activities as hobbyists devoted many hours and years in the intense pursuit of acquiring the skills and knowledge to perform these dances and music, creating costumes, and preparing foreign foods. They also frequently visited the countries of origin of the dances and music they adopted, seeking some degree of immersion in the local culture and the opportunity to view and, even more exciting, talk to and perhaps dance with "real" peasants.

## Economic Aspects of the Movement

This movement also had a financial impact, both on the participants and on those individuals from other ethnic groups, as well as an individuals in the countries of origin of the particular dance genre who sometimes established businesses catering to the new needs of mainstream Americans. For example, an enterprising Egyptian created a business, a three-story emporium in Cairo, that exclusively caters to costume needs of foreign belly dancers. Famed belly dancers exiting their performing careers, such as Nadia Hamdi, Nadia Gamal, and Nagwa Fouad, gain financial rewards and added fame by teaching foreign belly dancers. The Plaka district of Athens caters to the hordes of tourists flocking to the city in search of a "Zorba moment." Renowned tango dancers in Argentina earn a considerable revenue both in Buenos Aires and abroad through their teaching and stage performances in popular tango reviews, a practice that Savigliano notes began over a century ago when the tango was first introduced into Paris: "The tango was first performed in this fin-de-siecle environment of the Montmartre cabarets, which were now fully devoted to providing an escape from the ordinary and the conventional" (Savigliano 1995, 102). In Asia, special institutes and teaching centers have opened that cater almost exclusively to nonnative students.[4] All of this circulation of people, goods, cultural production, and travel contributes to the hybridization, transnationalization, and globalization of this search for exotic new personalities and identities through exotic dances.

In addition, hundreds of thousands of Americans go to considerable expense to take classes, buy or make costumes, purchase films and videos and music recordings, and attend workshops, nightclubs, dance classes, concerts, and other venues where they pursue their passions. Many of the individuals who undertake these different dance genres spend a great deal of money to travel to the countries of origin, sometimes staying for long periods, especially those individuals involved in learning Asian classical dance forms. I remember taking an annual trek for several years to the Balkans to attend folk dance seminars and journeys to Iran and Central Asia, which I felt were crucial to learning my art form.

## *Reflexivity*

It has been fashionable since the postmodern/poststructuralist era authors to insert their narrative within the various discourses of study, thus becoming both the subject and the object of the study. I think this is a positive academic and analytical move, for if nothing else the author's motives become transparent, allowing the interested reader to see where the author is "coming from." Such reflexivity reveals the author's personal involvement and viewpoint surrounding his or her participation in these activities. As I was in the thick of this phenomenon, indeed at the height of the period when "we were

Ethnic Dance Theatre of Minneapolis performs dances from Posavina, Croatia, 1998. Director Donald La Course. Photograph by Mischa Daniel. Courtesy of Donald La Course.

so easily assimilated," in Leonard Bernstein's and Stephen Sondheim's terms, I was too close and too involved in the artistic activities in which I participated as an actor and dancer to achieve the distance required for scholarly analysis. At that time I could do little more than occasionally wonder at the sheer numbers of my fellow Americans who peopled the Balkan and Middle Eastern worlds that I partially inhabited. So my personal narrative will form a part of these overall patterns of behavior that I describe and analyze.

In a sense, through my embodiment of various forms of dances from the Balkans and Middle East, the wearing of costumes, learning languages, living for significant time periods in those regions, I, and others like me, "naturalized" these dances. We came to "own" them as our own, until, in Roland Barthes's terms (1957 [1992]), they felt as "natural" as my native English language. To this day my body "knows" a Croatian or Iranian dance far more comfortably and more readily than it knows a fox trot or disco dance form; my body answers the strains of a Croatian *drmeš* or a Persian six-eight beat with a visceral reaction that no Western form can evoke. This construction of the naturalization of these dance forms for many individuals, such as that which Tomie Hahn, who devoted a lifetime to her chosen art form, describes and analyzes in her learning of Japanese classical *nihon buyo* (2007), constitutes an important aspect of this study.

Like several of the other individuals that I profile in this study, I straddled more than one form of creative expression.[5] As a teenager I was passionately involved in classical music, a career I thought that I would follow as a professional flutist. But like so many individuals found in this study and one conducted by Mirjana Laušević on participants in Balkan music and dance (1998; 2007), I discovered folk dancing when I entered college, and it changed my life forever. I participated in many immigrant group activities, differing from most of the American participants in the recreational international folk dance (RIFD) movement who were primarily interested in the social and recreational aspects of participation in the international folk dance clubs. While finding recreational folk dancing enjoyable, I was most passionate about the performances in the gatherings of the Iranian and Hungarian communities, and international folk dance festivals, as well as the "exhibitions," as formal, costumed performances were called, in the recreational international folk dance statewide conventions and other venues.

In 1956, with the appearances of Kolo, the Serbian State Folk Ensemble and Tanec, the Macedonian State Ensemble, and then Moiseyev Dance Company in 1958, as well as the sudden proliferation of recordings of Lado, the Croatian State Folk Song and Dance Ensemble, and the Philip Kutev Bulgarian State Ensemble, I entered a new level of artistic and aesthetic possibilities. It was in 1958 that I traveled to Iran and lived as a student and artist. Upon my return to America, I began my first choreographies and headed the UCLA Village Dancers, a group that had been moribund for several years, and in 1963 I changed the name of the group to the AMAN Folk Ensemble.

AMAN was indeed its own different village, and one that I largely choreographically created as an imaginary bucolic world filled with the wonder of music, dance, and costume. Our "village" saw real young love, marriage, love affairs and breakups, and (staged) peasant life cycle rituals. During our wedding from Croatia, the performers were so frequently caught up in the emotion we portrayed on stage that they cried. They believed themselves to be the "village virgin" (if for only a moment, according to Bonita Edelberg's interview, May 14, 2005) in our midsummer staging of *Ladarke,* made famous by Lado's recording on Monitor records and which attracted dozens of listeners to Balkan music and dance.

In some ways we embodied Gage Averill's critique of ethnomusicology department performances in American colleges and universities: "The meticulously imitative nature of most world music ensembles — at least in terms of the sound of the music produced, but also often of dress, demeanor, performance practice, and even pedagogy and transmission — reminds us that the aesthetic ideal to which they aspire (and never really reach) is the 'authenticity' of the model ensembles in their regions of origin" (2004, 100).

But if we did not achieve the sound and look of our favorite ensemble it was not for lack of trying. Many of the individuals that I interviewed or know undertook two or more dance traditions. Barbara Sellers-Young undertook classical Japanese dance and belly dance, in addition to modern dance, in the course of her career. Leonard Pronko, in addition to his long years of study of Japanese classical dance and theater, is equally involved in French and Spanish theater and language. Anne von Bibra Wharton undertook Balkan, German, and Javanese dance. In many ways my life was, in large part, carried out in Iranian or Eastern European environments, in which I felt culturally, linguistically, and choreographically naturalized.

## *Authenticity*

In those early years, I am chagrined to admit, I was a member of the "ethnic police," that is, those of us who were (self) charged with monitoring "authenticity" in the work of our own groups and, even more, of other people's performances. And of course we all lived in dread of other members of the ethnic police pointing accusing fingers at our offerings. But I was certainly not alone in the policing of authenticity. Speaking of the Balkan music and dance scene, Mirjana Laušević notes:

> Concepts of authenticity and preservationism are used to regulate the scene, to censor and evaluate. Scene members rarely if ever consider that their wrestling with issues of authenticity and preservationism is not particularly about Balkan culture, nor does it occur in the interest of this culture. These issues, rather, help scene members explain and validate their own involvement in Balkan music and dance [2007, 64].

Laušević's findings are not confined to the Balkan dance field. Bonita Edelberg, who participates in the Los Angeles tango scene, stated that "Tango is seething with issues of authenticity" (personal interview, May 14, 2005). "In the tango scene in Chicago, going to Argentina, taking classes in Argentina makes you 'more authentic'" (Lambreth 2007).

For fifty years, like my colleagues Dick Crum, Donald La Course, and Dennis Boxell, I created idealized worlds of Serbian and Iranian peasants and court dancers in which thousands of individuals took part, and hundreds of thousands of viewers witnessed, in performances that we created and performed across the nation. For the performers and for many of the audience members, those imaginary worlds took on a reality.

Ethnic Dance Theatre of Minneapolis performs a Tunisian folk dance, 1991. Director Donald La Course. Photograph by Mischa Daniel. Courtesy of Donald La Course.

However imaginary those performances were, they were often most enthusiastically supported by native audiences of the Balkans and Middle East, who loved our positive and spectacularized portrayals of their cultures, which most of them perceived as definitive and authentic.[6]

For the AVAZ International Dance Theatre, the ensemble I founded after I left AMAN, native Iranians overwhelmingly formed the largest percentage of our audiences in their search for a cultural touchstone in the wake of the Iranian Revolution. Dick Crum served as the choreographer of the Duquesne University Tamburitzans for several years, and his work served as the basis of that company's Eastern European presentations. His largely South Slavic audiences flocked to see his creative stagings of their dances. Thus, Crum's, La Course's, Boxell's, and my participation as creators of these imagined worlds differed from the performers who embodied those imaginary worlds that we created and which were first inspired by the performances of state folk dance companies. One of my dancers of Croatian heritage, who currently teaches the children at the local Croatian church, joined my ensemble, AVAZ International Dance Theatre, because of its reputation for the degree of authenticity of its performances. "My experience in AVAZ helped me want to find and teach the dances more authentically" (Heidi Wohlfahrt, personal interview, June 15, 2007).

In my own case, as a new member to the increasingly popular and largely recreational international folk dance movement in the United States, which began in earnest in the 1940s, the appearance of the Macedonian and Serbian State Dance Ensembles (called the Yugoslav Folk Ballet when traveling abroad) in 1956 sparked a deep division in the international recreational folk dance movement that resulted in the bifurcation of that movement along intellectual and generational lines. Many of the younger members, largely students or recent university graduates who were overwhelmed by the spectacle of the performances by the large scale state sponsored folk dance ensembles, opted to specialize in Balkan dances to the exclusion of the heterosexual, couple-oriented dances that characterized the repertoire of the international recreational folk dance movement. The emphasis among this younger group shifted from social and recreational environments — in which the dancers, throughout a single evening, danced thirty to forty three-minute dances from Denmark to Greece and Germany to Italy with little or no styling — to intensive rehearsals and informal evenings where the dancers attempted to perform polished, professional-level, "authentic" dances from the Balkans only.

## Social Bonding and the Performance High

Unlike the feelings of many of my performing colleagues, of bonding with or momentarily being peasants, which characterized a large number of the members of the Balkan dance community and was revealed by Lauševic's research (2007), my reactions were primarily aesthetic, not social. I think that in this way I differed from most of my colleagues, who seemed to respond primarily to the social bonding offered by our performances. Perhaps this was due to the fact that during my high school years I had lived on a ranch with no indoor plumbing or hot water and performed endless hours of backbreaking work. Having lived under some of the same conditions as peasants in the Balkans, I had no need or desire to relive those experiences.

But the social bonding was a significant element for most of the participants and even I was not totally immune to its magic. It is almost impossible to convey to the reader with no performance experience to what degree many of the performers in the large ensembles like AMAN experienced a certain ecstasy, Averill's (2004) "light trance," during those performances.[7]

Often, more than sixty dancers, singers, and musicians created a new and vivid world on the stage, cocooned in brilliant costumes, cut off from the world by the stage lights, whirling in circles. Until the applause signaling the end of the number, we were alone in our own place, bonded in a way that only continuous rehearsal and repetition can effect. To what degree that bonding came through the choreographies that I created and to what degree from the combined emotions and talents of the performers is difficult to say, but the magic and ecstasy that came from those performances was expressed over and over by members of the company as one of the key points of their lives. Audience members frequently commented that "It looked like you were having so much fun."

Daniel Strout remembers:

> My first real performance was with AMAN at the Greek amphitheater. I did get a spot in the first act closer, and rehearsed till I thought I had ground a rut in the floor. I remember terror entering the stage and staring into the black void with spotlights where an unnumbered audience watched. The dancer's first friend, motor memory, took over. A six-man bit, me wisely pinned near the middle, took front stage and I remember losing awareness of myself and for a time feeling like lightning must be streaming from me. I think this is what others have felt when they say "stage-struck" or the "rush" of performance. Heroin is for the ignorant and unambitious [personal interview, June 15, 2007].

Dance scholar Tomie Hahn describes a similar achievement of a type of altered state in the performance of classical Japanese nihon buyo: "Onstage, when mental and physical coordination effortlessly 'flow,' a dancer can use the heightened state of focused energy to project that awareness. I believe that this is the ultimate embodiment of dance" (2007, 165). Over and over, dancers in all of the genres described these peak moments of near ecstasy as a chief motivation for their years of participation. Marta Savigliano describes a similar phenomenon experienced by many participants in the tango scene: "The tango 'high' is a paradoxical state of abandonment and full control, of bodily awareness and mental disengagement" (1998, 104). Tango dancers in Chicago call it "a kind of spiritual connection," "nirvana" (Lambreth 2007).

The large companies that we created are largely gone or diminished now, which serves as an imperative to describe and analyze the phenomenon while it is still alive in the memories of those who lived through those heady times. Those who participated in those worlds all recall their experiences as the peak moments of their lives.

Several of the dancers in AVAZ expressed themselves after a recent 30-year reunion. "Dancing with AMAN and AVAZ was a truly wonderful experience and something I will never, ever forget" (Chrisy Whiting, personal interview, June 17, 2007). "AMAN was and, to some extent, still is my community. Some people go to church every Sunday to meet people and feel spiritually moved. I went to AMAN rehearsals (on Sundays) for the same reason.

Forty years later, former AMAN and AVAZ dancers are my community" (Trudy Israel, personal interview, June 14, 2007). In answer to the question-naire question What was the high point of your performing career?, Mark Angel responded, "Being in AVAZ!" (personal interview, June 15, 2007).

Betty Turtledove, former AVAZ dancer and singer, encapsulated the experiences of many of the performers who responded:

> It meant, as well as the high moments, moments of high comedy, of dreadful shared tragedy, when one of us died; memories of wonderful performances, ours, others, the fun we made together, the admiration and applause, the dreadful pain in the ass of multiple costume changes at high speed, the smell of grease-paint and the roar of the crowd; occurrences of the "AVAZ miracle" when, in defiance of logic, things magically fell together, the enduring friendships, the camaraderie and love. It has changed, shaped, and made my life [personal inter-view, June 15, 2007].

My participation, too, as the chronicler of these events, takes me into a new dimension of participation in the dance world: that of historian. For this pur-pose it required many years for me to take a step backward to review the events of my life, and those of countless others, to undertake this study and provide an intellectual context for those of us who would otherwise remain without a history.

## Theoretical Framework

Recent studies suggest several ways in which to conceptually frame this type of study. Theoretically, these identities might be conceived of as forming con-centric, overlapping circles in one model (Kitwana 2005, 69), or a circle of interconnected segments of different and music dance genres, through which individuals entered and were exposed and became involved in these new worlds of music and dance through contact between us and the genre from across the cultural "border" (Lauševic 1998, 26–36). Instead, I will call upon the concept of "narrative and identity formation" as developed by Margaret R. Somers and Gloria D. Gibson in order to build a theoretical framework for this study (1994).

The phenomenon that I describe and analyze constitutes, in Somers and Gibson's terms, an ontological narrative, and the important fact about the nar-rative, which I will describe, shape, and analyze in some detail, is that it is a new narrative and a new phenomenon — a major departure from past practices, if for no other reason than the mass scale of social actors who participated in the narrative. Although it is a basic premise of this study that identities are malleable and contingent, there is always a danger in forging new identities.

As social scientist Craig Calhoun notes, "It is a curious ideological development, and testimony to the power of the naturalizing discourse, that so many 'mainstream' Americans believe that any natural identity must be good, or at least acceptable, while free 'choice' is considered a weak basis for recognition" (1994, 36 n. 22).

The forging of new identities through the assumption of other personas — adopting foreign names, singing in foreign languages, and wearing costumes of the Other — was a choice we made and frequently a cause of wonder and negative comment among those who did not participate. Many of my informants commented that friends and family members thought their deep involvement in Balkan or other genres of dance odd; worried parents shook their heads over their offspring's desire to pursue a life on the stage not as a successful performer of rock music but as a Balkan peasant, rather than becoming attorneys or physicians. Today the issue of those involved in "exotic" dance traditions crops up in the news media as tongue-in-cheek novelty stories about groups of people who are perceived as eccentric and out of the mainstream of American life. (See, for example, Carpenter 2002; Flandez 2003; Timberg 2004. The headlines say it all.)

Thus the phenomenon of millions of Americans, most typically from the middle class although some came from working class backgrounds, who sought to assume the mask, identity, and cultural production of the Other, as far as I can tell and as I will attempt to delineate, is new. The movement to participate in the dances of other traditions, at least insofar as genres such as Balkan dancing, ballet folklorico, and Asian dance forms such as Kabuki, and Middle Eastern dancing, was largely triggered by the seemingly endless and frequent appearances of various national folk dance companies and classical Asian companies, especially during the period 1956–1967. The movement also coincided with the growth of ethnomusicology and later world dance or dance ethnology, as scholarly enterprises in numerous American universities and colleges, which included the establishment of exotic performing musical and accompanying dance groups on several American university and college campuses.

The "scene" still exists, but in a much diminished form.[8] Clearly this movement coincides with the 1960s and 1970s, decades that wrought huge changes in American life. To what degree did the politics and social turmoil that characterized this period create a context for this phenomenon? I think that they are all inextricably linked, and a portion of this study will attempt to understand those connections.

# *Appropriation, Hybridity, Transnationalism, Exoticism*

In addition, I will address issues of appropriation, transculturation, and hybridity, through the adoption and alteration of dances and music of the Other, which becomes an important theoretical consideration in this study. As Jane C. Desmond notes, "In studying the transmission of a form, it is not only the pathway of that transmission but also the form's reinscription in a new community/social context and resultant change in its signification that it is important to analyze" (1997, 34). A basic question arises in this mass movement: to what degree did the participants in this mass movement appropriate, and possibly misuse, the dances and music that they performed? Marta Savigliano's study of the tango suggests that the tango was commodified and colonized in an uneven movement from the developing world to the First World (Savigliano 1995).

Mirjana Laušević underscores Savigliano's point of appropriation and misrepresentation in the Balkan dance field:

> Many groups give concerts or lecture demonstrations in schools, often unaware that they are not simply *presenting* their group's repertoire, but *representing* Balkan culture to people who know little, if anything, about it. While some groups are very conscientious about their role in cross-cultural representation, others are often unaware even of the possibility of misrepresentation, and when confronted with the issue explain that "if it was not for [them] thousands of people would have never been exposed to Balkan music...." Some people even choose to perpetuate stereotypical views of particular Balkan cultures on the stage in order to cater to the preconceptions of their audiences [emphasis in the original text, 2007, 44].

The situation with oriental dance, in which the myriad orientalist images that abound in the United States are (mis)appropriated and perpetrated in performances of belly dance and Iranian dance, is even more widespread (see Shay 1999, chapter six).

Desmond further notes: "And, of course appropriation does not always take the form of the hegemonic groups' 'borrowing' from subordinated groups. The borrowing and consequent refashioning goes both ways" (1997, 35). Belly dancers in Egypt between the 1930s and the 1970s frequently appropriated movements, costumes, and other elements for their dances from Hollywood films. In chapter five I will suggest that combining these elements with basic movements from the traditional performers of the 19th century, the *'awalim* and *ghawazi*, dancers like Badi'a Masabni, Tahia Carioca, and Samia Gamal, created a new dance genre, a parallel tradition.

**Tango performed by Loreen Arbus and Alberto Toledano and Dancers, 1995. Courtesy of Loreen Arbus.**

Appropriation to some of the individuals who enter the world of exotic dance genres like belly dance or tango is a means of acquiring the identity of the Other, in a strategy that Barbara Sellers-Young and I characterize as "the vocabulary of the dance and its position in the framework of the West, especially the United States, as 'other' provide an 'empty' location, as in 'not part of my culture' for the construction of exotic new fantasy identities" (2003, 14). This style of appropriation and concomitant exoticism to fill the "empty location" and create "fantasy identities" can lead to Savigliano's characterization:

> Exoticism is a way of establishing order in an unknown world through fantasy; a daydream guided by pleasurable self-reassurance and expansionism. It is the seemingly harmless side of exploitation, cloaked as it is in playfulness and delirium. Exoticism is a practice of representation through which identities are frivolously allocated. It is also a will to power over the unknown, an act of indiscriminately combing fragments, crumbs of knowledge and fantasy, in disrespectful, sweeping gestures justified by harmless banality [1995, 169].

While Desmond and Savigliano make extremely important points, I suggest the issue of appropriation among such a large mass of individuals is extremely complex and in large part derives from the intentions of the participants. While some participants and choreographers in the flash and glitz world of belly dance, Iranian dance, and tango — in which participants frequently take a few dance lessons to playact the role of the other, and in some cases a parody of the other, as in anthropologist Jeffrey Tobin's description of some tango dancers "playing whorehouse" (1998, 96) — clearly embody Savigliano's description of choreographing the exotic insensitively. Many Americans want to consume dances like fast food. I call this "Mc-Tango" or "Mc-Kolo." They want to learn many dances and learn them quickly, a complaint that many teachers in the belly dance and Balkan dance field lodge. The rapid replacement of Latin American dances by the newest dance craze characterized the learning of Latin American dances in what I call the "Mc-Tango syndrome." Professional teacher and performer of tango Loreen Arbus said:

> Twenty years ago, when I was beginning, there was great excitement over the tango, just before and after the performances of "Tango Argentino." But Americans belong to a "Fast Food Nation" and so the large crowds wanting to learn tango faded within a year when they found out that you cannot learn tango quickly. Americans want to learn everything fast, but it takes years to learn tango. You must have formal training; you cannot pick up tango by watching as you can with other social dances [personal interview, June 28, 2007].

Others take their art seriously. Leonard Pronko, an exemplar of the art of Kabuki, has received the Order of the Sacred Treasure, Third Degree, from the Japanese government for his artistic skills in that genre. Like Pronko, many of the individuals that I will introduce in these pages undertook the study of the particular dance genre or genres that they inhabit with their whole beings and with great reverence and attention to details of representation. John M. MacKenzie notes: "And invariably artists developed a well-nigh reverential approach to the characteristics of oriental arts from which they believed the West could benefit" (1995, 212).

Ethnomusicologist Anne Rasmussen speaks to issues of appropriation that plague many of us who are not "native" or "heritage" performers:

> My hang-ups about playing the music of a people "whose blood doesn't flow in my veins" has pretty much dissipated after living in Indonesia researching Islamic musical arts for two years (1995–96 and 1999). In Jakarta I witnessed live performance of rock and roll, reggae, *nuevo flamenco*, jazz, oldies, Western art music, disco, pop-*musak*, Christian hymns, and Arab religious and pop music — to name just a few of the kinds of "foreign" music that Indonesians play professionally. Not only do Indonesians "cover" these musics, I believe they identify with them as their own. Their attitudes have done much to allay some of the insecurities I acquired through academic socialization about performing music of the "Other" [2004, 217].

Many Arab Americans and Arabs often deplore the way in which belly dance has become in the West an essentialized and orientalized symbol of their cultures and societies. However, many individuals in the Middle East and the Balkans, and immigrant groups from those regions living in America, often energetically supported the performative efforts of some of the Americans that we encounter in this study because they frequently made eloquent artistic statements and introduced these largely unknown forms to new and wider Western audiences. These performances were often a source of pride to individuals and their children of Middle Eastern and Balkan origin. Anne Rasmussen agrees: "Issues of affirmation are especially vital for many Middle Eastern communities in the context of America's often-hostile environment" (2004, 209).

One of the greatest sources of objection to Americans' participating in exotic genres of dance comes from other Americans, particularly those who assign themselves the role of ethnic police.[9] These individuals are frequently folklorists or anthropologists who undertook and embraced rigid notions of racial and ethnic purity as a litmus test for performance. Folklorist Barbara Kirshenblatt-Gimblett notes:

> *Difference does make a difference.* This is the basis for multiculturalism in its many forms.... Underlying much celebratory diversity is an affirmative racialism coded in the terms of culture. It reveals itself in the privileging of origins and originality, true character, precedence, preeminence, uniqueness, and authenticity, especially when linked to primordial claims. Add essence, spirit, genius, and purity. Keep in mind creative transformation on the part of those who borrow from those who create. What we have is a discourse of paternity and property.... Purity notions have dominated the history of the field (of folklore). The notion of hybridity ... starts with an assumption of diaspora and transnational flow of cultural material, rather than with provenance as the determinant of distinctiveness and distinctiveness as the grounds of identity. Borrowing is a bankrupt notion [1994, 236–237].

For years the Smithsonian Institution had strict rules about participation in their festivals and the bottom line was that you had to be a native performer. The San Francisco Ethnic Dance Festival created a small firestorm when they selected an American devotee of Iranian dance over a native Iranian because the American dancer was more "authentic" (Shay 2006). Kirshenblatt-Gimblett rightly characterizes these festivals as follows: "Quivering with issues of authenticity and iconicity, these events tend to make a clear separation between doers and watchers. Mainstream Americans are the designated watchers and the 'ethnics' and 'natives' are the doers" (1991, 424), at least in those situations in which American folklorists and anthropologists hold the reins of power.

As the director of a folk dance company, no matter how many of my dancers might have been of the appropriate ethnicity, I was frequently turned down for grant funding or for participation in a prestigious festival. This was because I was not of the appropriate ethnicity — I had impure blood. These decisions had nothing to do with the quality of my work, the research involved, or the degree of authenticity — whatever that term meant at any particular moment — that characterized my work. The issue always concerned *my* ethnicity. Thus, the discourse on appropriation, exoticism, inspiration, creativity, ownership, and ethnicity is a thorny one and not easily resolved. These issues, as I found, are not merely theoretical but affect individuals in personal ways.

## Narratives

This work will analyze the many narratives that will be needed to compose discernible patterns of identity formation and the act of assuming the guise or persona of the Other. I will call on many voices to weave this story. In this work I will suggest that this assuming the identity of the Other, to whatever degree, is an almost uniquely American preoccupation. This is not to say that individuals in other societies do not find an interest in the cultural production of other cultures. I could name several. However, in the U.S., the sheer number of individuals involved in various exotic dance activities that invite people to become someone else requires scholarly attention.[10]

In order to enrich this presentation I am going to draw from the concept of "ontological narrative" as presented by Somers and Gibson (1994). The concept of narrative as they present it provides this study with several important theoretical strategies, for in this study I must account for what appears to be an entirely new narrative — that is, the large-scale construction of new identities through the appropriation of the dance and music traditions of the Other, although as I will show the new narrative may well be woven, in part at least, from older ones.

Above all, one must account in this study for individual human agency, as well as the institutional formation that follows individual initiatives, such as the establishment of large-scale performing dance companies, orchestras, choruses, ethnomusicology department music and dance ensembles, and numerous solo performances (see Solís 2004). As Geertz notes, "Our formulations of other peoples' symbol systems must be actor-oriented" (1973, 14).

The accounting for individual agency is a crucial strategy because the description and analysis of individuals who undertake flamenco or belly dance and other genres requires care in description and analysis, for there exists a danger of essentializing "the" belly dancer, "the" Balkan dancer, or "the" *bharata natyam* dancer. In the same way that danger exists in characterizing entire ethnic groups by the behavior of a single person, I wish to demonstrate that individuals who enter these genres of dance, whether as dilettantes or full-blown creative artists in their own right, require an evolved and sophisticated framework to account for multiple patterns of human behavior within fields of representation. Moreover, I must account for the development of identity, for the construction of new, or altered, identities is crucial to the many macro and micro narratives that I construct.

Somers and Gibson state, "Every knowledge discipline needs an '*epistemological other*' to consolidate a cohesive self-identity and collective project ... that social life is itself *storied* and that narrative is an ontological condition of social life ... stories guide action; [and] people construct identities (however multiple and changing) by locating themselves or being located within a repertoire of emplotted stories, that 'experience' is constituted through narratives" (emphasis in the original, 1994, 38). The concept of narrativity permits us to address "the study of meaning, social action, social agency, and, most recently, collective identity" (*ibid.* 39), all of which are crucial to this study.

The element of agency in this study in which individuals choose to enter new worlds of the exotic Other is crucial "to develop a social theory that allows for human action which is nonetheless constrained by structural restraints" (*ibid.*). Somers and Gibson also warn that "Once we have acknowledged the potential significance of identity, however, we must reject the temptation to conflate identities with what can often slide into fixed 'essentialist' (pre-political) singular categories, such as those of race, sex, or gender...." (1994, 39), or Balkan dancer, or belly dancer, as if these terms constitute a single discrete bundle of characteristics.

Thus the use of the concept of narrative gives expression to people out of, and frequently alienated from, the mainstream of the metanarratives of American life. "Similarly, there are also groups and individuals who have been marginalized by our prevailing social theoretical accounts for why people act the way they do.... The new politics and movements of identity stress 'expressive' goals of 'self-realization'" (Somers and Gibson 1994, 53). They add that "In the task of rethinking theory and recognizing history we must also reconstruct and rebuild a sociology of action constituted on conceptual narrativity" (*ibid.* 58).

Crucial to my study is Somers and Gibson's discussion of narrativity:

> Above all, narratives are constellations of relationships (connected parts) embedded in time and space, constituted by causal emplotment.... Narrativity demands that we discern the meaning of any single event only in temporal and spatial relationship to other events. Indeed the chief characteristic of narrative is that it renders understanding only by connecting (however unstably) parts to a con-

structed configuration or a social network (however incoherent or unrealizable), composed of symbolic, institutional, and material practices.... Causal emplotment allows us to test a series of "plot hypotheses" against actual events, and then to examine how — and under what conditions — the events intersect with the hypothesized plot [emphases in the original, 1994, 59].

In other words, this narrative framework allows me to construct the way in which the phenomenon of hundreds of thousands of individuals in a specific time (1940–2007) in the United States chose the dances and music of exotic others to create new identities for themselves and how these "emplotments" can be tested against the history that I write, for "without attention to emplotment, narrativity can be misperceived as a non-theoretical representation of events" (1994, 60). Somers and Gibson identify four kinds of narrative: ontological narratives, public narratives, conceptual narrativity, and metanarrativity:

> Ontological narratives are the stories that social actors use to make sense of— indeed, in order to act in — their lives. Ontological narratives are used to define who we are; this in turn is a precondition for knowing what to do... Narrative location endows social actors with identities — however multiple, ambiguous, ephemeral, or conflicting they be.... To have some sense of social being in the world requires that lives be more than different series of isolated events.... Ontological narratives thus process events into episodes. People act, or do not act, in part according to how they understand their place in any number of given narratives — however fragmented, contradictory, or partial.... Ontological narratives make identity and the self something that one *becomes* [emphasis in the original, *ibid.*, 61].

Public narratives are those narratives attached to cultural and institutional formations larger than the single individual ... (1994, 62) while conceptual narrativity constitutes "the concepts and explanations that we construct as social researchers" (*ibid.*). The metanarratives constitute the master narratives — progress, enlightenment, etc., that postmodern scholars descry and deconstruct. Thus it is Somers and Gibson's first category, ontological narratives, which constitutes the framework within which this study is cast.

The framework of narrativity gives us the following flexibility to weave our micro and macro narratives: "That social identities are constituted through narrativity, social action guided by narrativity, and social processes and interactions — both institutional and interpersonal — are narratively mediated provides a way of understanding the recursive presents of particular identities that are, nonetheless, not universal ... [and] to transcend the fixity of the identity concept as it is often used in current approaches to social agency" (1994, 65). Somers and Gibson further elaborate the concept: "Narratives are not incorporated into the self in any direct way; rather they are mediated through the enormous spectrum of social and political relations that constitute our social world" (*ibid.*). This wide spectrum especially characterizes the web of relationships that individuals living in large urban environments experience, as the majority of those who entered the world of Balkan or belly dance did.

As to the availability of the concept of narrative aids in avoiding the trap of essentializing the motives, imperatives, and emotions surrounding an individual's appropriation and embracing of aspects of the culture of the other: "Our argument is that there is no reason to assume a priori that people with similar attributes will share common experiences of social life, let alone be moved to common forms of and meanings of social action, unless they share similar narratives and relational settings" (*ibid.*, 79). Thus, in this book I will weave micro and macro narrative elements into the fabric of the study to account for both the similarities and differences of the social actors that will narratively perform on these pages.

## Genres of Dance

It is important to grasp that between the various genres of dance which attracted different individuals there exist large differences. The first difference to be noted is the degree of technical difficulty in acquiring even the basic levels of competent performance. *Nihon Buyo* and Kabuki, Japanese dance genres (Hahn 2007; Sellers-Young 1992), and bharata natyam (O'Shea 2007) require years of practice and performance to achieve even a modicum of competence; there is definitely no "Mc-natyam."

By contrast, the techniques of Balkan dancing or belly dancing can sometimes be acquired with a modicum of exposure, and relatively rapidly for some individuals although even for these latter genres many individuals devote years of their lives to perfecting the intricate techniques these dances require for expert performance. Thus the Asian genres and flamenco, due to the demanding and exacting technical requirements, in general attracted far fewer individuals than other genres such as Balkan dancing, tango, and belly dancing, which could confer a basic competence after a few lessons.

Moreover, the Balkan dance genres and Latin American forms such as tango, for example, are most often performed in social settings in their native environments, and they are frequently large group activities. In contrast, flamenco and many Asian classical dance genres are essentially professional forms and, as such, are generally performed as a solo or, less frequently, in small groups by highly trained dancers and musicians, in theatrical or intimate café environments in which there are performing artists and viewers. In Western terms, they can be compared to classical ballet that is also not commonly performed in social environments.

Asian dance genres and flamenco frequently require intensive hours under the guidance of a master teacher, during which the aspiring student forms a master-student relationship, whereas belly dancing, tango and Balkan dancing were most often taught in large-scale classes sometimes no more than one or two hours in duration. Such classes could frequently produce what I call Mc-Tango or Mc-Kolo results with many dancers unable or unwilling to achieve even a modicum of styling.

Those dancers who wanted to achieve a higher level of performance, with proper styling, and who had the dedication frequently joined the professional level dance companies like AMAN or AVAZ, which required hours of rehearsal time each week in order to perfect their skills. Penny Baker noted that "In AMAN we performed the same dances like *Katanka* (Serbian) and the *Shope Suite* (Bulgaria) thousands of times. We never tired of it. We never needed to constantly have new dances like the recreational folk dancers and the coffee house dancers" (personal interview, October 29, 2005).

## Scope of the Study

No historical phenomenon occurs in a vacuum, and that includes the pursuit of dancing, even if the individuals involved have a sense that they are participating in a unique kind of event. These various dance scenes were the result of historical trends that led to their occurrence. For the purposes of this study I identify four threads that led to, or were part of, the phenomenon itself. In this study, I refer to these as "gateways," doorways that enabled individuals to enter their new worlds of exotic dance genres: Chapter one captures the first encounters with the Other, the first performances, visual images and sounds seen and heard by many of the individuals who entered these new worlds, and the first impressions that individuals received. These performances, which many participants cite as life-changing experiences, frequently empowered the individual to attempt to learn a new exotic dance or music genre. Dancer Linda Yudin stated, "I saw a performance of Pearl Primus that was so powerful that I knew that I didn't want to roll around on the floor anymore" (personal interview, January 15, 2006).

Chapter two explores the early performances, like those of the first women solo dancers at the turn of the century, that I identify as precursors to the exotic dance movement: Ruth St. Denis, Maud Allan, Isadora Duncan, and La Meri, who in addition to performing sometimes taught individuals who are still active in performance and teaching today. Chapter three examines the origins and development of the international recreational folk dance movement that attracted hundreds of thousands of adults during the depression years and after.

Chapter four charts the rise and development of world dance and ethnomusicology programs in universities and colleges across America that grew especially after World War II.

Thus, in the first four chapters of the book, I will look at these events and movements and link them to the mass dance phenomena that followed. Finally, I will devote a chapter each to the examples of exotic dance genres in which hundreds of thousands of Americans participated: Balkan dance genres, belly dance, Asian classical dance genres, and Latin American dance forms such as samba and tango.

# PART I: GATEWAYS

## ONE

# "I Nearly Swooned": Empowering Encounters of the Exotic Kind

ALMOST ALL OF THE INDIVIDUALS who took up one or more exotic genres of dance or music recall a seminal moment in which they attended a performance or happened on a dance class that was so moving or powerful that the experience empowered them to locate a group, a class, or a teacher from which they could learn. Sometimes an individual experiences more than one such performance over an artistic lifetime and these frequently serve to reinforce the original desire to learn and perform. These meaningful encounters with an exotic dance, costume, or musical sound can be varied and in this chapter I will address the ways in which participants became involved in their chosen dance tradition and which elements — social, sexual, or aesthetic — they found in learning and performing the dances and musical forms in which they participated impelled them to undertake this often arduous effort. Throughout this and other chapters I will provide space for numerous voices to share their experiences.

I remember as a child seeing my cousin, who was a few years older, playing the string bass in her junior high school orchestra. A year later, when I entered junior high school, I, too, took up the string bass — an experience that changed my whole life. In elementary school I had been taken on field trips to see the opera once and the philharmonic orchestra, but seeing someone that I knew participating in music empowered me to take up a practice that I otherwise might not have imagined doing. I found the sound of live music, new to me, absolutely overpowering.

## First Encounters

First, it is the enabling and empowering moment, the first meaningful, life-changing realization that interests me in this brief chapter, as well as those emotions and feelings they remember the most. Most of the people with whom I spoke about their experiences in the dance and music genres of other ethnicities talked, often passionately, of an empowering moment — a moment in which their lives were changed. Others have described their feelings and reactions in memoirs and studies.

Perhaps the most famous of these epiphanies were the two experienced by Ruth St. Denis:

> Ruth, too, had seen Sadi [*sic*] Yacco [1871–1946] and taken away an excitement so intense it inspired her first experiment in dance-drama. It was in 1900, after only a year with [David] Belasco, that she made a solo dance sketch in the Japanese mode — or at least in Japanese costume. She named the dance "Madame Butterfly," in honor of Belasco's new play, and she performed it with his permission in small vaudeville houses — even though she never mentioned this in later narrations of her career.... Mme. Yacco's attraction for Ruth was her "aura of stillness — so different from our Western acrobatics." Ruth had sensed that Sadi Yacco's art came from an older, more honorable source than Belasco's commercial formulas.... But in Sadi Yacco she saw the dignity this tradition gave the Japanese actress's motions [Kendall 1979, 47–48].[1]

St. Denis's second encounter is the more famous, always recounted in dance history classes and well known to historians, what dance historian Jennifer Fisher refers to as St. Denis's "cigarette poster moment" (personal interview, May 13, 2007). As dance critic Elizabeth Kendall recounts:

> A sign came to her in Buffalo of what she must do. She and a friend, drinking a soda in a drugstore, looked up to see a poster advertising Egyptian Deity Cigarettes. Under the brand name was a splendid picture of a bare-chested goddess, Isis, seated between two stone columns under a twilight sky, her head lifted, her hands resting serenely on her thighs. This was vision, stronger even than the Japanese, of the things Ruth wished for in her theater — control, serenity, Sphinx-like reserve, absolute feminine authority. For the rest of the tour she devoured books on Egypt in every available library. In San Francisco she had herself photographed as Isis, in a square black wig with a paper lotus flower in it, a band of silk across her chest, a draped skirt, and bracelets on her arms and ankles — the first of many costumes improvised by Ruth Dennis out of nearly nothing.... There was something about the angular Egyptian design, the severe and the sensual combined, that exactly matched the spiritual hedonism inside this rather fanatic American girl [1979, 49].

Ruth St. Denis was certainly among the first Americans who fell under the spell of the exotic other, and she lived her life through identities, like those of

Madame Butterfly and Rhada, that she created throughout her career. Her fascination with the Orient that characterized her entire dancing life is why I argue that she was not a pioneer of modern dance, but rather a pioneer of exotic dance.

Mark Morris, the famous choreographer, had multiple encounters and spent his most important formative years learning and performing flamenco and Balkan dances. But his other, later encounters with exotic traditions were also moving. In India as a performer touring with the Laura Dean company:

> I saw great great great dancing all the time. I would say that the thing that really knocked me out was a particular Kathak performance. It was in Delhi actually, and it was of course incredibly hot and the concert was incredibly long. But I was really excited because I felt like I got it.... It was actually frightening for me ... and then it would go on and on and on and on and get more and more fabulous and more and more thrilling. And I ended up going back to the hotel and sobbing all night. It wasn't jet lag. It was really one of the greatest things I've ever seen [1995, 200].

My own experiences of empowering performers were perhaps not as dramatic of those of Ruth St. Denis and Mark Morris, but they were no less life-changing. As a university student, before seeing the performances of Tanec and Kolo in 1956, I had regarded folk dancing as a joyous hobby. The performances of the Macedonian and Serbian national companies were the catalysts that moved me into dance as a serious lifelong pursuit. These types of striking or empowering performances enable an individual to imagine themselves on the stage. Throughout the 1960s and 1970s a parade of state sponsored dance companies arrived on American shores: Serbia, Macedonia, Bulgaria, the Soviet Union, Hungary, Croatia, Guinea, Senegal, Poland, the Philippines, Armenia, Mexico, Cambodia, Bali, Uzbekistan, Iran, and more, all sent their dance ensembles. Each of them was a thrilling revelation to a young American with absolutely no sense of ethnic identity with which to identify.

Linda Yudin, choreographer and artistic director of Viver Brasil!, a dance company that performs the African based dance traditions of Brazil said passionately:

> When I first saw Pearl Primus in 1977 at the University of Illinois I was a modern dance student in college. I didn't even hear the word "ethnic." That concert changed my life: I knew that I did not want to roll around on the floor anymore. But, it took a while. I went to Jerusalem to study for a year, but I was unhappy there. I was always interested in African culture and I was going to originally do my master's field work on the Felashas, the Ethiopian Jews. Then a dance group, Bahia Magia, sponsored by the Brazilian Tourist Ministry, came. I just connected: I engulfed myself in Brazil. I thought I would faint. I'm going to Brazil [personal interview, March 6, 2007].

LADO performing dancers of Slavonia. Choreography by Zvonko Ljevaković. Courtesy of LADO, Ensemble of Folk Songs and Dances of Croatia, 1990.

This encounter with African-based Brazilian dance engaged Yudin's life, and the African aesthetic she first saw in Pearl Primus's company inspired her, after some years, to enter the UCLA dance department to take up the study of ethnic dance traditions. The appearance of the Bahian group with which she had an immediate rapport decided her to change her master's project at the last moment and travel to Brazil instead of Israel with the encouragement of Allegra Fuller Snyder, her advisor. She mastered enough Portuguese in three months to function in the field and her experiences in Bahia served to intensify her interest. Her life is centered around the Brazilian dance group that she directs. Yudin's reaction to the Brazilian dance company reinforced her strong feelings and passion for what she calls "a black aesthetic."

Noted Balkan dance instructor and choreographer Dick Crum said: "When I saw Lado (the Croatian State Ensemble of Folk Dances and Songs) perform Slavonsko Kolo, I nearly swooned. It was then that I saw the possibilities for folk dance on the stage" (March 12, 2002).

Jason Webster describes his first encounter with flamenco music and dance:

> I am held by the music, as though any separation between myself and the rhythm has disappeared. A fat woman singing onstage, dancing in a way that seems as if she is barely moving, yet I feel she is stepping inside something and drawing me in with her. A chill, like a rippling sensation, moves up to my eyes. Tears within me begin to well up, while the cry from her lungs finds an echo within me and makes me want to shout along with her. The hairs on my skin stand on end, blood drains to my feet [2002, 7].

Sometimes the thrill of a first performance that is life-changing can occur at a very young age. "Then, when he [Mark Morris] was eight, Maxine took him to a performance of Jose Greco's flamenco troupe. Watching Greco and his company, Mark decided that he too would like to be a dancer — a flamenco dancer" (Acocella 1994, 20).

Daniel Strout, a former AVAZ dancer, remembers his first moment as if it were yesterday:

> I had taken on joining the Sierra Club as a way to combine the outdoors with broadening a narrow social life. After a Friday evening hike the group went to the (only) Greek Restaurant in town for dinner. The Plaka (now long gone) was also a folk dance café, and dinner included George, the owner, dancing with a table cloth in his teeth, much breaking of dishes, a belly dancer and a lot of people behaving in ways well outside reserved WASP upbringing.
>
> I had mumbled through a few obligatory shufflings on darkened dance floors as part of the mating ritual in college, but this was like finding a new color. I had never seen so much open laughter, so many unconscious attachments expressed in full-on bear hugs to simple gestures of contact on a dance floor in my life. This was dancing for the simple exuberance of living. Elegant, modest, sometimes saucy, movements in patterns exclusively for women, muscular, sweaty bravura in blatantly masculine steps for men: I knew I wasn't in Kansas anymore. And dance in mixed lines, joining in seemingly random DNA strands of a group relation. I had found the color that most suited my heart. Right then and there, I knew this was what I wanted a whole lot more of in my life. I have often looked back on that instant that changed the course of my life, but never with regret [personal interview, June 15, 2007].

Many who enter the world of the dance tradition of the Other are reluctant to attend the first class or see the first concert because of preconceived notions and assumptions based on popular culture images of a particular dance tradition.

> Images of Rudolph Valentino lurching across the dance floor with a rose between his teeth played in my mind. Quite frankly, the idea of having strangers pressed tightly up against me in some stiff dramatic mockery of silent movies was just something I had no curiosity about. But I was depressed, coming out of yet

another failed relationship, and had promised, just this once, to try it. I dressed in my most dramatic Tango ensemble (consisting completely of black, of course) and set off, prepared to employ guerrilla tactics on the dance floor if necessary. Instead, I found the Holy Grail [Siegmann 2000, 1–2].

Leonard Pronko, professor of theater and romance languages remembers:

I had researched Asian theater traditions to go and study in Japan. But I was unprepared for the total emotional impact and effect of a Kabuki performance. The color! Kabuki was the most exciting theatrical experience I had ever seen. I ended up staying six months in Japan in 1961 and 1962, and then returning in 1970. I studied dance in the Hanayagi school. And I still study. I really got into Japanese culture on that first trip [personal interview, October 13, 2005].

Loreen Arbus remembered her first experience of tango vividly:

It was at Helena's (Kalianotas) café, which was located in a terrible part of Los Angeles. She had brought Miranda Garrison, a choreographer and dancer, together with an Argentine tango dancer, Orlando Paiva from Rosario. He was a blue-collar worker who could not even speak English. Helena, an actress who was close friends with Jack Nickolson and Warren Beatty, announced that she had a surprise for us to watch. The real Argentine tango had fallen out of style, not even the Argentines in Los Angeles danced it. I never saw or heard anything like it in my life. Intense, intense. I was totally overwhelmed [personal interview, June 28, 2007].

Anne von Bibra Wharton noted wryly, "My first encounter with folk dance was a class at Louisiana State University by a teaching assistant who wore flip-flops and taught from a book. In spite of that, I was hooked" (personal interview, June 11, 2007).

## Spiritual Encounters

Some individuals feel a powerful sense of spirituality in the dances and musical forms that they undertake to learn. Through that spiritual nourishment the dance tradition they have chosen affords, they remain in that field all of their life. They return over and over to the country of origin of their field, drawn by the spirituality and magic they find in the form:

After five years away, I have returned, as I always thought I would. Back on the eastern coast, a flamenco connection once again. But different this time — another turn in the cycle. I am still fascinated by Spain, perhaps the only country, as Hemingway suggested. It is a labyrinth-like land, a place only partially influenced by the mechanical world, it seems. I always have the sense that, on turning any corner, or entering any village here, I might pass unexpectedly into an ancient fairy-tale world where earth spirits still reign [Webster 2002, 326].

Anne Von Bibra Wharton teaching a recreational international folk dance at St. Olaf College, Minnesota, 2003. Photograph by Patricia Von Bibra. Courtesy of Anne Von Bibra Wharton.

Many of those, for example, who undertake Japanese classical dance, *nihon buyo*, or bharata natyam and other Asian classical forms talk about their spiritual qualities as a subtext (see Sellers-Young 1992; Dox 2005; Hahn 2007). Others are so drawn to the land of origin that they organize tours in order to proudly show the land and its cultural expression to other seekers, like a proud parent showing their precious child, and to pay for the "fix" they must experience it on a regular basis.

Other individuals retain a sense of the spirituality of their dance form without the physical return to its country of origin and regard that spirituality as a precious gift the form has bequeathed to them. Barbara Sellers-Young feels that through her study of Japanese classical dance, *nihon buyo*, she was "on a path of developing *seishin* or inner awareness through the study of the form" (personal interview, May 13, 2007).

Barbara Deutsch, a musician with my dance company AVAZ International Dance Theatre, said:

> I was a student at Oberlin College studying classical music and playing clarinet in the orchestra. It was there that I heard my first Greek music. I nearly swooned. I wanted to know where they taught such music and someone told me UCLA

had an ethnomusicology department where they taught Greek music and I left the next semester and took a BA in ethnomusicology. Now I play in six or seven different orchestras: Greek, Persian, Romany, Polish, Hungarian, Macedonian, Bulgarian. I felt like I had come home, and even consulted psychics who confirmed my feeling that I must have been a Greek or a Persian in another life. When I play Greek music people come and speak to me in Greek, and Iranians come and speak Persian to me when they hear me play their music [personal interview, December 27, 2006].

Mirjana Laušević noted that many of her informants in the Balkan dance scene, like Barbara Deutsch, expressed strong feelings of having been another ethnicity in another life:

> As the response is immediate and happens on a "primal" or "gut level," it transcends the individual, cultural, and historical and is experienced as metaphysical magical, or cosmic. Hence, in keeping with contemporary "new age" philosophy, many people view their involvement in Balkan music and dance as a confirmation of reincarnation theory.... These ties are "found" in past lives [2007, 66].

Dance scholar June Adler Vail noted that several members of a Balkan dance group that she described and analyzed in Maine were attracted by the spiritual aspects of their belonging: "However, a few mentioned social, spiritual, or aesthetic motives, with comments such as, 'I love people, and any activity that brings people together in a holistic and spiritual way is very attractive to me,' and, 'Dance and music are a necessary part of living — we express cooperatively the love of movement and beauty. I like doing ethnic dance because it is what people have doing for centuries'" (1996, 314).

Dance historian Janet O'Shea observes of American modern dance students encountering bharata natyam in classes led by the famous Indian dancer Balasaraswati that "Modern dancers found in her assertion that individual, emotional experience articulated universal themes a corroboration of their own views on artistry.... Balasaraswati's foreign students found expressivity a lure because, for them, bharata natyam offered an avenue toward an interiority that the other dance forms they experienced lacked" (2007, 53).

Most Americans who sought spirituality equated it with the "ancient," and the "timeless," as Edward Said has described in *Orientalism* (1978). This timeless quality entices (as it did the Balkan dancer above who stated that "ethnic dance is what people have been doing for centuries") many Americans into performing and learning Balkan dance, belly dance, and classical Asian forms. "Enduring Orientalist viewpoints alongside a lack of familiarity with choreographic codes often lead non–South Asian viewers to assume that bharata natyam choreography, no matter how recent its composition, as 'ancient' and 'traditional'... (O'Shea 2007, 57).

Many of the participants expressed that their chosen genre of music and dance filled a void in their lives: "All at once it became clear; I should learn flamenco guitar, the musical heart and essence of Spain. It was colorful, exciting, and wild — everything my life wasn't" (Webster 2002, 4).

## Sexuality

Other individuals discover aspects of their sexuality or find that they can meet individuals with whom they can connect emotionally because they gain confidence in their attractiveness. Some individuals discover their bodies, and through their bodies a different kind of knowing: bodily knowledge. One participant noted:

> The heterosexual codes that were inherent in belly dancing helped me to become more socially adept and thus more consciously accepting of my lesbian identity. Learning the codes of socially accepted femininity I was transformed. Instead of feeling confused and concerned that my social behavior was clumsy because I was confused ... I could now read the situation and use the appropriate gender display. Thus, the feminine codes became something to either embrace or transgress depending upon the community. The more I understood the codes the more I understood myself and of course the understanding paved the way to the freedom to be me [October 20, 2006].

Long-time Balkan dancer Robert Leibman states that dancing liberated him from shyness and enabled him to meet women, a social turn that he had found difficult to negotiate in his youth:

> I was a fairly shy kid who never dated in high school and did not go to the prom because I did not know how to dance. At the beginning of my junior year at the University of Chicago, in 1961, I came upon the folk dance group doing a beginning-of-the-year showing for prospective members. I was entranced and stayed all evening. I soon discovered that I could dance. Line dances didn't require asking partners and the ethnic of generally accepting at least one invitation to dance per evening meant that I could ask women to dance with less fear of rejection. But I discovered that I was a good dancer and soon they were asking me. By my senior year I was dancing up to four times a week and often staying up all night — not a good year academically [personal interview, May 13, 2007].

Other individuals describe how they came to know their body through dance. This aspect of self knowledge characterizes individuals who were raised in choreophobic families or environments. Dance scholar Barbara Sellers-Young relates:

> Coming from a Baptist family that did not approve of dancing, I did not take dance classes until I was a university student. There I studied modern dance,

but quit once I graduated. Following the birth of my second child in 1973, a friend talked me into taking a belly dance class in order to get fit. I went to the first class reluctantly, but discovered that the movement suited my post-pregnant body. I also discovered that learning to move fluidly from the core of my body, the coccyx to the top of my head developed within me a deep satisfying centeredness that was complementary to the modern classes I had taken earlier. The limited vocabulary of the dance allowed me to explore my personal expressiveness and the sheer joy of moving from the core of my being. It felt as if I was not limited by a technique as in Graham, Humphrey, Cunningham, but was creating my own technique that was a true expression of my body [personal interview, May 13, 2007].

Anthropologist Julie Taylor observes of her bodily encounter with the tango:

I was in a world deeply familiar from my years as a dancer, a world that gave me back my body and the modes of learning with and from it that had formed my earliest perceptions. As the tango threw all this sharply into focus, I recuperated something that had been obliterated by years of rational argument. I recuperated ways of knowing, ways of knowing art, ways of knowing violence, ways of knowing fear — ways of knowing them to be bound up together in a body to which I could lay a tentative claim [1998, 20].

And all of us in our dancing create a somatic discourse with the Other that resonates throughout our lives, and lives only in our bodies. We feel it deeply, but only rarely can we find adequate expression in words.

## Social Encounters

The theme of individuals who were lonely or regarded themselves as social misfits or simply unable to easily socialize discovered that belly dancing or Balkan dancing allowed them to perform without having to deal with engaging in the potentially rejecting rituals that the heterosexual partnering required by many social dance forms like the tango or the lindy hop Robert Leibman described above. During evenings in which I participated in Balkan dancing on a social level, I noted individuals who were unable to speak to others around them but who were able to step into the line of dancers and, from the way in which they held themselves and the expressions on their faces, clearly felt that they were enjoying a social experience. Some were even transformed.

As Joan Acocella notes of individuals searching for social contact, "But this was the late sixties, the height of the hippie movement and most of Koleda's [Balkan folk dance performing group] members were counterculture types. According to Chad Henry, who was one of the Koleda musicians, 'It was about ninety percent misfits and spiritual homeless'" (1994, 27).

David Strout explains:

The perfection of popularity may be universally admired, but it is not universally achieved. Being one of the many lesser mortals to escape "being cool," I saw my younger self as strange and without any affiliation or approval. Performing part of a folk dance affiliation was like being part of the peacock's tail. I have never encountered another affiliation that drew so intellectually and socially diverse a population. They were all odd in wonderful intriguing ways that I never encountered in my "normal" life. And for reasons known only to God, I "fit in."
    Over time I have realized that these encounters and relationships have been among the most valued I have. Particularly, AVAZ became a network of the family you wished you could have grown up in [personal interview, June 25, 2007].

The sense of belonging on a social level impelled many individuals into the dance traditions they participated in, especially in group forms like Balkan dance. June Adler Vail cites one of the dancers in her Balkan dance group, Borovčani: "Performing brings joy to the audience, but really I like the costumes and being someone else" (1996, 210).

Mark Morris, the famous modern dancer, as a youth thrived in the socially accepting world of Balkan dance:

In 1970, at age thirteen, Morris was taken to a Koleda rehearsal by a friend, and for the next three years he more or less never left. To him, Koleda was a dream come true. First, it was dancing, all the time — the thing he most liked to do.... Koleda offered him the first social environment in which he wasn't an odd duck. However well he handled being "weird" in school, it can't have been that easy. The members of Koleda, on the other hand, were as weird as he, and this was liberating to him. "He was able to let his hair down and be completely wild," says Chad Henry, "because he had this safety net of adults around him" [Acocella 1994, 29–30].

Like Robert Leibman, who encountered his first Balkan dance experiences at the university, Laušević notes that 37 percent of her respondents first encountered Balkan dance in colleges and universities in which many of them were searching for a social environment in which they could comfortably fit: "At the height of the IFD [international folk dance] movement there was hardly a college in the United States that did not have a folk dance group, and, as some 97 percent of respondents are college graduates, it is not surprising that this was the location of many people's first exposure" (2007, 26). My findings and experiences parallel the results of her study.

## Aesthetic Encounters

Many individuals experience a visceral reaction to the movements of the dance or the sounds of the music. Folk dancer Ann Howe says: "A friend of mine at the University of Michigan talked me into going to the dance. Once I heard the music I was hooked" (personal interview, May 13, 2007).

Some of the individuals who undertook the study of exotic dance genres had a more cerebral reaction or holistic reaction to their first encounters. Barbara Sellers-Young, who took up nihon buyo, a form of Japanese classical dance associated with Kabuki, remembers: "Nihon Buyo was a very different experience [from the visceral one that I had with belly dance]. It is much more tied to my love of structure and continuity of the relationship with the Sensei. In this sense it was the opposite of the free flowing expressionism of belly dance" (May 13, 2007).

I had a similar reaction with solo improvised Iranian dance. When I first experienced it in the early 1950s, my reaction was very different from the encounter I later had with Balkan dances. Iranian dance was a more nuanced movement tradition and I sensed that it had an underlying geometric structure that I immediately responded to on a deep aesthetic level, and which I later saw in Islamic art forms. Similar to Sellers-Young, I responded to the structure and beauty, in which I found a special feeling of serenity. As so many informants have stated, finding this dance form was like coming home. It was where I belonged.

# TWO

# *The Early Exotic Dancers*

IN ORDER TO UNDERSTAND and locate the performances of the early dancers, nearly all women who began their careers at the end of the nineteenth and the beginning of the twentieth centuries, we must understand the conditions under which they performed and the worldview and visual environment, in many ways radically different from our own, that informed their creative experiments. I suggest that in many ways the performances of exotic dances by the so-called barefoot dancers, Maud Allan, Isadora Duncan, Loie Fuller and Ruth St. Denis, at the turn of the twentieth century presaged the later mass movement to perform exotic dances that I describe and analyze in this study.[1] In fact, in this work I claim these figures as the mothers of exotic dance genres more than as pioneers of modern dance, as is commonplace in many dance histories (see, for example, Bentley 2003, 57–58). "It is popularly believed that these creators of a new dance were rebelling against 'the ballet.' But none, during her formative years, was in a position to see any ballet worthy of the name" (Reynolds and McCormick 2003, 2). I suggest that these early dancers, with their interpretations of exotic places and historical time periods, paved the way for the performances of exotic dance genres that followed throughout the twentieth century.

## *The Age of Darwin*

As a background to these performances, the mid-nineteenth century ushered in the Age of Darwin that created a paradigm shift in the way people in England and the United States and Canada viewed their world. Today it is frequently thought that the introduction of the theory of evolution by Charles Darwin (1809–1882) and others was received with shock and horror by the general public, and it is imagined that a pitiful group of beleaguered scientists struggled against the stubbornness of the common herd to make the concept of evolution finally understood and accepted. The current concept of the struggling nineteenth century scientist is certainly fueled by recent memories of the Scopes trial found in PBS programming and current attempts by the more retrograde religious fundamentalists of all stripes to insert creationism in the curricula of the public school system in their attempts to keep the twentieth century out of the American home. However, social sciences scholar Jane R. Goodall points out that "The mid to late nineteenth century was a period in which Europe and North America developed an acute consciousness of themselves as the modernizing nations, the leaders of the industrial revolution and therefore the generators of progress for mankind in general. The rise of evolutionary thinking was a shaping influence on this self conscious sense of modernity and progress" (2002, 3).

This evolutionary concept gave rise to a concomitant scholarly and popular interest in ethnology and the accompanying curiosity about the "lower" races. More darkly, it also served as a justification for colonizing them, often brutally, for their own good, not to mention the economic benefits for the metropolitan centers in raw materials for the burgeoning economic development fueled by the industrial revolution. Dance was among those raw materials.

In a series of spectacular world exhibitions, beginning with the Crystal Palace exhibition in London in 1851, natives were put on ethnological display to contrast their "primitiveness" and "savagery" With the newest inventions and technological prowess of the industrial West that were exhibited alongside them, a practice that continues today in a somewhat altered form (Shay 2006).

Religious and political leaders created the "civilizing mission," through which England, France and the United States saw themselves in the role of bringing the "white man's" civilization and Christian values to the benighted populations of Asia and Africa. The metropolitan centers supported, sometimes militarily, missionaries as well as government officials in this overarching endeavor (see Dunne 1996). The civilizing mission served to partially mask the violent and odious colonizing efforts of England and the United States through the seemingly *noblesse oblige* humane generosity to what were widely perceived as savage and primitive natives, an idea that is still alive and well in Washington, DC. In aiding the colonial project, and the accompanying civilizing mission, scientists masqueraded in a cloak of philanthropy and, very probably sincerely, "saw their role as involving a duty of care towards inferior races, whose regressive slide might at least be halted through Christian education and some training in agriculture" (Goodall 2002, 80).

Evolutionary thought provided an even stronger underpinning for the rampant racism that coursed through British and American societies and became manifest in the many world exhibitions and their native displays that dominated public life in the United States and Europe. Perhaps less well known is the fact that the Smithsonian Institution and the United States Congress funded and supported these racial displays in the many exhibitions in Chicago, St. Louis, and San Diego, for example.[2]

The public loved these "ethnological" displays of exotic and lesser humans, and millions of people in the nineteenth and early twentieth centuries flocked to these displays of native peoples in their "authentic" villages and towns set up on the midways of the world fairs, those "natives" wearing colorful costumes, going about their "ordinary" work activities, performing dances and reenacting their savage warlike activities. Show business producers like Buffalo Bill Cody, Sol Bloom, and the great circus entrepreneurs Barnum and Bailey (who promised 100 rude and savage representatives! Fanatical and pagan idolaters! Bestial and fierce human beings! Ignorant and warlike barbarians! (Quoted in Goodall 2002, 98) responded to this avid interest, which rewarded them richly, by providing ethnography as entertainment. All of these events — colonialism, imperialism, ethnological displays and world exhibitions — whetted the public appetite, more than ever before, for the consumption of the exotic. Entertainment and "science and knowledge" were irretrievably blurred in these exhibitions: "Dances and races were clearly the crowd-pulling ingredients" (Goodall 2002, 99).

More importantly, well-known anthropologists of the time like Fredrick Ward Putnam, director and curator of the Peabody Museum of Harvard, and his assistant Franz Boas, headed the Ethnography and Archeology of the Chicago World Fair and promoted dance as a means of educating the visiting throngs. "In defending the great anthropological lessons of the fair, Putnam at one point suggest that certain tolerance had been instilled where dance was concerned, due to the great variety on display in Chicago. It is an interesting consideration that dance played such a large part in the ethnographic exhibits, but the public evidence does not bear out Putnam's hopeful assertion" (1991, 361). They often found them vulgar and unexciting. As one observer noted, "One hardly expects to find any great beauty" in the Indian Ocean" (*ibid.*). Belly dance scholar Paul Eugene Monty describes in detail the public response to these dances, which covered a wide spectrum of views, most of which were a negative reaction to culture shock. The feeling most frequently expressed was that "It was not dancing as we understand dancing" (Monty 1986, 52). What the dancing and exotic displays did incite was an interest in seeing these dances as interpreted a few years later by Western women such as Ruth St. Denis and Maud Allan.

## *Women's Work*

A less well-known aspect of Darwinian thought was the notion that woman was inferior to man — morally, physically, mentally. The embodied figure of the ballet girl, the sylph, a mid-nineteenth century cultural icon, was located at the intersection of cultural anxiety over the clearly physical strength, not to mention the displayed sexuality, required in order to dance and the supposed and highly valued frailty, passiveness, and weakness of the female body. "While some social Darwinists (including Darwin himself) claimed that, as the less evolved of the two sexes, women were closer to the condition of animality than men, the sylph provided a model of the higher feminine as further away from this condition...." (Goodall 2002, 194).

The public performance of dance in this period was linked to prostitution. The worst fate imaginable for the middle and upper classes was the possibility that a son might marry an opera dancer or, worse, that a daughter might "trod the wicked boards." Thus, one of the tasks of the new generation of barefoot dancers was to negotiate the shoals of revealing costumes and exotic, sensual dances and respectability at a time, in the 1890s, when show business was attempting to clean up its act and become respectable and thereby tap into the new and growing middle class market by attracting families. By calling them barefoot dancers, I emphasize the ambiguous position that they occupied, since the exposure of the bare foot was considered indecent at that period. These early dancers were fully cognizant of their ambiguous position. Their attempts to be considered serious artists, removed from the vaudeville in which all of them participated at some point in their professional lives, was a lifelong struggle.

In the 1890s a group of reformers created a counterrevolution to the earlier ideal of the corseted weak women and gained strength. A concern over improving women's physical health through exercise, looser clothes, and fresh air inspired a number of middle class women involved in social work to find suitable physical activities for young women. "In fact, 'the physical' and 'the artistic' were the two realms where American women's new capacities for self expression were exercised. Dancing was the synthesis of those two realms" (Kendall 1979, 8). This search coincided with the appearances of the early dance pioneers like Ruth St. Denis and Isadora Duncan, who rode on the tide of this emancipatory movement and, indeed, served as exemplary models for the "New" Woman. It was also at this time that the promotion of international folk dance as a suitable vehicle for exercise for young girls in the public school system grew, which is a topic for the next chapter.

In order to contextualize the performances of the early dancers (who I argue served as the precursors to the mass movement in America toward performing exotic dance genres, especially the popularity of belly dance), I think it is valuable to look at the entire issue of orientalism as it pertained to that time period. In addition, to fully understand the performances of these early dancers, the role of spiritualism and the state of dance in the theater also need to be briefly addressed. Like the theory of evolution, these aspects of American and European high and popular culture alike constitute an important background for the development of dance, in all its forms, in America.

## Orientalism

I do not wish to rehearse the entire issue of orientalism as put forth by Edward Said and his numerous followers and critics, since they are well covered elsewhere (see Said 1978; MacKenzie 1995; Shay 1999; Turner 1994). Needless to say, Said's concept of orientalism constitutes a polemic which accuses many members of the literary and scholarly establishment of eighteenth-, nineteenth-, and twentieth-century England and France of constructing the "Orient" in one-dimensional terms — abject, passive, overly spiritual, unchanging, sexually overwrought, in fact, everything that the West was not — creating a timeless, feminized location that needed to be dominated and brought to order. In other words, according to Said, these scholars and writers paved the way and enabled England and France to colonize the Middle East. Said claimed that the Orient was "an imaginative geography ... Europe's collective daydream of the East" (using Kiernen's characterization, quoted in Said 1978, 52). Said's main point is that orientalism was, "in short, a Western style of dominating, restructuring, and having authority over the Orient" (1978, 3).

Said's "orient" was, in fact, the Levant since he was Palestinian. However, as the rich concept of orientalism, an idea whose time had come, was mined by other scholars and writers, the meaning was quickly expanded to include North Africa, the Middle East, Central and South Asia, and the Far East. Like many polemical works, *Orientalism* contained many home truths, particularly regarding the construction of the "Other" in Western societies and in academia and, most importantly, spawned an entire and crucial discourse that continues today.

Said's book and the writings that followed hit academia at ouch a time that it created a furor, particularly in anthropology and related departments like sociology, history, literature, folklore and ethnomusicology, and caused an outpouring of "mea culpas" and soul-searching. In many ways the concept of orientalism paved the way for alternative ways of establishing new modes of research and scholarly writing. This achievement alone requires that *Orientalism* be considered one of the most important scholarly books of the twentieth century. One cannot minimize the importance of this discourse. Said's examples focused entirely on elite literature, one of the points that his critics quickly pounced upon, but other scholars took up his cudgel and began deconstructing the films, the visual arts, music, and dance as well as politics and economics of the turn of the century.

However, orientalism was a feature of both highbrow and lowbrow art, which Said did not address, and, as such, orientalism formed an integral element in popular culture, particularly from the period 1890–1930, an important point missed by many scholars and one that is crucial to some of the arguments that I put forth in this study. Lewis Segal notes that "Oriental-themed ballets such as La Bayadere and Scheherazade, some of which are still performed made a huge impact on audiences in the West" (personal interview, July 23, 2007). Art historian John M. MacKenzie notes that "A full understanding of Orientalism requires some comprehension of the extensive range of artistic vehicles through which representations of the Orient were projected. Ideally these need to be analyzed in terms of production, intention, content, audience and specific historical moment" (1995, 10–11). Thus, this discussion will involve the view of several scholars.

According to political science scholar Marta Savigliano's magisterial account of the construction of passion through the circulation of exotic dance genres between the West and the underdeveloped world, belly dance became the first of many scandalous dances that lubricated the machinery of exoticism and orientalism that was constructed from performances of oriental dances at the world exhibitions (1995, 99–107). The popularity of exotic and scandalous dances like belly dance paved the way for the dance fads that followed, like the tango craze.

Two outstanding recent analyses by dance scholars of the performances of these early dancers in light of Said's later concept of orientalism require our attention. The first, by Jane C. Desmond (2001), describes and analyzes Ruth St. Denis's performance of *Radha*, her signature choreography of 1906, which set the model for many of St. Denis's later works, some of which she performed almost to the end of her life, and the second, an essay by Amy Koritz (1997), addresses Maud Allan's famous choreography *The Vision of Salomé*, performed two years later in 1908.

*Radha* certainly fulfills the current concept of orientalism. St. Denis's choreography constitutes an essentialized India filtered through western eyes. It consisted largely of simple movements constructed from *bourrée* turns, poses, the manipulation of her skirt and a series of orientalist props, and Delsartean gestures, all of which were part and parcel of the choreographies of all the barefoot dancers. The choreography came no closer to India than the musical score by Leo Delibes, with selections from his equally orientalist opera, *Lakmé*.

Desmond characterizes the orientalism of St. Denis's choreography: "*Radha*

Ruth St. Denis performs "Rhada," Denishawn collection. 1906. Photographic postcard. Jerome Robbins Dance Division, The New York Public Library for the Performing Arts, Astor, Lenox and Tilden Foundations.

projects a vision of the east as a site of imaginary pilgrimage both for sensual indulgence and physical awakening.... We can see *Radha* as a portrayal of Western desires and ambivalences displaced onto an orientalized, gendered body" (2001, 263). Desmond adds that "In white Western discourse, both nonwhites and non–Westerners are coded as extremely or excessively sexual" (2001, 265), a factor that applies equally to the performance of Maud Allan's *Vision of Salomé*. Both used the same types of simple but sensuous movements, like snaking arms and other similar elements such as the revealing bare midriff costume pieces, a considerably daring strategy in the corseted age in which they lived.

Maud Allan's *Vision of Salome* was only one of several versions of the Dance of the Seven Veils that titillated and scandalized European and American audiences from 1905 until the end of World War I. In historian Andrea Deagon's characterization, "The Dance of the seven Veils was a key marker for the transgressive interweaving of sexuality and the sacred.... By the end of this period, it had been through comic and burlesque versions as well; separated from its high-culture origins, it remained a fee-floating signifier of ancient and oriental degeneracy, chaotic feminine sensual power, and all of the things that made these both threatening and amusing" (2005, 243).

Maud Allan's version of Salome's dance came after several other dancers had been censored in the previous decade since Richard Strauss' opera and Oscar Wilde's play by the same name had created a scandal. Censorship supposedly centered on the treatment of biblical subjects, but in fact it was the visual sexuality portrayed onstage that caused the stir. The single performance of the opera *Salome* had created an uproar in New York, where it was closed down after a single performance (Deagon 2005; Kendall 1979). However, in making the decision to portray Salome as an innocent victim of her mother's scheme to execute John the Baptist rather than Salome as an oversexed nymphomaniac thirsting for John's head because he had sexually spurned her, Maud Allan made history in the role and performed "an unprecedented run of over 250 performances" in the London season (Koritz 1997, 133).

Dance historian Amy Koritz characterizes Allan's impact in *The Vision of Salome*: "This Orientalism (in Edward Said's sense of the term) in turn depended upon a rhetoric that characterized as female those attributes that denoted the inferiority of England's colonized peoples.... The attributes of English, or, more generally, of Western women, however, had to be distanced from those of both the feminized and the female native" (1997, 133). In fact, the audiences of the time preferred the American or English white dancers to any native performers. Authenticity was not a concern, because for the overwhelming majority of Americans and British the Orient — Morocco, India, or Persia — was one entity. They wanted their exotica filtered through American bodies. "It was to Ruth's [St. Denis] advantage that she wasn't Indian or trained by Indians; the audience preferred her to be American, like their home brand of Orientalia" (Kendall 1979, 78). This is an important point, because "The stereotype of the Oriental woman enacted by Allan embodied anxieties about women and Orientals while also affirming the mastery of both by a Western and male-defined truth" (Koritz 1997, 138).

The performances of actual native dances of the Middle East viewed in the frequent world exhibitions were now fixed in the public mind as vulgar. These performances were now linked to the Coney Island performances of the Hootchy-Kootchy, which had been closed down by the New York City police and the courts, and which had been performed by native Egyptian dancers from the Chicago Columbian Exhibition.

In reviewing Maud Allan's performance, "The *Times Literary Supplement* asserted that 'authentic' Eastern dance would have been offensive to respectable British sensibilities. Particularly in the case of belly dancing, it explained, Eastern dancing was 'something lascivious and repulsively ugly'" (Koritz 1997, 140). Koritz characterizes Allan's use of orientalist tropes:

> Allan's performance could thereby be abstracted from the explicit expression of sexuality assumed to characterize Eastern dance as practiced in Cairo or Tangier, while at the same time the authority of her rendition can be maintained because of its accurate portrayal of some essential "truth" about the east. This process serves two interrelated functions. First, it reaffirms the West's authority, since it takes a Western woman to understand and represent the essence of the East. The Orient, as Said notes, cannot represent itself. Secondly, it reaffirms the spiritual nature of (middle-class) womanhood, as posited by the still dominant separate-spheres ideology [1997, 141].

Allan and St. Denis, and their followers and imitators, accomplished this tightrope act not only through the avoidance of actual Middle Eastern and East Indian dance practices, of which they were often ignorant, or as Lewis Segal notes of Ruth St. Denis, "She did study with natives but rejected the specifics of what she learned" (personal interview, July 23, 2007). More often than not, they created a generalized and vague "orient" rather than a specifically regional or national genre of dance from Egypt, Algeria, or Turkey. They used music in minor keys by Western composers that conveyed some faint whiff of the exotic Orient and a frisson of forbidden excitement to their western audiences. Their costumes owed more to orientalist tropes of the degenerate sexualized East, later popularized by Leon Bakst for the Ballets Russes and Hollywood films (and still with us today in *Kismet* and *I Dream Jeannie*) or in classical ballets like *La Bayadere*, but they actually exposed much more flesh, or simulated flesh through the use of skin toned tights or net, than a native Egyptian or Turkish dancer would have done at the turn of the century.

In fact, in all of these performances the early dancers, since they were

Maud Allan as Salome, kneeling beside the severed head of John the Baptist. "The Vision of Salome," 1907. Jerome Robbins Dance Division, The New York Public Library for the Performing Arts, Astor, Lenox and Tilden Foundation.

virtually untrained, invented the dance vocabularies that they utilized in portraying the Orient or the glories of Ancient Greece. Dance writer Lincoln Kristen noted that the Ancient Greece Isadora brought to the stage could be more accurately characterized as a "native expression of Californian pantheism" (quoted in Reynolds and McCormick 2003, 11).

Dance writer Elizabeth Kendall notes that Ruth St. Denis "Could only have emerged in America.... Ruth knew more than the other solo dancers about the popular theater and less about dance training, so that a significant part of her dance inventions derived from theater and the techniques of tragic actresses of her day" (1979, 12). Her movements, and those of many of her contemporaries, were Delsarte-based technique poses learned from viewing Mrs. Genevieve Stebbins, a popularizer of Delsarte movement technique whom she had seen as a teenager. St. Denis had been a vaudeville performer for many years and utilized the skirt dancing, a form of jig and clog dance that she had performed on the vaudevillian stage for several years and which she now used to advantage in the finale of *Radha*, in which "Ruth's old skirt-dancing instincts came back to her in a series of high kicks, backbends and tour-de-force twirls with gauze skirt rippling up and down" (Kendall 1979, 51).

Dance historian Iris Garland notes of Desmond's and Koritz's analyses: "Desmond and Kortiz applied Said's analysis to the Oriental dances of St. Denis and Allan, and indeed, found both guilty of appropriation and complicit with imperialism" (2000, 193). And while Garland's characterization of the analyses of Koritz and Desmond appears harsh, historian John M. MacKenzie notes that it is not uncommon for postmodern deconstructions of the past "to fall into all the pitfalls the historian constantly warns students, the public and himself to avoid: reading present values into past ages; passing judgments on entire previous generations" (1995, 38).

Dance historian Susan Manning also challenges the analyses of both Koritz and Desmond for focusing on orientalism as a key to the popularity of the performances of dancers like St. Denis and Allan, especially with female audience members, rather than on their movement practices:

> What both Koritz and Desmond overlook, however, is the kinesthetic dimension of Allan's and St. Denis's performances ... their own movement vocabularies that drew on methods of physical culture — aesthetic gymnastics and Delsartism — widely practiced among middle-class women of the time. Unlike spectators of nineteenth-century ballet, whether male or female, who rarely had direct experiences of the movement techniques presented onstage, many female spectators of early modern dance did have such direct experience, which surely intensified their kinesthetic response to the performances they witnessed. Although few women wrote reviews of early modern dance, more than a few recorded their enthusiasm in letters and memoirs, and these sources suggest that they viewed the kinesthetic power of early modern dance as a metaphor for women's heightened social mobility and sense of possibility. It may well be the case that the representational frames of Orientalism were less central to the responses of contemporary female spectators than they were to the response of male reviewers of the time [1997, 162].

However, was it the kinesthetics of the dance to which women spectators primarily reacted? Film historian Gaylyn Studlar suggests that "In this context, the fan magazine's sympathetic reliance on dance iconography as a cultural production traditionally associated with female performers, and more recently associated with female audiences, reminds us of an important fact sometimes overlooked, that women's spectatorship during these years worked primarily to sustain female stars" (1997, 113). Desmond's, Koritz's, Garland's, Manning's and Studlar's positions demonstrate that the popularity of the early dancers was complex. I suggest that orientalism was, in fact, a key ingredient in spectatorship analysis, but I also suggest that male gaze theory, for the analysis of many heterosexual male viewers, is also useful. Audience spectatorship theory tends to the essentialist, when in reality audience reactions are complex and contingent.

I would suggest that for many of the heterosexual male viewers, since Manning is attempting to significantly challenge the overarching theoretical position of the male-oriented gaze, while the female audience members may have responded viscerally to the movement vocabulary as well as the orientalist images, for the male members of the audience the scanty orientalist costumes, and the sensuality of the early dancers, hardly ever seen in public before that time, might have offered more interest since, in the view of one contemporary, it "pleases men of simply carnal minds" (quoted in Monty 1986, 53). As Koritz notes, some "observers did not hesitate to characterize Allan's Salome as a 'hot-blooded, sensual Oriental'" (1997, 139). Thus, theorists must account for multiple audience reactions.

I do agree with Manning that certain aspects of the kinesthetics of these performances have frequently been overlooked by scholars, but even more importantly, the specific charismatic qualities of performers like St. Denis, Duncan, and Allan were also overlooked. Without the charisma of the original performers one cannot imagine someone like Maud Allan commanding a stage as a solo dancer for over 250 performances by merely performing simple gestures. Ruth St. Denis was noted as a singularly savvy stage personality: "In the course of the dance she took her audience into her confidence with a smirk, a wink, a signal of infectious self-delight that put them at ease with the 'artistic' side of the dance" (Kendall 1979, 83). Isadora Duncan's' biographer, Victor Seroff, a musician who knew Duncan personally, notes that Isadora possessed a magic power on the stage (1971, 45–46). "In her performances, through her powerful personality and musical intuition, she not only did present visually the spirit of the composition, but actually compelled her audience to feel and see with her the spirit of music" (1971, 120).

But Manning, too, by concentrating on the movement vocabulary familiar to women spectators, fails to understand the enormous impact of orientalist images on women of that time period. The overwhelming reception of the popular film *The Sheik* (1921) and other oriental-themed stage and film performances, which followed St. Denis's and Allan's performances, came from female viewers who could create their own sexual imaginaries through the highly orientalist images present in the film, with its white western heroine. Film theorist Gaylyn Studlar observes, "We know that the relationship of women to Orientalism was a culturally pervasive one, both long-standing and complex ... [and] dance played a crucial role in Hollywood's visualization of an imaginary Orient identified with unleashed sexual desires and women's fantasies." Studlar's observation supports my suggestion that orientalism was not a mere fad, but a long, lasting feature of popular culture in the United States and Europe.

Studlar concludes: "Dance, I will argue, was associated in the early twentieth century on a number of cultural fronts — including film — with a feminine desire to escape bourgeois domesticity's constraints and to create other, transformative identities that were convergent with those qualities of the New Woman that disturbed social conservatives" (1997, 105–106). In reference to the early dancers Studlar notes that "fan magazines offered portraits of Denishawn graduates and other female stars in highly stylized, dance-derived poses" (1997, 114).

More importantly, I think that all of the writers overlook the degree to which orientalist images pervaded the visual world of the turn-of-the-century dancers and their audiences. Not only the Salomania craze during which women dressed up in wildly imaginative exotic clothing, but theaters, new movie houses, and other popular buildings of the period were ostentatiously rigged out with Orientalist designs and architectural features, and paintings, rugs, and the decorative arts flooded middle class homes at this time. Ultimately, orientalist motifs formed one of the most important underpinnings for the Art Deco movement that followed:

> With the decorative arts, however, the influence of oriental forms, motifs and colourings, together with the practices and techniques of Asian craftsmen, became increasingly influential as the nineteenth century wore on. Eastern styles, however modified in the process of transfer, became central to the development of interior decoration, fabrics, carpets, ceramics, metalwork, jewellery, even furniture.... These interests often feed into the revulsion against industrial, machine-made products [MacKenzie 1995, 71–72].

Many women had "Turkish corners" in their salons that they decked out in orientalist exotica. These were frequently furnished with souvenirs that were available at the world exhibitions and other emporia. "Ruth's East Indian skits were perceived as the very spirit of the Turkish corner, expressions of a refined sensuality new to the American palate" (Kendall 1979, 78).

The famous story of Ruth St. Denis seeing an Egyptian Deities cigarette poster that changed her life, in 1904 in Buffalo while touring with a David Belasco vaudeville show, is retold in virtually every description of her life. "It pictured Isis as an imposing goddess, hieratical and with chest bared — a serene, mysterious, eternal figure. Ruth wrote that 'my destiny as a dancer had sprung alive in that moment'" (Reynolds and McCormick 2003, 23). What enabled St. Denis to encounter such a poster was the vast proliferation of orientalist decorative art that characterized that period. In other words, St. Denis's, Duncan's and Allan's decisions to perform orientalist exotica through

**Nazimova in the role of Salome. Lobby cards. 1992. Billy Rose theatre division, The New York Public Library for the Performing Arts, Astor, Lenox and Tilden.**

their choreographies were much more hard-headed business decisions than they were the spiritually inspired created artistic productions their authors claimed in their publicity and program notes. Orientalism was a driving aesthetic and popular-culture force of the period in which they lived.

## The Wicked Stage

I suggest that one of the important reasons for the difference in the numbers of individuals who performed exotic dances in the late nineteenth and early twentieth centuries and the late twentieth century was public attitudes toward the theater and women's appearances in public arenas:

> Most Americans associated the dancer's art with tawdry showpieces featuring plump women in tightly laced corsets who were massed together in routines resembling military drills.... In short, dancing existed to titillate, decorate, or entertain — never to edify. And to dance was considered virtual prostitution. It

was this prevailing state of affairs, rather than "the ballet," that drove the early dancers to evolve an art of self-expression, spiritual significance, and dignity [Reynolds and McCormick 2003, 2].

Far more than in Europe, the austere religious climate in America produced deep choreophobic reactions that militated against dancing careers for either men or women. As Jane Goodall notes, "In America at this time, theatres were still struggling to achieve respectable status in the face of Puritan opposition to all forms of theatrical representation" (2002, 34). Against such public prejudice, how many families would permit their daughters to "trod the wicked boards"? It is clear from reading the biographies of these women that dire economic necessity as much as the need for self-expression drove them to the stage, supported by their mothers. It was one of the few professions in which a woman might earn considerable fame and fortune. Dance historian Toni Bentley notes of Maud Allan: "Always eager to counteract any hint of salacious publicity, Maud was ever present at charity fund-raisers for worthy public causes. She continued to walk the precarious line between the vulgar and the acceptable. The Edwardian sensibility needed someone to embody sex, and Maud received in return for this service what she most needed, fame and fortune" (2003, 66).

One conclusion that I draw from the performances of these early dancers is that they made it possible for future generations of dancers to perform in public in a more relaxed social and cultural atmosphere. They also participated in a major way in the formation of the image of the New Woman, and current generations of feminists and dancers are inheritors of this liberating transformation.

## *Spirituality*

Spirituality is always mentioned as an aspect of the performances of early dancers. I suggest that in the United States at the turn of the nineteenth century spirituality was as pervasive as orientalism, but not on the overwhelming visual level that characterized the latter. Delsarte, the most frequently cited movement practice of the period, was a spiritually based practice. "Although the press would later point to (and exalt) Greece as her [Isadora Duncan's] inspiration and would frequently cite the similarity of her poses to figures on vases, in reality her vocabulary owed more to a response to nature and to the American fad for Delsarte" (Reynolds and McCormick 2003, 11).

In many ways the period of 1890–1918, in which the early dancers flourished spirituality, transcendental, Christian and especially Eastern spiritual ideas penetrated American society, and these spiritual ideas were eagerly sought by many individuals in the form of tracts, books, and lectures, which, according to all accounts, characterized all of the early dancers. Isadora Duncan's biographer, Peter Kurth, commented: "This was the era of the table-rappers, of theosophy and Christian Science, but it was also the era of Darwin, whose *On the Origin of Species*, far from curtailing the wilder flights of spiritualist thought, instead gave birth to the most unscientific developments in popular culture" (2001, 30–31).

> Like the other late Romantic Isadora Duncan, St. Denis read the American Transcendentalists and agreed with Ralph Waldo Emerson that natural facts are signs of spiritual facts, that the artist must penetrate to the spiritual truth beyond physical appearances. She also studied the techniques of François Delsarte and Emile Jacques-Dalcroze who explored the correspondences between movement and expression, movement and music [Shelton 1981, xv].

Maud Allan held the "conviction that dance was the 'spontaneous expression of the spiritual state.' This belief in the spiritual value of dance enabled Allan to situate the public display of the female body within the terms of the separate-spheres ideology" (Koritz 1997, 146).

Like her mother, Ruth St. Denis read widely in areas of spirituality and religion throughout her life:

> The young Ruth saw glory and light — a vision — and desired it. Her imagination was so hungry that it seized on even the few crumbs of exotica to be found in such a religious tract.... Lacking a dance education, she invented one, a kind of dance prehistory culled from her visions of antique and sensual civilizations and some scraps of information from public libraries. But she believed it. She never doubted she was giving her audience an ideology as well as a performance [Kendall 1979, 26 and 13].

In this way, through spiritualism, orientalist themes, and a desire to create "art," although Iris Garland does not mention it, the parallels that she draws between the early part of the twentieth century and the latter part of that century in which dancers looked to the Orient for exotic dance genres have similarities. Both periods are characterized by the claims and beliefs in the spiritual aspects of the East that were strongly believed by many dancers to adhere to those dance traditions that they had appropriated.

In the early period, "For Ruth St. Denis East Asian dance performance would come [to] symbolize the ultimate synthesis of theatre and religion: dance being one of the oldest forms of ritual" (Tenneriello 1999, 280). For the latter part of the twentieth century performance studies scholar Donnalee Dox notes: "Spiritual belly dance, as a specific adaptation of belly dance, draws heavily on imagined reconstructions of the origins of Middle Eastern dance in matriarchal societies, goddess-oriented cultures, and rituals that pre-date institutionalized religion" (2005, 304).

Claims of spirituality also contributed to an assumed respectability and authenticity of purpose. "Several other ladies of the day who dared to show too much flesh and too little piety in their entertainments were arrested for indecency. But Mata Hari, in her spiritual disguise, received only ever more prestigious invitations, performing on one occasion for the recipients of the Legion of Honor...." (Bentley 2003, 101).

Thus, although Garland did not remark upon this aspect of the parallels that she draws between the interest in exotic forms in the beginning and end of the twentieth century, I suggest that spirituality as a backdrop and a major ingredient of these performances indelibly links these dancers of different generations together.

Dance historian Nancy Lee Ruyter makes the point that Genevieve Stebbins, a Delsarte teacher and lecturer:

> Identified what she taught with the kinds of expressive movement she felt existed in the sacred dance of the Orient and the art of ancient Greece. She thus directed attention to sources that would inspire the first two artists of the new dance — Ruth St. Denis and Isadora Duncan. Associating the new dance with remote cultures of the past and of the mysterious East gave to dance a high tone and a sense of serious purpose as well as providing a metaphysical and philosophical rationale for dance as an art [1979, 23].

Claiming that there was a spiritual, quasi-sacred aspect to their dancing enabled dancers like Ruth St. Denis, Isadora Duncan, and Maud Allan to negotiate the slippery slope of appearing in public scantily clad and performing sensual movements at a time when dancing was equated with prostitution. As dance historian Susan Manning notes of Isadora Duncan, "Reviewers often noted that Duncan's dance, daringly costumed for its time, projected a spontaneous sensuality rather than eroticism" (1998, vol. 2, 454). By claiming, and sincerely believing in many cases, that their dances were imbued with spirituality, one of the major components of orientalism, they were able to claim the cultural high ground for their performances. Such claims and an entire discourse on spirituality surround current belly dance practices as Donnalee Dox suggests.

Duncan's Ancient Greece, a land and culture she was unfamiliar with until after the creation of her first dances, which she soon abandoned after her first appearances in London, also resonated with turn-of-the-century audiences. "The Greeks in their excavated form — sculpted bodies of white marble — were racially pure and aesthetically pleasing to everyone, not only to Delsarteans but to dress reformers, to hygienists, to eugenicists, to artists, poets, philosophers, politicians, educators, 'classic' dance enthusiasts" (Kendall 1979, 110).[3] Confronted with the reality of turn-of-the-century Athens, like many Westerners before her, she reluctantly abandoned her deep-seated admiration for the "glories of Ancient Greece" (Seroff, 1971, 56–62; see also Shay 2007 introduction).

A common feature of all of these dancers was their constant reading of books available in public libraries and the objects from Ancient Greece and Egypt found in museums. "Like Duncan, St. Denis spent time in museums, her Egyptian dances were based not only on a great deal of reading but on the photographs in museums and art books. As she remarked, 'All I had to do was take the best poses, the most meaningful ones, and set those poses dancing'" (Reynolds and McCormick 2003, 28). Like their contemporaries (not to mention ours), these women found the sacred in the Orient, the spiritual in Ancient Greece. Later oriental dancers like Jamila Salimpour and Morocco (Carolina Varga Dinicu) are also avid readers of every book that pertains to their lifelong study of Middle Eastern dance traditions (personal interviews at various periods).

Another reason for claiming St. Denis, Allan, Duncan, and Fuller, who produced several other important ethnic dancers from the Orient, is that none of them left a teachable technique. That came with the true founders of modern dance, Martha Graham, Hanya Holm, Doris Humphrey, and Helen Tamaris. Irma Duncan described Isadora's attempts at teaching: "Her method consisted in demonstrating the sequence of a dance perfectly executed by herself. Then, without demonstrating step by step, she expected her pupils to understand immediately and repeated it" (quoted in Seroff, 1971, 183). Seroff notes that "she arrived at the depressing conclusion that she did not know how to teach" (*ibid.*, 182).

La Meri (Russell Meriwether Hughes) was a direct descendent of the pioneer exotic dancers. She came a generation after Ruth St. Denis and constitutes a link between them and the massive dance movement of the 1950s and after. I personally know two individuals, one from the Balkan movement and one from the belly dance field, who are still active teaching and who studied for a significant time with La Meri. La Meri dates her love of exotic dances from seeing a concert of the Denishawn company "sometime around 1915" (Ruyter 2009, 215). La Meri appeared successfully on the concert stage, and like her predecessors gave solo concerts of exotic dance forms, but she never achieved the fame and fortune of the earlier generations, not because of any lack of artistry but because changing tastes in America had turned away from these types of concerts, which meant that Ruth St. Denis's fame and popularity were beginning to fade, so La Meri experienced this appearance at the zenith of St. Denis's career. I think that La Meri was as much struck by St. Denis's undoubted charisma as by the content of the performance, which fed into La Meri's own burgeoning imagining of an exotic Orient.

Like her predecessors, La Meri, like St. Denis, read widely about exotic places and gave performances of her interpretations of these places in her childhood. She also performed and choreographed interpretations of the exotic genres that she imagined and later learned more carefully during her travels. For example, La Meri studied with a professional dancer for a brief period in Morocco and later performed the dances that she had learned from her. Like the other early dancers her choreographic works were accompanied by music by Western composers, frequently played on the piano. At the time, through reading and imagination, like her predecessors she constructed her concert dances because nothing else was available (see Ruyter 2005 for a description of her Middle Eastern dances). However, she differed from the earlier generation in that she had a genuine interest in learning authentic materials from native dancers in a way that never interested St. Denis and the others. In this way she provides the link between the earlier generation of dancers like St. Denis and Allan and their interpretations of oriental dances and the later dancers in the latter half of the twentieth century with their thirst for learning and performing authentic movements. The belly dance community revered La Meri and she was profiled frequently in *Arabesque* and *Habibi*, the two largest journals of the belly dance community.

La Meri worked with St. Denis from 1940 and shared a studio with her for some years in New York City. "They met after one of La Meri's concerts. Ruth bounded back to her dressing room and announced that they must collaborate" (Shelton 1981, 251). La Meri remained a lifelong friend to St. Denis, but clearly their teaching methods differed: "Ruth had the notion that at long last she wanted to study authentic oriental dancing. She would summon La Meri to her studio and ask her to demonstrate some step she had noticed in her work. 'I taught her the Kathak turns because she fell in love with them,' La Meri said, 'and she was a very quick study. But when she put them into her dance it became something else again" (*ibid.*). La Meri also attempted to learn from St. Denis that unfathomable charisma and genius that dancers like Ruth St. Denis and Isadora Duncan brought to the stage. But, because St. Denis's movements, gestures, and intuition were so idiosyncratic, learning these proved as impossible for La Meri as learning and retaining authentic movements were for St. Denis (Shelton 1981, 252).

The two women also appeared together in several concerts. On one occasion at least, La Meri would perform an authentic dance followed by St. Denis "with her own romantic interpretation of its style" (Shelton 1981, 252). The leading La Meri dance scholar, Nancy Lee Ruyter, sums up La Meri's contribution to the evolution of exotic dance genres to later generations of dance enthusiasts:

La Meri's presentation of herself in the dances of cultures not her own differed significantly from the superficial adoption of orientalist "signs" found in some of the Western theatrical dance of the late 19th and 20th centuries. In the beginning, she was following that path, but as she became more deeply interested in the cultures that she studied and in the whole process of understanding and acquiring new dance languages, her work demonstrated an attempt to render the dances in a more seriously "authentic" way or to be honest about adapting aspects of them for her own original choreographies. She provided a major contribution to culture on a global scale by introducing the dance languages of many parts of the world to audiences around the world; to students in the United States and Europe; and to readers of her books on various aspects of world dance [2005, 219].

However, like St. Denis, La Meri, searched for the essentialist and spiritual "Orient." For example, La Meri discusses the use of western music in place of authentic music: "This has proven to be good theater, for the average audience is not conditioned to the sound of Oriental music (including, until very recently, flamenco) and often resent it to the point of staying away from the theater" (Hughes 1977, 40). Thus, for La Meri, "oriental" music is all of a piece. La Meri uses the nineteenth century term "race" to mean "ethnic": "The term ethnic dance designates all those indigenous dance arts that have grown from popular or typical dance expressions of a particular race" (1977, 1). She was first and foremost a performer of what she called "ethnological," or ethnic, dance, a form of art dance for the stage as opposed to folk dance, from which she claimed art dance was developed.

For an American wishing to perform the dance of other ethnicities La Meri advises: "Like the Oriental we must submerge ourselves in the art and express the primal motivations clearly, fairly, and honestly" (*ibid.*, 12). And this honesty and truth is achieved through mystical and spiritual means: "for the art of ethnic dance is neither an amusement nor a means of self expression. As the pundits have taught us, it is a means to taste *rasa* (sentiment or feeling) ... and to find God" (1977, viii). In spite of her essentializing the Orient, and what appear to the careful scholarship that followed, La Meri clearly serves as a bridge between the completely interpretive performances of Ruth St. Denis and the more authentic manner of learning the various foreign dance genres of succeeding generations of dancers.

In the same way, modern belly dancers seek to use the spiritual elements that they find in belly dance practices and its perceived ancient spiritual and ritual origins, as a means of endowing an undoubtedly sexualized and sensual movement practice, with its associations with strip tease and exotic dancers, with a respectability and artistry that moves their movement practices to a higher plane. In this way, through the strategic use of spirituality, they fulfill Iris Garland's hypothesis that the two movements, at a century's remove from one another, have a good deal in common, and through this commonality demonstrate one of the reasons that it is important to establish the historical roots of the current movement.

# THREE

# The Recreational International Folk Dance Movement

LIKE THE APPEARANCE of the pioneer interpretive dancers, the growth and development of the recreational international folk dance movement contributed to and provided a second gateway for the mass phenomenon of the 1960s, when individuals sought new identities through immersion in exotic dance genres. I suggest that recreational international folk dance (RIFD) often served as a gateway for many individuals to enter the more specialized realms of dance that I address in the chapters relating to specific dance genres.[1] In my beginning involvement with traditional dance, I spent several years in the Gandy Dancers, a recreational folk dance group from Southern California that was well-known for its high level of exhibition performances in the RIFD movement. For a few years I attended many folk dance festivals sponsored by the California Folk Dance Federation, regular evenings of dancing with the Gandy Dancers, and occasionally I danced with other clubs.[2]

As many social, religious, and political movements grow they frequently fissure into special interest groups, and the Recreational International Folk Dance movement was no exception. The Balkan dance movement was only the first. Later, Hungarian, Scandinavian, Polish, and other divisions appeared. Many individuals bridged several of these special interest areas as they continued to participate in RIFD, while others chose to devote their full time to their special interest(s). As Balkan and Middle Eastern dance became increasingly compelling to me, I, like many others, largely left regular RIFD activities for more intensive immersion in my chosen fields to devote full time to directing and choreographing dances from the Balkans and the Middle East.

In this chapter, for analytical purposes, I identify three major periods of the development of the recreational international folk dance movement.

The first period was from the beginning of the twentieth century to 1939, during which folk dance largely served as a branch of physical education activities for children and for use in settlement houses and international institutes as a vehicle for assimilating immigrant populations into American life and providing an alternative to attending dance halls.

The second period began in 1939–40 and extended to 1956, a period in which new teachers gained popularity and visibility in classes in folk dancing that they held for the public attending world fairs held in New York and San Francisco. The well-publicized appearances of these teachers spread folk dancing as a hobby to hundreds of new enthusiasts. During this period these new teachers, Michael Herman in New York, Vyts Beliajus in Chicago, and Song Chang in San Francisco, introduced folk dancing as a recreational form — wholesome, fun-to-do, and cheap — to meet the needs of adult men and women during the depression, through the war years, and in the decade following. This period was the zenith of the recreational international folk dance movement, its period of highest attendance and participation.

The third period, from 1956 to the present, is marked by the appearance of the first national state folk ensembles to perform nationally in concert halls throughout the United States, and the subsequent attraction of hundreds of thousands of young Americans to specific dance genres such as Balkan dance genres. During this period, the performing, rather than the recreational, aspect became more important and ascendant for many new and young dancers. In addition, different from the past, musicians also entered these fields in large numbers. Many of the new adherents to these genres either left the RIFD to focus their attention on the new time-consuming activities of rehearsals, costume preparation and performances, or they directly entered Balkan, Mexican, Brazilian, Polish, Greek, or Hungarian dancing. In other words dancers in this period enter specific genres of folk dance via other means than the RIFD, into such scenes as folk dance coffee houses or the proliferating world dance and music programs that mushroomed on college and university campuses after World War II. During this period new, more sophisticated teachers like Dick Crum, a protégé of Michael Herman, and later the Canadian Yves Moreau, who danced in Koleda ensemble, appeared and traveled nationally to teach authentic dances from Croatia, Serbia, Macedonia, and Bulgaria to ever-growing numbers of enthusiastic young dancers.

I also characterize this period as the graying of the recreational international folk dance movement. The California Folk Dance Federation South held several meeting in the 1980s on the topic of how to attract a new generation of members, a problem which worried, and continues to concern, some of the leaders of the movement. The situation formed a major topic of conversation among many participants in a recent folk dance festival that I

Donald La Course teaching an international recreational folk dance class, 1999. Photograph by Joan Elwell. Courtesy of Donald La Course.

attended in San Antonio, Texas (March 9–11, 2007). It is a problem for RIFD that remains unsolved.

## The First Period — 1900–1939: Dancing for Health and Morals

At the turn of the twentieth century the teaching of folk dancing was addressed to two audiences: urban immigrant populations and school children. Several useful studies exist that give a great deal of detailed information concerning individuals involved in the development and creation of the recreational international folk dance movement (Casey 1981; Getchell 1995; Houston 2006; Lauševic 1998, 2007; Tomko 1999; Wagner 1997). Some of these studies (Tomko) focus on the beginning period (1890–1920), or describe the history in a specific region such as California (Getchell). And while Lauševic's study provides the most complete overall picture of this movement, she frequently laments the lacunae in documentation that plagues any overall study of this movement because it had several origins on a national level. In attempting to construct a history of international folk dance in the United States, folk dance instructor Betty Casey remarks:

> It would be impossible for any one person, or even a group of persons, to delineate and detail specific stages, chronologically or otherwise, in the development of international folk dancing in the United States. Unrelated programs conducted at the same time but in different geographic and ethnic areas only became significant in the overall picture when later programs pooled them together [1981, 7].[3]

Beginning in the last decade of the nineteenth and especially the first decades of the twentieth centuries, several Anglo American individuals, many of whom were female social workers in settlement houses, and international institutes like Elizabeth Burchenal and Mary Wood Hinman worked with large and diverse immigrant communities. They found several uses for folk dance in the immigrant populations: to provide an alternative to the dance halls that were spreading in urban areas, to provide a pride in heritage through these dances to give the younger generation of source of pride for their parents and grandparents, and to provide a suitable exercise for immigrant workers who frequently sat for hours in backbreaking labor in crowded, airless workshops.

The efforts to work with immigrants often lay in a moralistic attempt to prevent young working class men and especially women from attending dance halls. Prompted by religious and social leaders, the evils of dance halls had become a rallying cry for social workers of the Progressive era (1890–1920). As dance historian Ann Wagner points out, the core issue that exercised conservative

Christian groups from the seventeenth century to the present are: "associations of drinking, dancing, and brothels [that] figure prominently in the anti-dance literature" ( 1997, xvi). She not surprisingly adds, "Dance detractors by and large laid the responsibility for morality solely at the feet of women" (*ibid.*, 243).

Above all, the activities in the settlement houses were to assimilate the immigrants into American life:

> Folk dance work thrived because it performed cultural work on the thorny issue of immigration. In the settlement's view, the dancing, music, choruses, and national songs at that [1906] event "lifted all up above their little patriotism and blended all hearts in the neighborly spirit of our American international citizenship." This interpretation of the festival's Americanizing effect is full of transcendental hope and pragmatic faith in neighborliness as a nexus for interaction among differing peoples. It's not at all clear that immigrant neighbors shared this interpretation of the event, nor that the new spirit of citizenship lasted beyond the event itself [Tomko 1999, 170].

Dance historian Linda Tomko shrewdly adds, "Seen from a Foucauldian point of view, however, such settlement house intervention clearly aimed to 'discipline' immigrant people to American ways" (1999, 85).

## Folk Dance for Physical Education

Many of these same individuals who taught in settlement houses also helped to spearhead the burgeoning physical education movement for girls in public education systems, and thus they found a second use for European folk dances. During that period, only European dances, preferably from northwestern Europe, were deemed proper for American (white) children to learn. These dances included both those folk-derived character dances created for the urban populations and authentic rural dances that these women teachers often personally researched in Europe and published in the new and booming market for folk dance manuals. Thus, the first use of folk dance was a method for social workers to encounter and provide a means of "Americanizing" immigrant populations and the second use taken up by educators was for purposes of providing physical education for American girls, and less often for boys.

The drive to utilize folk dance for children's physical education can also be located in the Darwinian worldview that I alluded to in the Introduction. In that evolutionist viewpoint children were perceived to be on the same mental level as savages and peasants; they embodied the "traditional European ideas of savages as child races" (Goodall 2002, 66). Thus, "as with respect to individuals, there is a progress from infancy to maturity; so there is a similar progress in every nation from its savage state to its maturity in arts and sciences" (*ibid.* 67). In this era the popular notion of the peasant as Noble Savage and childlike (Jean Jacques Rousseau's examples were Swiss peasants) led to the conclusion that peasant folk dances were childlike and thus pure and wholesome, and therefore suitable for children to learn.

And underlying the total vision of folk dancing in the later development of the recreational international folk dance movement was that it was wholesome and fun, a theme that continues unabated today. Those folk dancers who perform those dances regard them nostalgically as linked to a simpler, more wholesome lifestyle of uncomplicated peasant existence.

Dance historian Linda Tomko stresses the role of women in teaching dance in both the settlement houses and in the physical education movement in her important study, and clearly women were preeminent in the history of the settlement house movement. However, other historians indicate that in the physical education movement men were equally prominent and through their writings and positions in the administration of large public school systems like that of New York they supported the efforts of individuals like Elizabeth Burchenal. As Tomko and historians of the early interpretive dancers point out, dance became a profession, whether for teacher or performer, that provided women with a new-found agency in that turn-of-the-century period when few creative employment opportunities existed for women. "This empowered female instructors under Burchenal's direction to gain and claim expertise as folk dance educators, thereby making inroads into the male-preponderant ranks of athletics and dance teachers. Like Burchenal, numerous women writers found publishers for folk dance, singing game, and rhythmic play instruction books gauged to children's needs" (Tomko 1999, 208). I will look at those manuals below.

The first group, the educators, characterized by Dr. Luther Halsey Gulick, Dr. Thomas D. Wood, Dr. Ernest C. Moore, Mary Effie Shambaugh, Helen Frost, Mary Wood Hinman, and Elizabeth Burchenal, enthusiastically pushed for the teaching of folk dances in the public school curriculum for girls. At the turn of the century, as physical education programs for girls were expanding in the United States, folk dance (with its communal rather than competitive character) rather than sports was regarded as a suitable physical exercise for girls. As I noted in the previous chapters, this Progressive era was characterized by the notion that women needed improved health standards through looser clothes, fresh air, and suitable exercise. To counter the prevailing choreophobic atmosphere of the turn of the century, high moral standards found in folk dance activities were stressed: "Gulick also promoted folk dance festivals and wrote prodigiously on the value of dancing, athletics, play, health, and morality" (Wagner 1997, 252). And always the emphasis was on improved morals.

The schoolteachers who taught folk dancing organized popular park fetes in the month of May in New York City, in which as many as 50,000 girls from all over New York City participated.[4] Some enlightened male educators, such as Ernest C. Moore of UCLA, pushed for the idea that boys should also participate in folk dance activities (Shambaugh 1929, 10). By the time I attended elementary school in the 1940s folk dances were taught to both boys and girls and we performed them for the Parent and Teacher Association meetings on May Day.

It is important to grasp the central idea that these early pioneers in the teaching of folk dance viewed these dances primarily as a vehicle for healthy and wholesome physical exercise particularly suitable for young girls. As the many manuals of instructions they produced for teaching folk dance suggest, they were interested in folk dance almost exclusively as a vehicle for physical education. Even though these teachers spearheaded the public presentation of these dances in May Day fetes and festivals, the dancers were a means of demonstrating the values of physical education. The teachers were not interested in the artistic presentation or authentic reproduction of the dances that characterizes most contemporary folk dance presentations. Costumes were not worn and music was provided by pianos or, in larger park settings, by brass bands.

## Early Folk Dance Manuals

Early pioneer teachers such as Frost, Burchenal, and Shambaugh produced many books with instructions for the performance of these dances and they personally conducted field research in Europe (see as examples Burchenal 1913, 1924; Frost 1930; Shambaugh 1929). Nevertheless, the authors of these volumes were not concerned with the elements of authenticity that characterized the research beginning to be published in Eastern Europe, such as the meticulous research that Serbian dance scholars Ljubica and Danica Janković conducted chiefly among the Eastern Orthodox (Serbian, Montenegrin, and Macedonian, 1929–1960) populations of the former Yugoslavia. Later, when "authenticity" (or what we thought was authenticity) became an important issue in the presentation of folk dance, choreographers and folk dance groups in the period from the 1960s came to value this latter type of research by European researchers like the Janković sisters. By contrast the books of the earlier American researchers began to appear quaint and, above all, unauthentic. For example, there are rarely comments on the contexts of the performance, who dances them, and who does not dance (frequently women who were married or had a first child ceased dancing in public events); the dances were presented as decontextualized only as a series of movements and steps.

In the books that these early American instructors published, the authors did not reproduce the actual music that accompanied the dances in the field, rather, they utilized piano scores with Western harmonies. The lyrics to the dance songs, when they were included, were almost exclusively in English rather than the original language. The young students, as well as many of the newly minted instructors, most likely had no idea of what the actual music that the peasants danced to sounded like.

Unlike the Janković sisters of Serbia, who intensively focused on small ethnographic districts, attempting to document all of the dances and their variations in the selected region and the contexts in which they were performed, the books written by Burchenal and Shambaugh for American teachers covered many countries of Europe. They largely focused on north western and central Europe, with one or two dances from each country, although Burchenal also produced books on specific (German and Irish) countries.

European dances were sought after because of widespread belief in that period that Americans did not have a culture and dance tradition of any value because the country was perceived of as being too young to have developed any deep tradition. Little or no information was provided concerning the ethnographic or anthropological contexts in which they were performed. Also, the Janković sisters were deeply concerned with the individual dancers who served as their informants, and they frequently cited outstanding local performers. They were also committed to carefully describing in detail the style of the dancing that they observed and notated.

In a sense, the books by the American educators can be conceived of as "cookbooks" for dance, that is, the books provided instructions or "recipes" for performing the basic steps and movements through step-by-step dance descriptions. Also, through their written descriptions, they were unable to convey even the most basic information about the style of performance such as whether the demeanor of the dancer should be grave or happy or whether the carriage of the body should be erect or relaxed, a topic which the Janković sisters described in some detail. This produced a mechanical and pale reproduction of the original dances. Since they were teaching physical movement as physical exercise, the style of the dances did not seem to have interested them.

The authors, at least judging from the published results, seemed to be interested neither in the context of the dance performance nor in the performers themselves. In fact, Dick Crum, who had extensive access to Burchenal's diaries, found that she had no interest in the peasants who danced for her:

Recreational folk dancing in the AVAZ International Dance Theatre's 30th Anniversary celebration, June 2007. Photograph by Edward N. Brown. Courtesy of Edward N. Brown.

She mostly hobnobbed with the elite. In one case, a Prussian noble had his peasants dance for her. She took her notes from this performance as well as a photograph. Context meant nothing to her. She was clearly a New England patrician matron with little feeling for the dancing beyond its use as a vehicle for her physical education program [personal interview, March 11, 2002].

The single, primary goal of these instructors was to produce manuals that would be of use to physical education teachers in the United States and aid in the spread of folk dance activities in schools.

In the early period at the turn of the twentieth-century, the teachers did not instruct their students to use costumes or any kind of authentic regional music. Indeed, they domesticated and homogenized the dances for use by Americans for recreational and physical education purposes. Therefore only the movements themselves were important in these performances. Piano was the most common form of musical accompaniment used in these early classes. The recordings of folk dance orchestras that Michael Herman promoted and that characterized the second period of folk dancing did not yet exist.

The early instructors, Shambaugh, Frost, and Burchenal, reflecting the ethnocentric and racist attitudes of the time in which some ethnic groups such as Greeks were perceived as nonwhite in many American locations, focused almost exclusively on dances from northwestern Europe in their books (see Shay 2006, 94). "The bulk of the folk dances presented in park fetes were drawn from northern and western Europe — not from southern and eastern Europe" (Tomko 1999, 204). Thus,

> Folk dancing confirmed the political priority assigned to people and practices of Anglo-Saxon derivation, granting only occasional place and thus status, to dances from Italy, Bohemia, or Russia. In failing to acknowledge black and Asian peoples and practices as folk sources for the work of cultural construction, Girls' Branch dancing reinforced the contemporary social and political erasure of these people [*ibid.*, 205].

These dance manuals published as a series by A.S. Barnes for public physical education teachers also reproduced and perpetuated the racial prejudices of the era. For example, Helen Frost's *Oriental and Character Dances* (1930) contained "negro" derived dances composed by Frost entitled "Juba," "The Carolinas," "On the Levee," "Cotton Pickers," "Sweet as Sugah," "Cole Black Dandy," and "I'se Trablin.'" In her instructions for "Plantation," she wrote the following: "In the country, 'way down south,' plantation negroes have barn dances. A jolly carefree group ... takes turns jigging to the strum of a banjo" (74).

These dances were typical of the minstrel shows that characterized the era. "One important popular source defining 'whiteness' was minstrelsy entertainment, an institution that the political scientist Michael Rogin uses to decipher 'the centrality of notions of black and white in American identity'" (King 2000, 42). Minstrel shows were a feature of American life into the 1940s. Thus it is crucial to examine such seemingly innocent cultural productions as "folk" dances that were taught in schools across America with some care to examine to what degree they were complicit in contributing to the racism that afflicted the United States.

Folk dance movement historian Ron Houston summarizes the contributions of the early period: "With a few notable but ineffective exceptions, the halcyon days of educators Hinman, Burchenal, Bergquist, Crompton, and Crawford had developed into a community of 'muscle mechanics' maintaining a self-perpetuating repertoire only remotely connected to RIFD" (2006, 5).

## Origins of the Recreational International Folk Dance Movement (RIFD)

The teaching of folk dance to children eventually led to the beginnings of recreational international folk dancing activities for adults that slowly gained momentum during the depression years of the 1930s, rapidly grew in the 1940s and through the next decades developed into the recreational international folk dance movement we are familiar with today. The linkage between the development of the adult recreational folk dance movement and the activities of the early instructors of folk dance for girls, such as Elizabeth Burchenal and Mary Wood Hinman, have not been studied in any great detail, but Betty Casey, who chronicles what she calls the "international folk dance movement" in the United States, credits Burchenal as an early leader (1981, 7).

Mirjana Laušević also points out that Mary Wood Hinman began to question the way in which folk dance was being taught in the public schools system: "What Hinman was implying was a shift from bodily exercise to the creation of fun, from folk dancing as a drill, a means of achieving physical vigor, to folk dancing as an engaging social activity. In its then new incarnation, folk dancing was not to discipline, not to shape the bodies and educate the foreign and the poor, but to entertain.... Here the agency is in the hands of participants" (2007, 136).

Dick Crum, who was active in the recreational folk dance movement for over sixty years, confirms my findings of the probable connection between the settlement house and physical education teachers and the origins of the adult recreational international folk dance movement. He stated that "Mary Wood Hinman was Michael Herman's mentor" (personal interview, March 11, 2002). Michael Herman was one of the main figures in pioneering folk dance as a recreational activity for adults.

The Americanization of European folk dances continued into the adult recreational folk dance movement that began to slowly grow in the 1930s; participants only gradually incorporated dances from other parts of Europe, chiefly because Michael Herman and Vyts Beliajus were of Eastern European background and they helped spread the dances from that region. Later, one or two Americanized, folk-derived "Mexican" dances also found their way into the recreational repertoire (Casey 1981, 201).

Three seminal figures, Michael Herman (1910–1996), Vyts Beliajus (1908–1994), and Song Chang (1891–1974) can be identified as seminal figures in the development of adult recreational folk dancing. Each of these men began their work in the 1930s, most likely unaware of each other's activities, at least in the beginning.

## Michael Herman

Michael Herman was born in Cleveland the son of Ukrainian immigrants and learned Ukrainian dance from Vasile Avramenko (1885–1981), the most important figure in the teaching of staged folk dance (from the 1920s) in the diasporic Ukrainian communities of the United States and Canada (see Nahachewsky 1998, volume 6, 233).[5] In addition to the formal training he received in Ukrainian dance (like his protégé Dick Crum), as a youth he learned dances from the many ethnic groups in the Cleveland area. He became an accomplished musician, unusual in a folk dancer at that time.

In the 1930s Herman was active in the New York City area where he attended folk dance classes in a variety of settings and assisted Mary Wood Hinman in her teaching. He became the major figure in folk dance teaching and organizing beginning with the 1940 New York World's Fair where he taught thousands of people on a daily basis. He was a charismatic teacher always exhorting fair attendees to participate. "This vision of humanity, joyful and harmonious, was very attractive and many were eager to participate in its creation" (Laušević 2007, 159). From among these people Herman created the impetus for the classes that he and his wife, Mary Ann, held in a variety of rented halls until they were able to establish a major center for folk dance in New York, Folk Dance House, which he and Mary Ann ran for decades starting in 1951. This was the heyday of recreational international folk dance in New York.

As both Casey and folklorist Robin Evanchuk observe, throughout its history the recreational folk dance movement was largely peopled by individuals who promoted the Folk Dance Federation ideal that learning folk dances from a variety of cultures "promoted one's deeper understanding of peoples of the world, which exemplified for them 'the American way' of doing things'" (Evanchuck 1987–88, 117). This sentiment links the members of the recreational folk dance movement to the turn-of-the-nineteenth-century social workers of the settlement houses who also viewed folk dances as a means of providing entrée and inclusion into the American way of life.

Herman's most important influence on the national folk dance movement came through his producing, playing, and distributing over 300 records specifically for folk dancing on the "Folk Dancer" label.[6] This recorded music enabled folk dancing to spread everywhere, and was a major change from the piano accompaniment that characterized the earlier period, bringing a more immediate sense of what the actual music for dancing must have sounded like. For this purpose he formed his own folk orchestra, "Michael Herman's Orchestra," and also hired some other ethnic orchestras like the Banat tamburica orchestra, a group of Serbian musicians from the Romanian Banat area (Dick Crum, personal interview, March 11, 2002). These records were among the first to which I danced and they remain popular among folk dance groups today.

Recreational folk dancing at Pamela Baker's wedding party, 1980. Courtesy of Pamela Baker.

## Vyts Beliajus

Vyts Beliajus was born in Lithuania, came to Chicago as an immigrant and became one of the most colorful and influential figures in the recreational international folk dance world over a teaching and publishing career that spanned six decades. Like La Meri, he was clearly impressed by exotic dance genres performed by Ruth St. Denis. In his youth he dressed up in the exotic and theatrical garb of Hindus and Hassidic figures and performed highly impressionistic dances in concert settings. "Dick Crum saw Vyts as a follower of Ruth St. Denis and Ted Shawn...." (Lauševič 2007, 146). Like Herman, Beliajus began his teaching career in the parks and possibly the settlement houses of Chicago. Beliajus claimed that "By 1940 he'd taught at over two hundred universities, colleges, and institutions and had sparked nationwide interest in folk dancing" (Casey 1981, 12).

His most lasting contribution was the founding of *Viltis* (first a mimeo-graphed newsletter in 1942) in 1944 that served as the nationwide, and indeed international, clearinghouse for news, information, dance descriptions, recipes, and activities of RIFD. For his years of editing *Viltis* and his widespread teaching activities Vyts Beliajus is considered a major and seminal figure in the world of recreational international folk dancing.

## Song Chang

Song Chang is the least well-known of the three pioneer figures in the RIFD movement, in part because his involvement in RIFD lasted no longer than a few years; but also no careful and accurate records were being kept at the time. According to longtime folk dancer John Filcich, "Chang, who was active into the 1960s, was quiet and reserved" (personal interview, March 12, 2002). Both Herman and Beliajus were very outgoing and never shied away from publicity, and both of them had journals (*The Folk Dancer* and *Viltis* respectively) in which they extensively reported their activities. Song Chang had no printed vehicle to trumpet his activities. In February 1938, according to the official history of RIFD in California by Larry Getchell, Song Chang and his wife, Harriet, taught Scandinavian and other folk dances and waltzes to three other couples (1995, 1–2).[7]

In 1939, like Michael Herman who taught dances at the New York World Fair and attracted a large number of new dancers, Song Chang and his dancers appeared across the country in San Francisco at the Golden Gate International Exposition World Fair on weekends and holidays, attracting large crowds. In that same year the group formally organized as Changs International Folk Dancers. According to Vilma Matchette, an early member of Changs, the emphasis in the group was on the quality of dancing and performing; they soon formed beginning, intermediate, and advanced groups, with the latter participating in the many exhibitions they performed. "Changs was the most important group in San Francisco and to be a member gave one a special cachet as a dancer" (personal communication, April 26, 2000).

Within two years of that night in February 1938, when eight individuals led by Song Chang began to learn their first steps, the number of folk dance groups all over the Bay area exploded. Within four years the California Folk Dance Federation was formed, and by 1952 the number of folk dance clubs in California had reached 400. Moreover, classes in New York City were attended by hundreds of enthusiastic dancers, and folk dance clubs, according to the listings found in *Viltis*, proliferated throughout the United States. In the following section I will describe the types of activities these folk dance clubs sponsored.

## Anatomy of a Recreational Folk Dance Club Event

As I indicated above, the clubs in California quickly organized on a number of levels. Most of the clubs took on names that followed their location, e.g.,

The Berkeley Folk Dancers. But folksy and down-home names like the Polky Dots, Hollywood Peasants, and the Fun Club were also popular.

The federation soon established a research and standardization committee, which insisted that each teacher provide a written dance description and that once a dance was taught it must be performed exactly the same throughout the federation clubs. The rationale for this rule was that if Mr. and Mrs. Folk Dancer should visit another dance club while on vacation, they would have the comfort of knowing that when the music began they would know how to perform the dance in the same way as they did in their home club. For the serious dance researcher, this clearly flies in the face of how dance is performed in the field, in which dancers often perform differently than one another in the same location within a stylistic framework, and improvisation is common, desirable, and admired and breathes life into dance traditions that would otherwise die.

Each evening in most of the clubs, as well as at local and statewide festivals, the program chairman or committee posted the evening's program of some forty dances, with perhaps a few empty spaces for requests. "In 1945, RIFD had perhaps less than 1% non-partner dances" (Houston 2006, 8). In the period prior to the 1960s, these largely Anglo-American recreational dancers happily interchanged the heterosexual partner dances of Germany, Denmark, Sweden, Italy, England, France, and Austria as one homogenized folk dance, which they performed during the course of an evening with little or no stylistic differentiation. The dances were short, less than three minutes due to the technology of the 78 rpm phonograph records of the period, enabling recreational folk dancers to perform dozens of dances in one evening.

John Filcich, an early folk dance instructor of Balkan dances, noted that "the older generation of recreational folk dancers that I knew in the San Francisco Bay area, those who were over 40, were generally very resistant to learning line and circle dances from the Balkans. They only wanted to perform couple dances from Western Europe" (personal interview, March 12, 2002).

Clearly this use of partner dances, a perusal of the federation's programs, as well as my early memories, indicate that the overwhelming number of dances, like those in the first period, came from northwestern Europe. The overall quality of the dancing was mediocre because the emphasis was on how many dances a person could perform in an evening rather on the technical level of performance. Except for a few clubs like Changs and the Gandy Dancers, which gave exhibitions, little emphasis was placed on the styling or the technical quality of the dancing. Rather, the emphasis was on having fun. Vyts Beliajus and his style of teaching epitomized this attitude, while taking a sly poke at teachers like Dick Crum:

In "olden" days many leaders tried to maintain authenticity while doing and
enjoying the dances. Some went overboard, while others viewed authenticity as
a minor factor. The joy of dancing and the companionship it afforded was
deemed uppermost for the hobbyist and recreational dancer; fortunately this
idea prevails [Quoted in Casey 1981, 99].[8]

Thus, folk dancing was marked as a location of heterosexual socializing and
fun, frequently accompanied by coy badinage between the sexes. The women
wore peasant-like blouses and full skirts with petticoats and frequently brought
tote bags in which they carried tambourines, scarves, and other props to give
a bit of spice to an Italian or Spanish dance, and the men wore loose shirts
and slacks, sometimes with a sash, and often a towel tucked in at the waist
to wipe away the perspiration.

Beginning in 1940, folk dance enthusiast Jane Farwell established a folk
dance retreat held in a campground (later taken over by Michael and Mary
Ann Herman), and by 1950 folk dance camps became popular places to invite
well-known teachers and for the dancers to absorb many new dances. These
camps became popular places to socialize, spend a vacation, and frequently
pick up college credits (for teachers). The idea of the folk dance and music
camp is still popular today; however, they are frequently devoted to single
genres like Middle Eastern dance and music camps, or Balkan music and
dance camps. And today Balkan and other line dances constitute a larger portion of the general recreational folk dance repertoire than was the case in the
1960s.

According to Getchell, by the early 1950s the Folk Dance Federation
clubs were already beginning to experience the problems of an aging population: "During the Forties, folk dancing attracted the youngish crowd. Those
who had stayed with the movement were now up to ten years older" (1995,
74). I remember joining the Gandy Dancers in the mid–1950s and noted that
I was one of the few young people. Getchell describes the 1952 Statewide Folk
Dance Festival in Oakland as "the high water mark" for RIFD in California
in terms of activities and the numbers of participants.

A quick study of the "folksy" and homey language used in *Viltis* and
Getchell's history indicate that this is a movement that became mired in 1950s
Disneyesque images of *Green Acres*. For many individuals like me, the cloy-
ing folksiness, the sterile camaraderie, and the hobbyist attitudes of the federation folk dance clubs became an increasing source of discomfort:

Distanced from their cultures of origin, folk dances were reduced to the single
category "fun." As "contributions" to the "world of fun," folk dances did not
belong to the people that created them or danced them, but to everyone.
Responsibility to original sources, or even interest in them, was not an issue
here. The details of a particular style were of little interest to the musicians and

folk dancers alike, and the significance of the dances as "international" was primarily symbolic [Lausević 2007, 161].

Above all, it was this trivialization of the dances and cultures I was increasingly embracing which drove me away from spending time with dancing as a leisure or recreational activity. These precious choreographic and musical traditions had in many ways become my art form and, in an important sense, the core activity of my life.

Nevertheless, for many current folk dance hobbyists recreational folk dancing constitutes a major activity in their lives. Recreational folk dancer Ping Chun stated that:

> I was in my thirties when I discovered folk dancing. I used to jog in New Jersey for my health, but in the winter it got dark early and people let their dogs out. Several times I was chased by a big Doberman Pinscher. One of my co-workers suggested folk dancing. It was a win-win proposition. You got your exercise to music and dance, and besides there was wonderful companionship. I gave up the jogging. Now I travel to Maine for camp, go to Rumania for folk dance tours, and also dance in Hawaii [March 8, 2007].

Ping Chun is illustrative of the many hundreds of devotees who travel the United States and abroad seeking the recreational folk dance experience. Jimmy Drury, a long-time folk dancer, alternately despairs because of the fewer numbers of people participating in recreational folk dance on the one hand, yet somehow manages to enjoy his folk dance experiences on the other. He runs a folk dance group in San Antonio, but recently only one or two dancers appear at the regular Friday night meeting. "I would like to travel more but if I leave the group will die" (March 10, 2007). Drury agrees that recreational folk dance is on the wane: "Here in San Antonio only English Country Dancing remains popular" (March 9, 2007). However, these individuals rarely seek other identities through their hobby. For them the joy of seeing old friends and dancing a wide variety of dances from many countries constitutes the drawing power of recreational folk dancing and keeps them pleasantly engaged. Thus, most of the individuals in the RIFD movement do not seek alternate, exotic identities through their dancing. It is within specific genres of dance, such as Balkan dance, that we find those searching for a more satisfying experience.

Also, as witnessed in a recent concert in San Antonio, the difference between recreational folk dance groups and immigrant community groups is palpable: the average age of the participants in recreational international folk dance groups were thirty and forty years older than the teenagers who participated in the Mexican and Serbian groups that were based in ethnic communities and who were representing their own ethnicity in public performance supported and accompanied by their parents and members of their community (March 10, 2007). As Peter Zovak, a first-generation Croatian American, told me: "My parents insisted that I dance in St. Anthony's church group, and so I put in my four years, and then got out" (personal interview, June 3, 2007). By contrast, the mainstream American folk dancers were performing because they loved what they were doing without parental prodding.

The environments in RIFD changed, characterized by a largely generational division. The recreational folk dance evenings, typical of so many recreational activities in the 1950s, took place in the sterile spaces of community centers and gymnasiums. With the rise of Balkan dancing on a large scale, large cities across the United States saw the appearance of coffee houses that catered to these activities. These became trendy hangouts for the young, sexually active, cool and hip dancers who found the coffee house environment congenial to their new personae. Specific nights were given over to Israeli, Balkan, and Greek (considered by the participants as something apart from the dances of Bulgaria and Yugoslavia) dancing, with some more social nights featuring dances from all of these sources. The specialized nights featured teaching by specialists and traveling guest instructors in town for a few days and their presence sparked special interest and increased attendance. In Los Angeles there existed at one time six or seven such establishments in the 1970s.

The heyday of this latter activity spanned the years 1956–1990, peaking in the late 1960s to the early 1980s, after which the large numbers that participated in these activities slowly waned. Much of the excitement among many eager young dancers was generated by the rise of performing groups like the AMAN Folk Ensemble of Los Angeles, Westwind Ensemble (in both San Francisco and Los Angeles), Ethnic Dance Theatre of Minneapolis, Komenka Dance Company of New Orleans, Khadra of San Francisco, AVAZ International Dance Theatre of Los Angeles, Mandala of Boston, and many others which rose to national prominence and a professional level of performance and whose dancers achieved a certain cachet by virtue of their membership. AVAZ dancer Art Aratin said of his years in the company: "It was the sense of being part of something important" (June 14, 2007).

I suggest that the major cause for the original fragmentation of the recreational international folk dance into ethnically specific conclaves began with the state supported folk dance ensembles that first appeared in 1956, Tanec from Macedonia, Kolo from Serbia, and, in 1958, the Moiseyev Dance Company from the former Soviet Union. The spectacle that unrolled on the stage during their performances gave many of us a vision of the future. Suddenly, everything that we had performed in our exhibitions appeared quaint and inadequate. Now the possibility of performing not a single dance for a RIFD festival, which we had rehearsed for weeks between recreational dancing, gave way to the vision of a full evening of dances performed in brilliant costumes and accompanied by live music. Thus, while RIFD served as a gateway in my life and the lives of many others to the activity of dancing, the performances of Kolo and Tanec and other ensembles that came later served as the empowering moment of our artistic lives.

An important aspect of the performances of the national companies was the demeanor of the professional dancers from Macedonia and Serbia: they appeared as serious adult artists performing authentic folk dances rather than as ever-smiling extras from the "Song of Norway."[9] Within weeks of those performances, a group of dancers left the Gandy Dancers and other RIFD groups and formed the Yosemite workshop. After weeks of intensive rehearsals, we were performing these dances in the same way that we learned from the members of the state ensembles. The exhilarating experience that we lived and felt has been documented by Robin Evanchuk (2007). A similar movement away from RIFD clubs took place in San Francisco, as enthusiastic dancers formed the Sokoli group. The intense camaraderie of the performing experience is difficult to describe to those who have not had such an experience. The exodus had begun.

# FOUR

# *Ethnomusicology and Dance Ethnology*

A FOURTH GATEWAY provided many enthusiasts either the opportunity to enter the world of new and exotic forms of music and dance for the first time, or provided those who had already entered that magical realm a second gateway that offered them the opportunity for a more intense degree of immersion and involvement. This gateway, for the most part, opened after the late 1950s when ethnomusicology and, later, dance ethnology courses offering advanced degrees and intense intellectual and performance experiences blossomed on campuses across the nation. Ethnomusicologist Jeff Todd Titon noted: "University courses in world music have increased dramatically since World War II" (1992, xxi).

The first serious and extensive ethnomusicology department in the United States opened at UCLA in the late 1950s during my years as a student there, and expanded in the early 1960s under the direction of Mantle Hood, with classes and full-scale performing ensembles from West Africa, Bali, Iran, Greece, and Mexico. These ensembles gave highly publicized, well attended public performances that, like those of the earlier performances of the Kolo and Tanec ensembles, were empowering experiences and drew many students into the ranks of performance and scholarship. In many parts of the United States university campuses, like those in Indiana, Hawaii, Washington, Illinois, Virginia, New England, Ohio, Illinois, Oregon, Texas, and other locations, became a means through which many mainstream American individuals heard world music genres for the first time. Not only did these Americans encounter new forms of music and dance but also the artists who performed them.

This gateway provided contact — sometimes the first contact, depending on where they came from — with exotic individuals from romantic locales for these students of American backgrounds. Ethnomusicologist Anne Rasmussen notes: "I mention the significance of university [ethnomusicology] ensembles not because of the quality of their performances but simply because of the sheer numbers of people from the Middle East and from Middle Eastern-American communities and music scenes that intersect with these groups" (2004, 218). Ethnomusicologists Ted Solís observes: "Ensembles also provide vehicles for students and community members to 'act out' their perceived and chosen heritage, however constructed and reconstructed" (2004, 5). In other words, these ensembles provided another venue in which American enthusiasts could construct new, exotic identities.

## A Brief History

Like the previous gateways that I have described in this study, those of the examples set by the interpretive dancers of the turn of the century, and the expansion of the recreational international folk dance movement, ethnomusicology and dance ethnology, or world dance and music as it is often called today, underwent crucial changes of philosophy, theoretical conceptualization, and emphasis that characterize today's programs.

A detailed description of the history of ethnomusicology and dance ethnology is beyond the scope of this study; however, a brief description of the history of these disciplines reveals that many of the ways in which they evolved constitute parallel developments with the other, earlier gateways. These changes included the idea of the students' becoming immersed in the performance and mastery of the style or styles of dance or music they undertook (see Solis 2004). This type of performance experience and an emphasis on field work experience for the serious scholar, like one of its parent disciplines, anthropology, became a hallmark of ethnomusicology and dance ethnology studies as it had become earlier in anthropology. I suggest that it is important to gain an understanding of the world view of the disciplines' predecessors because such an understanding is crucial to grasp the ways in which world music and dance are regarded and practiced today as well as historically.

The modern field of ethnomusicology is the older of the two disciplines by a period of one or two decades. The Society for Ethnomusicology was founded in 1955, whereas many dance scholars regard the Third Conference on Research in Dance (CORD), held in Tucson, Arizona, in 1972, as the seminal moment for the recognition of dance ethnology as a conceptual field of scholarship and the historical moment of its founding. From its inception, the very nature of the study of ethnomusicology required some attention to dance, since dance was frequently an integral part of the performances of many of the musical traditions of Africa, Asia, and Mexico that first attracted the serious students of ethnomusicology. In the early period of dance ethnology, the *Journal of the Society for Ethnomusicology* was one of the few available spaces for publishing scholarly dance research. It is significant that Alan Merriam, one of the editors of the *Journal of the Society for Ethnomusicology* and a supporter of many early dance ethnologists, gave the keynote address at the 1972 Tucson conference.

## Early Music Collectors

The very term "ethnomusicology" is recent, dating only from the 1950s. Prior to that time, from the mid-seventeenth to the late nineteenth century, various individuals, often avid amateur enthusiasts who were frequently travelers, missionaries, or civil servants in colonial regimes, collected musical samples from different parts of the world, such as China, India, among Native Americans, and African or European villages. From the 1880s musical scholars interested in "exotic" music developed the discipline of "comparative musicology," the predecessor of ethnomusicology.

The endeavor of widespread collection of music among the peoples of the world was spurred by two technical inventions: Thomas Edison's invention of the phonograph in 1877, which enabled the researcher to record in the field, and Alexander J. Ellis's invention of pitch and scale measurements, by which the octave was divided into 1200 equal units. "This finding brought into question the assumed superiority of Western tempered tuning and led the way to open-minded cross-cultural comparison of tonal systems" (Myers 1993, 4). However, such open-mindedness to embrace other musical traditions as equal to Western music, characterized by the tempered scale, proved to occur in a systematic way only many years because studies like Alan Lomax's study of cantometrics and choreometrics of the 1960s, as we will see, were still based on evolutionary theoretical concepts.

Many studies of dance, for example Curt Sachs's *World History of Dance* (1937), which unfortunately is still occasionally cited in dance studies, placed Western classical ballet and modern dance as the apex of an evolutionary pyramid below which various dance traditions from historical periods and other geographical locales were located. For many years into the twentieth century Western music and the tempered scale were perceived as the final evolutionary stage of music, while the musical traditions of Africa and Native Americans, as well as peasant traditions of folk music, were subsumed under "primitive" music. Both ethnomusicologists and dance ethnologists had their work cut out for them, and in some arenas they still struggle with old and hoary evolutionist attitudes.

The increased pace of the collection of folk music and folk songs throughout the late nineteenth and early twentieth centuries was spurred by multiple impulses. In Eastern and Central Europe, folk song collection evolved from the Romantic era of nationalism, and as such derived from folklore studies as exemplified by the collection of folk tales from the Brothers Grimm and Johann Gottfried von Herder, in which such musical luminaries as Bela Bartok and Zoltan Kodaly of Hungary collected voluminous numbers of folk songs throughout Hungarian-speaking regions. In Eastern Europe the music and songs of the rural population was seen as the primordial repository of the "true" national spirit, unchanging and unspoiled. The music and songs were collected as so many collectible items; the context and performers were of relatively little interest to many of the collectors. Before the invention of the phonograph, song texts were frequently collected without the accompanying music. In that period, some collectors considered the linguistically based song texts more important than the music.

These songs and music also furnished the raw materials for Bartok, Kodaly, Antonin Dvorak, and other composers of the area who, imbued with strong nationalist feelings, composed many works based on folk music. While frequently one is familiar with this practice from famous nineteenth century nationalist composers like Dvorak, Smetena and Chopin, in the early twentieth century, as nationalism intensified with the creation of independent national states like Czechoslovakia and Poland "in art music, the use of rural musical themes — already common in the early nineteenth century — became far more common at this time" (Noll 1991, 146).

The so-called Child ballads, *English and Scottish Popular Ballads*, a collection of some 305 Anglo-American songs by Francis James Child (1825–96) which sustained the intellectual and scholarly attention of dozens of researchers in the field of folklore over the next decades, came from the antiquarian impulse of collecting "ancient" and very old materials before they disappeared. This antiquarian approach characterized much of the research of Great Britain in the eighteenth through the early twentieth centuries, and later in the United States where residents of areas like Appalachia also sang them. One of the chief areas of theoretical contention in the study of ballads, particularly those of the Child collection, revolved around the issue of whether folk songs were communally composed or whether they had a single composer instead. The Child ballads, like folk tales, were collected as musical and literary items with little reference to the contexts of performance; the song took precedence over the singer and his or her performance among antiquarian folk tale and folk song collectors. They were seeking early literary connections. Many individuals in the folk dance world still unreflectively believe that folk dances are communally composed, continuing the notion of a singing-dancing horde dancing and singing around a fire under the moonlight sometime in antiquity.

In the United States, many individuals — prominent among them many women like Alice Cunningham Fletcher, who notably and courageously fought against racism, and Frances Densmore, who was responsible for the collection one of the largest bodies of Native American music — began to collect the traditional music of the Native Americans. This impulse came not only from the idea that an important body of tradition would disappear but also from the idea that the Native Americans themselves, as well as their traditional ways of life, were disappearing.

In addition, many American amateur enthusiasts collected numerous regional folk songs from Anglo-American populations through motives of regional pride for newly established state folklore societies. These musical collection projects were salvage and rescue operations to collect the songs before they were forgotten or "lost." Thus there are four intellectual impulses which drove the massive collection of music that occurred before World War II: (1) antiquarianism: that is, looking for ancient sources in modern folklore, (2) nationalism, (3) regional pride, and (4) rescuing music before it disappears against the onslaught of industrialism and other modern forces. And while many individuals went into the field to collect music, much of the analytical work was done in laboratories by musicians, without reference to actual performances, especially in Germany and Central Europe but also in the United States.

## Darwin and Evolutionary Theory

As I indicated in the introduction, the Darwinian evolutionary concept, which permeated both the intellectual and popular spheres of the late nineteenth and early twentieth centuries, also influenced the thinking of many of the individuals involved in the early field of comparative musicology. Many of the comparative musicologists studied exotic musical genres in order to prove the superiority of Western art music over other world musical traditions.

The American John Comfort Fillmore, who notated some of the music collected by pioneering musical collector Alice Cunningham Fletcher from the Omaha Indians, "embraced the evolutionary perspective of his day, developing a theory of musical analysis that assumed a common harmonic foundation of all music, European and exotic. He attributed Indian deviations from the diatonic scale to an 'underdeveloped sense of pitch discriminations'" (Lee 1993, 23). In other words, if the Indians were as advanced and on an equal cultural level with white Americans or Europeans they would sing on pitch, as designated by the tempered piano and orchestral instruments of the symphony orchestra.[1] Many native performers struggled to "modernize" their musical traditions to bring them in line with Western practices. When I began studying Iranian dance, I remember Iranian individuals who hesitated at using authentic music to accompany their dancing because Americans would not understand or like the microtones that characterized it. These attitudes were part of a colonial or postcolonial mindset.

## Colonialism

The effects of colonialism were in many ways devastating to the colonized, not least in the ways that the British colonial authorities colonized the minds of the upper classes of Egypt through educational and administrative practices, and the application of the "civilizing mission" (see Armbrust 1996; Dunne 1996; Mitchell 1991; Shay 2002). I characterize colonialism as "the gift that keeps on giving": the effects of the colonized mind far outlasted the actual colonial period and have shaped intellectual and cultural life in countries like Egypt and India right up to the present. In short, in this process, many of the colonized individuals accepted, and continue to accept, and even exaggerated the denigrating opinions of themselves and their forms of cultural expression held by the representatives, both private individuals and officials, of the colonial powers long after the physical presence of the colonial administrators and their supporting military powers have physically departed and changes imposed under colonialism have become standards of behavior and execution.

The negative way in which the overwhelming majority of English and French travelers and officials regarded the colonized populations are readily available in the plethora of travel journals that enjoyed enormous popularity in the seventeenth through the early twentieth centuries. Even the most liberal of them compared the music of the Middle East to caterwauling and found the dances utterly without redeeming value. English observer Fredric Shoberl characterized Persian music: "The music did not play out of tune, but still the effect of the whole sounded not unlike a concert of cats" (1828, 174). Persophile Edward Browne, who wrote a still highly regarded history of the Persian literature, characterized Persian dancing in his memoirs: "Dancing boys ... more remarkable for athletic skill than grace" (1893, 120). "His evolutions were characterized more by agility and suppleness than grace and appeared to me rather monotonous" (*ibid.* 320). And these were the opinions of relatively favorable observers who spent many years in the Middle East. The majority of observations of European and American travelers were far more harsh and ethnocentric, reflecting the superiority with which they regarded themselves and Euro-American culture in light of evolutionary theory.

Ethnomusicologist Ali Jihad Racy demonstrates how long-held British and Western colonialist opinions of the inferiority of Egyptian culture surfaced in 1932 in an Arab music conference held in Cairo that was attended both by Egyptian musicians and intellectuals and by Western comparative musicologists. One of the stated goals of the Egyptian government for organizing the conference was "to discuss all that was required to make the music civilized...." (1991, 69):

> The Egyptian assumptions echoed countless nineteenth and early twentieth-century writings by Western travelers and Orientalists who had made disparaging remarks about Arab music and musical instruments. Many European musical scholars had contended that the "primitive" music of Africa and Asia and the "semi-civilized" music of "Oriental or high civilizations" were similar to the early and less-advanced historical manifestations of European music.... Egyptian belief in Western historical superiority within a dualistic world context led to the acceptance of Western music as the ideal referential model [Racy 1991, 82].

By this time, however, several of the new generation of European comparative musicologists had distanced themselves from such evolutionary concepts and ethnocentric and orientalist thinking: "Their pluralistic attitude was combined with a relativistic openness, as they attempted to challenge the Egyptian belief in European musical superiority in favor of a nonjudgmental and nonutilitarian perspective that deemed all local musical profiles legitimate and equally valid" (*ibid.* 87). These new attitudes of openness toward the music of other parts of the world constituted the new field of ethnomusicology that expanded after World War II.

## Modern Ethnomusicology

The 1950s is the era that proved to be a benchmark in the field of ethnomusicology when the term ethno-musicology (the hyphen was dropped in 1957) was used for the first time because it marked a major shift in the way in which the field was perceived. The Society for Ethnomusicology and the *Journal of Ethnomusicology* were founded in 1955, and departments and institutes were established in several universities throughout the United States. In the decade between 1955 and 1965, UCLA's Institute of Ethnomusicology had produced a large number of outstanding scholars who were hired in newly established ethnomusicology departments or chairs throughout the United States.

Indonesian Performing Arts Association of Minnesota's Sumnar gamelan, 2003. Director Joko Sutrisno. Photograph by Petronella Ytsma. Courtesy of Anne Von Bibra Wharton.

The newly established field was composed of two major strands: anthropology and musicology, which did not always mesh comfortably. According to ethnomusicology historian Helen Myers, "By the late 1950s, American ethnomusicologists had divided into two camps: those with anthropological training, led by Alan Merriam (1923–1980), and those with musicological backgrounds, led by Mantle Hood (1918–  )" (1993, 7).[2]

Mantle Hood "envisioned that long-term study in the field with master artists would result in a mastery of the musical idiom akin to a second language.... Hood's apprenticeship model can lead to a deep understanding of the terminology, cognitive structure, rules, and aesthetics of a second musical language" (Averill 2004, 96). Thus Hood championed the intense learning of music. On the other hand, Alan Merriam championed a more holistic approach to the learning of another culture *through* music. Ethnomusicologist Ricardo D. Trimillos characterized the intense discourse as "the reductionist debates between 'Hood-ites' and Merriam-ites at the end of the 1960s" (2004, 24).

Today "Ethnomusicology includes the study of folk and traditional music, Eastern art music, contemporary music in oral tradition as well as conceptual issues such as origins of music, musical change, composition and improvisation, music as symbol, universals in music, the function of music in society, the comparison of musical systems and the biological basis of music and dance" (Myers, 1993, 3).

It is notable, and germane to the topic, that I address in this study that "Often ethnomusicologists study cultures other than their own, a situation that distinguishes this field from historical musicology" (*ibid.*) in the same way that many mainstream American individuals in dance ethnology pursue interests in exotic dance forms, unlike dance historians of Western theatrical dance traditions who largely document the history of the dance traditions of their own culture.

As late as 1991, ethnomusicologist Stephen Blum observed: "We cannot restrict ethnomusicology, in principle, to studies of non–Western societies, conducted by Western scholars, for use within the West. Attempts to limit the scope of ethnomusicology (whether to 'orally transmitted,' 'traditional,' 'non–Western,' or 'ethnic' music) have run up against the realities of musical practices that move across these categories" (Blum 1991, 17).

A related issue that I find a problem is the way in which ethnomusicology as a field has established a canon that has a stranglehold on ethnomusicology studies that is only recently being challenged. This canon privileges older versions and more "authentic" musical traditions over any traditions deemed to be "contaminated" by the West, however that is perceived:

Dancers of the University of California Santa Barbara, Middle East Ensemble (Scott Marcus, Ensemble Director; Alexandra King, Dance Director), perform a khaliji (Persian Gulf) dance. Choreography by Cris Barzellay (based on the teachings of khaliji dance specialist, Kay Campbell) in a performance at UCSB in March 2007. Courtesy of Scott Marcus.

It is important to point out that the great bulk of ensemble activity in ethnomusicology programs was devoted to court musics (Javanese gamelan, Imperial Japanese *gagaku*, Hindustani and Karnatic chamber music, Ewe and Ashanti drumming), which emerged as an ethnomusicological canon of sorts. This elitism inexorably shifted ethnomusicological attention toward structurally complex, high-status, theorized, ensemble traditions, and away from the alternatives ... thus reproducing or reinscribing along the way a Euro-American fetish for sophistication even while purporting to stand for its negation [Averill 2004, 97].

This Western ethnomusicological fetish has found eager welcome in conservatories from Turkey to Japan where those advocating the support of "pure, classical, authentic" musical forms have been supported in their efforts by American colleagues to exclude from their institutions the study of folk and, more particularly, music from popular sources, no matter how old or authentic those traditions may be. Averill notes that "Hood's institutionalization of the ensemble approach and its dissemination throughout North America by his disciples has had real implications for scholarship. Ensembles have provided formative experiences for young scholars, many of whom have taken up research in areas linked to their ensemble interests" (2004, 97). I would add that the implications in nations like Iran and Turkey for native ethnomusicologists who attempt to study outside of the "classical" canon have been severe since American scholars in ethnomusicology have provided the protectors of the "pure classical" tradition the ammunition they need to stave off attempts by anyone to study the "vulgar" popular musical traditions that they, and their North American and European colleagues, overwhelmingly denigrate (see, for example, During, Mirabdolbaghi, and Safvat 1991; Fatemi 2005; Shay 2000).

In no way do I wish to undermine or undervalue the sincerity and enormous contributions made by individuals who promote and are sympathetic to the rich spectrum of forms of world dance and music. But, in many ways, perhaps unconsciously, the establishment of ethnomusicology and dance ethnology courses appears to perpetuate the colonialist notion and division of "the West and the rest." Ethnomusicologist David Locke is more blunt: "World music ensembles inexorably are affected by the world's imperial, colonial past" (quoted in Solís 2004, 10).

Through courses conceptually separated from the intensive multiyear Western art dance and music courses offered at most American universities, world music and dances courses, frequently only a semester long, provide only the briefest exposure to beginning gamelan and Balinese dance classes or bharata natyam. This privileging of Western forms, such as modern dance, underscores the old colonialist attitudes of the superiority of Western traditions over others.

These brief world dance and music courses neatly divide and package the production, analysis and consumption of the exotic, giving what I call only a "sampler" exposure to musical and dance traditions that, like their Western musical and dance counter parts, require years for their mastery. And while it is theoretically possible to view Western art music and dance from the viewpoint of ethnomusicology and dance ethnology, such studies are rare. Joann Kealiinohomoku's seminal article, "An Anthropologist Looks at Ballet as a Form of Ethnic Dance" (1970), has never been equaled, expanded, or used as a means of looking at Western art dance in the same way in which exotic dance forms are viewed and studied since it was written over three decades ago.

## The Birth of Dance Ethnology

Nearly two decades after the establishment of ethnomusicology as a discipline, a small group of dance scholars gathered together and founded the Conference on Research in Dance (CORD) in 1967, the same year that the first MA program was established at UCLA in dance ethnology. Like the ethnomusicology field, dance, too, was divided between a group of historians of Western dance traditions and those scholars who were dance ethnologists. It has proved an uneasy alliance that continues today, although the CORD organization has taken care to create a tent large enough to hold all of its members; nevertheless, a group of scholars who felt that their interests were insufficiently represented broke away from CORD to found the Society for Dance History Scholars (SDHS).

Unlike the fate of the ethnomusicologists, many of whom found ready employment in welcoming university and college campuses, dance ethnologists faced a field in which two decades before the development of dance ethnology an army of modern dance teachers promoted by universities like UCLA and armed with only a BA or an MA degree, gained a stranglehold on the university and college system of dance education throughout the United States. These modern dance teachers, many of whom have little scholarly knowledge of the field, overwhelmingly support the evolutionary notion that modern dance is the pinnacle of human dance creation. There is little or no room for classes in the teaching of world dance, or perhaps worse in the current age of multicultural impulses frequently supported by college and university administrations, a grudging concession to one or two classes per semester or quarter in bharata natyam, Mexican folk dance, or some form of West African dancing are provided with outside instructors to comply with new university standards. But serious programs of dance ethnology with tenured faculty are rigidly excluded from all but a few programs in the United States.

Allegra Fuller Snyder, who, together with Elsie Dunin, developed the UCLA dance ethnology program, which was effectively in place by 1970 with "a clearly structured sequence of classes," details the conceptual issues that confronted the establishment of the program (1992, 4). Snyder stated that in its beginnings "It is difficult to imagine how tenuous, alone, and undefined our horizons were when we first started.... It required a new way of thinking. It was the field of music, primarily ethnomusicology, that largely nurtured and finally midwifed this field. The field of anthropology was a more passive participant at the birthing" (*ibid.*, 5).

Adding to the problem of establishing a field of study was the paucity of scholarly literature. The first major article, "A Panorama of Dance Ethnology" by Gertrude Kurath, was published only in 1960. That article was seminal to the field. Allegra Snyder commented: "I still find this an amazing article because of the courage embedded in it. Kurath writes as if a field existed, but she was the field" (*ibid.*, 7). In reality, as Snyder observes, the basic extant literature existed of "limited 'case studies' and collections which lacked any comprehensive perspective." Kurath's article along with those case studies "was the field when we embarked on the program" (Snyder 1992, 7). Thus, the CORD conference of 1972 was critical as the beginning of the appearance of a critical mass of scholarly publications that now constitutes dance ethnology studies.

Snyder describes a series of theoretical and conceptual frameworks within which the instructors in the department ordered the orientation of their courses. The first of these was the conceptualization of dance. Folklorist Robert A. Georges developed the concept of framing in his seminal article, "Toward an Understanding of the Storytelling Event" (1969), and, following upon his important concept of framing an event in order to look at multiple aspects of performance, the audience reactions, the content of the story, etc., as a holistic event, dance studies largely followed the framed event of contextualization rather than focusing only on dance movement descriptions. But Snyder worried that through the contextualization model that was taken from anthropology that, by 1982, "we were losing our unique identity through too rigorous an adoption of that discipline's theory and methodology. Were we moving too far afield from the study of dance as a critical fact of human culture? I became concerned that too strong an anthropological position might eventually tip the balance away from dance altogether" (*ibid.*, 10–11).

Snyder's concerns echoed the musicological/anthropological debate that characterized the contestation in the field of ethnomusicology between Alan Merriam and Mantle Hood three decades earlier. The UCLA program placed an emphasis on students who could dance in order to kinesthetically feel the dance and this experiential aspect of dance became an important element of

Dancers of the Indonesian Performing Arts Association of Minnesota take a bow, 2003. Photograph by Petronella Ytsma. Courtesy of Anne Von Bibra Wharton.

the program. Other conceptual models derived from studies in linguistics and somatics were also explored.

Theresa J. Buckland notes of the dance ethnology program at UCLA: "Unlike studies of dance conducted from within departments of anthropology, here there was greater use of literature from the European disciplines of ethnology, ethnography, and folk life studies" (2006, 6). UCLA also differed from European dance ethnology programs: "In European ethnographic studies of dance, it was not necessary to question what conceptually constituted dance, since the object of inquiry was the dance of one's own culture. Another characteristic of European ethnographic study was the status of the past and its continuing relevance to the present" (*ibid.*). Also, Americans in the UCLA dance ethnology program, as well as those within American anthropology programs, unlike European, Middle Eastern, Asian, and African scholars, American students most often studied dance traditions that were not their own.

Dance ethnology, outside of the program at UCLA, never gained a secure place in academia, and for years the UCLA program offered only a MA degree to its students. Until recently, there was no Ph.D. program that was dance-centered in any American university until the University of California Riverside opened its Ph.D. program in 1993. Moreover, at this time the dance ethnology program at UCLA, like the rest of the dance program, was subsumed under the World Arts and Cultures program, which effectively diluted the dance ethnology program. This can be seen in the cessation of the *UCLA Journal of Dance Ethnology*, which had marked the vibrant activity of that department under Allegra Fuller Snyder's direction.

In addition, many dance departments on university and college campuses have a schizophrenic composition of classroom scholars and studio instructors. The twin goals for their faculty to produce performing dancers for the theater dance market while at the same time providing enough scholarly education to justify a university degree simply cannot be met in an equitable fashion. Thus, the dance departments experience tensions regarding where to place their financial and other resources in meeting these twin goals, that of the conservatory model preparing performers for professional ballet and modern dance companies and the university aim of producing scholars.

## Evolutionism Continues

Evolutionary concepts continued to plague both ethnomusicological and dance studies well into the post–World War II period. Ethnomusicologist Alan P. Merriam describes several studies made in the 1950s (1964, 284–286). Joann Kealiinohomku in 1969, as dance ethnology was forming as a discipline, lamented the widespread use of Curt Sachs' *World History of the Dance* (1937), a book that is notorious for its evolutionary organizational scheme that was out of date when it was published: "It is time for Sachs' book to be relegated to its proper place as a necessary but outmoded part of the history of dance scholarship in the western world" (1969, 90). Unfortunately, Kealiinomo-homoku's plea went unheard. More than thirty years later, Sachs' book is still found in both serious and popular dance writing (Shay and Sellers-Young 2005, 10–11; Shay and Sellers-Young 2003, 18–23).

Thirty years after the appearance of Curt Sachs' work, Alan Lomax produced his work on choreometrics (1968), a well-funded project reflecting Lomax's influence in the Smithsonian Institution's organization. Dance scholar Anya Peterson Royce characterized Lomax's questionable findings:

> Most of Lomax's conclusions support an evolutionary scaling of dance styles, from simple to complex, which is correlated with mode of subsistence. Pre-agriculturalists fall into the simple reversal type of transition, while agriculturalists employ more looping transitions. Lomax also finds that "primitive people employ a smaller number of body parts at any given moment in dance and everyday life than do people of complex cultures," (1968, 243), and that there exists an "extraordinary uniformity of movement style in any non-complex society" [*ibid.*, 230; [1972, 64].

Thus, in its beginnings, serious scholars had to wade into battle against the ghosts of quaint ideas and theoretical frameworks that would make contemporary scholars smile.

## Defining the Field of Dance Ethnology

In the field of dance ethnology, in which scholars found themselves in societies in which dance occurred but had no specific linguistic designation because dance activities were so entwined and deeply enmeshed in ritual, musical, and social events that the individuals of that society did not conceive of dance as a separate activity divorced from its context, scholars had to confront new ways of looking at and labeling dance and movement activities. Thus, for the first decade of dance ethnology, dance scholars expended a great deal of energy attempting to define what constituted dance and what constituted non-dance activities that were rhythmic and/or accompanied by music in a spectrum of varied societies, some of which had no word for "dance" (see Royce 1977), Chapter one of Royce's book summarizes the many thoughtful definitions of dance that would permit research in a cross cultural perspective. However, today the topic of what constitutes dance in crosscultural perspectives has largely been abandoned as an intellectual issue in dance studies.

Over the past thirty years, a number of scholars of a new generation produce works that span a wide spectrum of important studies that reflect both dance in the field and highly theoretically and conceptually sophisticated scholarship that is poised to make an impact in other areas of the social sciences and humanities.

# PART II: GENRES

## FIVE

# Kolomania: Balkan Dance as American Expression

FOR OVER TWO CENTURIES people in the West, that is, those few who had ever heard of those regions, regarded the Balkans as a site of primitiveness, wildness, and mystery. Before the nineteenth century most of the Balkans were backward outposts of either the Hapsburg or the Ottoman empires, and as such attracted no particular attention. But in the early nineteenth century, as revolutionaries in Serbia, Greece, Romania, and Montenegro established tiny impoverished kingdoms, their presence intruded, often annoyingly, into the arena of great power politics. The only bare knowledge of these remote regions came from little-known travel journals of a few intrepid travelers and adventurers, often on their way to Istanbul; their destination was not the Balkans.

That all changed when Lord Byron, the infamous British poet ("mad, bad, and dangerous to know"), traveled to Greece in the 1820s and championed the cause of the Greeks against the Ottoman Turks.[1] His contemporary, the poet Shelley, expressing solidarity with the cause of the rebellious Greeks that was a widely held sentiment in the West, said "We are all Greeks." Like many Western Europeans schooled in Ancient Greek literature, he was imagining the contemporary Greeks as the inheritors of the glories of ancient Greece struggling against the oriental Ottomans in his poem "Hellas" (Crompton 1985, 86).

In this chapter I will lay out the ways in which the Balkans came to be

imagined and perceived in the West.[2] This background constitutes a necessary viewpoint for understanding the way in which many of the Americans
who became involved in the Balkan folk dance movement created colorful
new identities for themselves.

The nineteenth-century reality of the Balkans appalled Byron, and a
multitude of other literary figures after him, who at first looked to find in
Greece the descendents of the glory of Classic Greece. Instead, they found
impoverished peasants and discovered that the highly vaunted local *hajduks*
and *klephts* were not the brave mountain revolutionaries of local epic poetry,
but rather common, vicious bandits who fought the Turks and plundered
and victimized their own ethnic kinsmen indiscriminately. As historian Maria
Todorova points out, "In practically every description, the standard Balkan
male is uncivilized, primitive, crude, cruel, and without exception, disheveled"
(1997, 14), thus establishing the Balkans as another region over which the
superior West might establish intellectual and political dominion. Another
Byron contemporary, the French viscount Chateaubriand, quipped, "Never
see Greece, Monsieur, except in Homer. It is the best way" (quoted in Todorova 1997, 94).

AVAZ International Dance Theatre performs dancers of Šumadija, Serbia, 1982.
Choreography by Anthony Shay. Photography by Darrell Young. Courtesy of
AVAZ IDT.

In the late nineteenth and early twentieth centuries a kind of orientalizing literary trend established the Balkans as a site for comic opera settings for novels, operettas, and poetry. Historian Larry Wolff comments: "One might describe the invention of Eastern Europe as an intellectual project of demi-Orientalization" (1994, 7). One must not forget the Gothic novel and the films derived from them, either. Bram Stoker's *Dracula* (1897), set in a mythologized Transylvania, emphasized the wildness of the peasant-strewn, superstition-bound landscape, further promoting the Balkans as a site of mystery and primitiveness. By the second half of the twentieth century the Balkans metamorphosed into a gritty battleground of the Cold War, a fertile site for adventure and spy novels by British authors such as Eric Ambler and John Le Carré.

Since the 1950s, especially after the 1956 appearances of Tanec, the Macedonian State Folk Dance Ensemble, followed in a few months by a major tour of Kolo, the Serbian State Folk Dance Ensemble, the first national folk ensembles from the Iron Curtain countries to perform regularly in the United States, hundreds and later thousands of young mainstream Americans discovered Balkan music and dance.[3] The dancers in these national ensembles were distinctly not disheveled, but clean-cut, dashing examples of Balkan manhood, appealing to many men in their audiences who wished to emulate their vibrant masculinity through the performance of heroic looking dances of Macedonia, Greece, and Bulgaria. In the wake of the appearances of the state supported dance ensembles in Los Angeles, San Francisco, New York, Boston, Seattle, Minneapolis, and other cities several mainstream Americans founded large-scale performing dance ensembles, singing groups, and orchestras, further popularizing the dances and music of Croatia, Bulgaria, Serbia, Macedonia, Greece, Slovenia, Romania, and Albania.

These performances provided many of the young Americans, experiencing a lack of ethnicity and roots in the mass post–World War II move to the suburbs, with their own "Different Village," in ethnomusicologist Mirjana Laušević's terms (1998). Performing in these ensembles was a life-changing experience for many of the participants, leading some of them into careers of teaching, performing, and scholarship. It is crucial to emphasize that these new American-Balkan ensembles were among the largest dance companies ever established in the United States; to perform Balkan dances "it takes a village," to paraphrase the old African saying. Most of the other exotic dance traditions that I describe and analyze in this book did not require such large numbers of performers for their successful evocation of other times and places; most of the other genres — tango, Asian classical forms, belly dance, flamenco — are solo or couples dance forms. For the most part these latter traditions constitute urban rather than rural village forms. Balkan dances, on the other hand, valorize peasants and rural life, which appealed to many in the "back to the earth" movement of the 1960s and 1970s.

Dick Crum was one of the pioneer teachers of dances from the Balkans in the United States, and throughout his fifty-year teaching career, which included numerous research trips to the Balkans,[4] he became preeminent in the large international recreational folk dance movement as a teacher and as a major source of knowledge and information about Balkan dances.[5] Frequently during his teaching he admonished the dancers who showed signs of "going native" that, however much they learned the dances and the language, ate the food, and steeped themselves in Bulgarian folklore that they could never become Bulgarian. Large-scale classes in which Crum as well as many others taught proliferated throughout the United States, including summer camps devoted to the teaching of folk dance and folk music, which became the emotional lifeblood of many of the participants (see Laušević 1998, 336–456).

Dick Crum was a product of the recreational international folk dance movement, as were many of us who entered the Balkan dance movement. Laušević noted that 37 percent of her respondents in her study came through the Recreational International Folk Dance movement and ended by specializing in dances of the Balkans. The process seemed at the time a natural step up into a more advanced stage of recreational folk dancing, but in fact it was qualitatively very different. It was intense rather than casual, and for most participants occupied far more time and effort.

## Ethnicity and Nationalism

Folklore, the "true" and "authentic" expression of the "people," became a major cornerstone in the production of nationalist mythologies of ethnic origins and their accompanying historical and territorial entitlements. This late eighteenth-century romantic concept, most forcefully enunciated by Johann Gottfried Herder and felt to our day, endorsed the study of folklore as the primary means for understanding the basic ethos of each specific ethnic group. In this concept the peasantry constituted the true, uncontaminated source of knowledge of a nation's history and origins, a continuation of romantic thought.

This philosophy of the Romantic period of the late eighteenth century, and throughout the nineteenth century and into the twentieth century, inspired the massive collection of tales, songs, beliefs, music, and, lastly, dance throughout Central and Eastern Europe that continues unabated today. Governments (national, regional, and local) throughout the Balkans, on both sides of the Iron Curtain, established national dance companies following the Moiseyev model of the USSR, and supported massive amateur dance and music activities and festivals to demonstrate folklore. The national companies of all of these countries, under the careful guidance of the state apparatus, produced sanitized picture postcard choreographies that underscored the positive image of each titular national group, while frequently suppressing or distorting the images of undesirable minorities (see Maners 2006; Rice 1994; Shay 2002).

Clearly, the performance of folk songs and dances, whether by a professional national state ensemble, one of the many state-supported amateur dance companies, or by peasants in regional folk dance festivals, serves to underline the unique ethnic character of particular ethnic communities, justifying their right to occupy the "original" homeland in which these forms of music, dance, and costumes, widely perceived as timeless, primordial, and unique to a specific ethnic group, occur. This body of cultural expression constitutes icons of national and ethnic identity.

## The Generic Balkans

Thus, identity in the form of ethnicity and nationalism quickly assumes an important sociological and historical dimension of any study of Balkan folklore. Sometimes the performance of music and dance, in specific regional costumes, attains an iconic status of ethnicity, and sometimes it can assume the representation of the nation state. Presentations of folk dance in the Balkans are never about the Balkans as a generic location, but about specific ethnicities and nations. However, and this is crucial to an understanding of the American participation in this genre, for most Americans performing dances from Balkan regions, particularly in the beginning phases of learning them, the dances and music often remained and continue to be generically "Balkan" rather than belonging to a specific ethnicity.

Ethnicity, in the sense that we currently use it — a cluster of elements defining a collectivity of individuals such as, but not limited to, a specific name and identity recognized by both insiders and outsiders, specific languages, a common ancestry (often mythological), a common historical territory, a common religion, and shared folkloric expressions of tales, music, dance, and costumes — is new. According to historians of nationalism John Hutchinson and Anthony D. Smith, the modern concept of ethnicity is recent and only "first recorded in the Oxford English Dictionary in 1953" (1996, 5). In the Balkans folk dances are regarded as ethnically specific rather than generically "Balkan" in folk dancers' parlance. Thus the performance of dances and music of the various regions of the Balkans constitutes a different meaning when American performers become Balkan peasants.

# The Nation and Nationalism

Nationalism in the Balkans frequently descends to jingoism and murderous chauvinism, as the recent breakup of the former Yugoslavia demonstrates. Nationalism constitutes a stage beyond ethnic consciousness — a demand for territory with all of the panoply of the nation-state: armed forces, state controlled educational systems, national languages, as well as less attractive characteristics of obedience to the state such as forced adherence to a state sponsored religion, banning linguistic use of other than officially approved languages, wearing special clothing, etc. In the Balkans the establishment of nation states came late compared to Western Europe.

Thus, for people in the Balkans, as in many areas of the world, the research through dances and music, costumes and folk tales establishes a patrimony, a primordial link with the "original" settlers of their land, which in turn establishes their authentic claim to the territory they inhabit: a nation of their own. Cultural historian Alexander Kiossev says of folklore studies: "It was taken for granted that the spatial span of the national 'fruits' coincided in a natural way with the boundaries of the imagined homeland. Thus these academic disciplines in fact reaffirmed the national mapping (and the official national identity) and were even used to justify territorial claims" (2002, 176). The search for the historic moment that a particular ethnic group put its collective feet on the national territory constitutes a major aim of historic and folkloric research — the basis for national identity — and occupies much of the scholarly output from the various Balkan countries. People ignore, or are ignorant of, the fact that ethnicity is historically contingent and malleable, not the fixed identity that they believe.

# The Balkans: Orientalism and Balkanism

Edward Said (1979) and Michel Foucault (1972) exposed the construction of the imaginary, for example the Western imaginary of "The Orient," as a systematic means of knowing, a means of establishing a sense of superiority and dominating the "Other." The Western imaginary of the Balkans, less well known than that of the Orient, has taken two distinct forms, what I will call the "comic opera" and the "noble (savage) warrior peasant" who will commit violence only in defense of his nation and his hearth. They both stem from the Romantic images of the Balkans created by Western travelers and writers, and both images feature singing, dancing peasantries. These two threads occasionally meet. The origins of this romantic turn can be traced to the comic-opera–like career of George Gordon, Lord Byron, who literary scholar Vesna Goldsworthy characterized as "by far the most important figure in the Romantic discovery of the Balkans in English literature" (1998, 16).

It has become fashionable for some scholars to characterize the western perception of the Balkans as a sort of orientalism known as "balkanism." While sharing some of the characteristics of orientalism, such as essentializing the Balkans so that, Agatha Christie, for example, could create the tongue-in-cheek comic-opera "Kingdom of Herzoslovakia" (1987) for her mystery novel *Secret of Chimneys* and Anthony Hope's mythical Ruritania became shorthand for the comic opera Balkan state. I have already mentioned Bram Stoker's *Dracula* and the films made from the novel, which contributed to the fuzzy image of the Balkans as a location of deep superstition and Hollywood-garbed, generalized Balkan peasants.

Nevertheless, there is a major difference between orientalism and balkanism: The Orient is a feminized place, epitomized by veiled women and the harem. The Orient is fecund and sexually available, largely created through the male gaze of such authors as Gustave Flaubert (see Karayanni, 2004). By contrast, the Balkans is a masculinized place, peopled in Byronian terms by brave and true (preferably mountain dwelling) warriors, as venerated and largely created by Rebecca West, Olivia Manning, and Edith Durham through what I suggest we may characterize as the "female gaze." Women hardly appear in their accounts; it is a man's world.

Another crucial difference exists: Major visual artists went in great numbers to North Africa, Egypt, the Holy Land, and Turkey and painted a vast array of romantic paintings, followed by Broadway and Hollywood orientalist productions like *Kismet* and *The Sheik*, from which westerners could construct orientalist views. No such corpus of works exists for the Balkans, thus creating an empty space for the construction of fantasies and images.

The comic opera image of the Balkans has been an enduring aspect of adventure novels like Agatha Christie's *Secret of Chimneys*, modeled loosely after the lurid events of 1903 in Serbia, during which the Obrenović dynasty was literally thrown out of the palace window by members of the Black Hand (the Red Hand in Christie's oeuvre), who hacked the king and his commoner wife, Draga, to pieces in a sensational *coup d'état*. It is not only contemporary Eastern European scholars who object to this orientalist approach to depicting the Balkans and reducing its inhabitants to quaint peasants. In 1913, when Franz Lehar used Montenegro as a "model for the comic Ruritanian-style kingdom of Pontevedro" in *The Merry Widow*, Montenegrin students in Vienna angrily demonstrated at its premiere in Vienna (Ash 2006, B11).

The other literary line of the Balkan imaginary is best characterized by the novels of Eric Ambler: the cold, skulking, lurid world of spies. In these novels, Sofia, the Bulgarian capital, frequently serves as the model for the typical Eastern European/Balkan sinister locale for the gray world of Cold War espionage and treachery.

Goldsworthy points out that the famous writer Lawrence Durrell demeaned the Balkans with the creation of Vulgaria, which he describes as "an unspeakable place full of unspeakable people" (1998, 142), and that "Durrell's stories are, in fact, fairly ruthless in exploiting a multitude of prejudices about the Balkans" (1998, 143). Needless to say, this aspect of Balkan life was of little interest and remained largely unknown to the majority of young Americans who were enthralled with Balkan dance and music.

## Balkan Music and Dance

It would be difficult to characterize the dazzling variety of choreographic and musical diversity found throughout the Balkans from Slovenia in the northwest to Turkey in southeast and Romania to the north and the Greek Islands in the southwest. While solo forms of music and dance exist, these forms and music dance are overwhelmingly communal. It is the great variety of these choreographic and musical forms found in a comparatively small area that many observers and participants find so compelling.

The most widespread choreographic form throughout the Balkans are group dances characterized morphologically by closed and open circle dances and line dances, mostly featuring short choreographic footwork sequences. These are called *kolo* or *horo(a)* in most of these regions. In some areas such as Croatia, Slovenia, the Greek Islands, and Romania couple dances are also popular. These latter forms tend to be historically newer forms, including polkas and waltzes, but many indigenous forms are also found throughout the Greek and Croatian coastal regions and islands, for example.

Solo forms such as the *çifte telli* (Turkish), *tsiftetelli* (Greek), and *čoček* or *kyuchek* (Serbia, Macedonia, Bulgaria) constitute a popular urban genre of solo improvised dance, and a musical genre, a legacy of Ottoman culture, that many subsume under the belly dance genre (Shay and Sellers-Young 2005, 2). This solo improvised dance form's association with the Turkish and Ottoman past, and its contemporary association with the Roma (Gypsies) create ethnic and generational tensions in the Balkans, especially since young people are frequently rebelliously attracted to these solo dance genres because of their negative erotic and ethnic connotations. Alexander Kiossev notes: "In the last decade ... a new mass taste for the old belly dance developed, new-old small taverns and kafanas opened, a new type of arrogant Balkan intimacy haunted the air. The most important symptom of this process was the lack of popular will to be Westernlike" (2002, 184). And, of course, the solo *zembekikos* performed by Anthony Quinn in *Zorba the Greek* remains an icon of Balkan dance, in all of its heroic and earthy aspect, for many tourists who flock to Athens for the "Zorba experience."

Of great musical and choreographic interest and excitement for many in the West is the spectacular proliferation of asymmetric rhythms — 5/4, 5 × 5/4, 5/8, 7/8, 9/8, 11/16, 13/16, among others — that characterize many dance and musical genres of the Balkans. While largely associated with East and South Serbia, Macedonia, Greece, and Bulgaria, they can also be found in Croatia and Romania.

Musically, in addition to the rhythmic varieties, unique harmonies in non-tempered scales have created worldwide interest, especially with the information age popularization of the "Voix Bulgares" Bulgarian female vocal ensemble through numerous live concerts throughout the world and CDs. Unique harmonies not familiar to most Westerners can be found in Croatia, Bosnia, Bulgaria, and Macedonia, among other regions. Familiar Western harmonic forms are also found in those costal regions of Greece such as the island of Corfu, where the men perform a vocal genre known as *cantadhda* and Croatian Dalmatia where men's groups perform vocal *klapa* music, both Italian derived musical forms that show the centuries-long political domination of Venice in these areas. Many solo forms, such as the musically sophisticated urban *sevdah* genre of urban Bosnia, with its complex melismas, showing Turkish influences, as well as natively developed solo vocal and instrumental genres also exist in profusion.

The unusual aspect of rhythmic construction of various Balkan musical and choreographic forms attracted many young American dancers with backgrounds in mathematics and engineering. Laušević found that 43 percent of the men in her statistical cohort had science/engineering/computer professional backgrounds (1998, 372). I vividly remember listening to the lively discussions among dancers, especially males, who listened with fascination to the newest recordings and attempted to parse the rhythmic breakdown of a new Bulgarian or Macedonian dance melody.

## Balkan Music and Dance in America

One of the incidents that inspired me to write this study occurred in Bulgaria in 2005. I found myself on a folkloric tour with a group of aging Balkan dancers and enthusiasts, among whom I must count myself. As our bus pulled out of the relative sophistication of Sofia, the capital, some of the women began donning embroidered blouses, head scarves and other items of peasant clothing. At every hotel stop, someone took out a boom box and most of the members of the tour performed Bulgarian folk dances for the nearby Bulgarians, many of whom seemed considerably startled but by no means displeased by the vision of a group of Americans performing their dances. We were on our way to the small mountain town of Koprivshtitsa where a pan–Bulgarian folklore festival is held every five years. It is a Mecca for the American Balkan dancer. An absolute feast of dancing, singing, and music from all over Bulgaria was served like a smorgasbord for a hungry crowd of Balkan dancers. The festival organizers built a special stage, somewhat away from the main performance area, for the foreign groups who performed Bulgarian music and song. Except for one entry from Japan and one from Australia, the rest of the Balkan enthusiasts were Americans. They danced with peasants in the mountain fields, hotel lobbies and courtyards, and the town square — wherever they could indulge in their beloved dances. And here in the heart of Bulgaria some of them could feel themselves to be Bulgarian

One morning as we were eating breakfast, one of the aging Balkan hand-maidens of the tour leader came to breathlessly announce, "Today we are going to visit a village and see real Bulgarians." "Do you mean to tell me that all of the people that I have been seeing in the streets are fake Bulgarians?" I inquired. The acolyte looked at me scornfully: "I mean we are going to see *real* peasants."

Thousands of young Americans not only undertook learning the dances, songs, and music that they heard and saw performed by national dance and musical ensembles of the Balkans, they sometimes eagerly embraced learning the languages, embroidery patterns, cuisines and other pleasurable aspects of Balkan life as well. They frequently fantasized being Balkan peasants, whom many Americans imagined to be near kin to Rousseau's "noble savage." The Age of Aquarius, which *Wikipedia* characterizes as "the Heyday of the Hippie and New Age 'movement' of the 1960s and 1970s," was epitomized by the anthem-like song, "The Age of Aquarius" from the 1967 blockbuster *Hair*. Many young people of that period were facing a Brave New World, rejecting what they regarded as the repressive, stultifying, and antiseptic 1950s. Balkan peasants appeared to many disaffected young Americans as an alternative to a gray existence: noble, stoic agriculturalists, primitively attired in stunningly colorful costumes and dancing and singing their lives away in quaint villages to celebrate bountiful harvests and fruitful weddings: in other words, "real people," untainted by the city, an image promoted by the national dance ensembles. Many of the people on the tour I described above were from that generation and still fervently clung to this belief.

This period was the inception of the "New Age" and one could conveniently forget about the unpleasant and insalubrious sanitary arrangements, backbreaking field work, illiteracy, and bitter poverty that was the lot of many of the actual Balkan peasants. The imaginary, as portrayed on the stages on which the national ensembles performed, trumped reality. After all, it was well known that Americans were notoriously ignorant of geography, and courses in Balkan history and geography were only rarely taught even in graduate programs in American educational institutions, and thus the "empty space" of the Balkans provided many individuals a site onto which they could inscribe their own fantasies and images.[6]

This was a time a period when many middle class youth sought alternative lifestyles and founded communes (in total ignorance of agricultural science); thus "village life" was celebrated for its simplicity, its pristine innocence, its avoidance of empty materialism, and, above all, its connections to the soil.

It is important to note that in the beginning of the period in the late 1950s and early 1960s, Balkan dance was an essentialized dance genre with "Croatian" or "Macedonian" variants for many eager young hobbyists. This concept was made manifest in a film, *Balkan Dancing*, created by dance teacher Mario Casetta, in which the young narrator, Steve Murillo, talks about "Balkan" dancing throughout the documentary that featured dances from Croatia, Bulgaria, Macedonia, and other regions.

One informant declared that "I envied the closeness and warmth of the Greeks" (Louise Anderson-Bilman January 26, 2003). This sentiment was echoed over and over again by many individuals involved in learning and performing Balkan dances and they eagerly embraced an exotic form of cultural expression in an effort to obtain the warmth they thought characterized Balkan village life. Ethnomusicologists Mirjana Laušević documents many of her American informants involved in the performance of Balkan dance and music expressing a sense of anomie and searching for a more colorful and "authentic" way of life filled with warmth and exciting music, dances, and costumes twenty-five and thirty years after my similar experiences (Laušević 1998).

By the 1960s an explosion of recordings by the Philip Koutev Ensemble of Bulgaria and LADO, the Ensemble of Folk Songs and Dances of Croatia, among a myriad variety of performances by Eastern European dance and music ensembles, increased the visibility and popularity of folk dances and music of the Balkans to the point that many college and university campuses and civic locations throughout America became sites for its performance. Enthusiastic individuals in some large cities founded coffee houses devoted to teaching dance, particularly Balkan dances, but also featured related forms of circle and line dances such as Greek and Israeli dances. "A couple of friends took me to Zorba's (one of the Los Angeles coffee houses) and I became hooked" (Stephanie Cowans). My own experiences in the Bay area and Southern California showed that hundreds of young men and women pursued this passion for Balkan dance night after night in these venues and other locales.

AVAZ International Dance Theatre performs dances of Pokuplje, Croatia, 1985.
Choreography by Anthony Shay. Photography by Darrell Young. Courtesy AVAZ
IDT.

While many young American men, who were frequently peace activists,
were overwhelmingly attracted to the machismo of the showier men's dances
in a Walter Mitty fashion, young women, occasionally frustrated by the sec-
ondary role of women in many dances, carved a feminist niche in the vocal
production of many Balkan musical genres such as Bulgarian and Croatian
songs, which featured unique harmonic and rhythmic elements that were
popularized by the performances of the Koutev ensemble and LADO. The
recordings of these ensembles inspired the founding of many women's singing
groups specializing in Balkan musical genres in America over the past half
century.

As ethnomusicologist Timothy Rice eloquently wrote of his own early
experiences of Balkan music and dance:

> In this world [the world of "international folk dancing"] we manipulated Bul-
> garian music, and particularly our dancing to it, as symbols that helped us
> establish new friendships, demonstrate our attractiveness and attractions to oth-
> ers, enjoy the physical and mental exertion of maintaining repeated aesthetic
> patterns in the body, and create a sense of small-scale community within the
> vastness of American society [1994, 4].

The intensity of this community feeling, especially for those in performing ensembles who spent many days a week in each other's company, is difficult to convey. Joan Acocella, in her description of the company of Balkan dance in which modern dancer Mark Morris participated as a teen-ager, writes: "Koleda [a Balkan dance company directed by Dennis Boxell] was like a sixties commune, and the project on which they were embarked was itself a symbol of community. Holding hands in a circle, dancing and singing in harmony, they made art out of friendship and friendship out of art" (1994, 29). The members of all of these companies bonded in a psychological manner that, in their minds, approximated the closeness that one must surely feel for one's fellow villagers if one lived in the Balkans: "'Koleda was like a little village' says one of its former singers, Jill Johnson" (Acocella 1994, 27).

This feeling of closeness was enhanced by the weeks of performing and touring for those of us intimately involved in concert work. Tomie Hahn describes the energy flow that came from audiences in Japanese *nihon buyo* performances: "Onstage, when mental and physical coordinations effortlessly 'flow,' a dancer can use the heightened state of ultimate embodiment of dance" (2007, 165). *Nihon buyo* is a solo form of dance, while Balkan dance builds its stage presence and "flow" through large numbers of performers interacting. The flow and the ensuing closeness and the feeling of being bonded

AVAZ International Dance Theatre performs dances of the Thracian region of Bulgaria, 1982. Choreography by Anthony Shay. Photography by Darrell Young. Courtesy of AVAZ IDT.

among the performers, and the energy which results from that ensemble closeness, projects to the audience: "It was like someone turned my electricity on
high" (Chrisy Whiting, personal interview, June 28, 2007).

A former member of AVAZ, Daniel Strout, recalls his performing experiences and how close the performers were. The bonding forged a unit of the
AVAZ members:

> Spend ten hours a week rehearsing with a group of twenty or so people for a
> few years and things form. The closest English word for this psychic group
> intuition is empathy, but it shorts the reality. After months of collective needle-
> work, a new set of dances from Pokuplje [Croatia] was ready for the stage and
> the suite was made part of that tour's program. (The women's headpieces were
> these amazing encrustations of beading and tiny mirrors that no fingers, male or
> female, escaped from working on.) The performance that evening was going
> well. The opening slow women's circle dance under a downlight bounced
> enough light from those headpieces to impress the blind. It ended, the on-stage
> band picked up the music for the men's entrance and we were off and running.
> At the end of the men's entrance pattern the band members somehow dropped
> four full bars of the choreographed music. And without a blink of hesitation or
> a moment's cross glance, the twenty-one people on stage instantly dropped the
> matching four bars of choreography and picked up at the exact same spot of the
> dance. The on-stage fix was so instantaneous it was invisible to the audience
> and suspected by only some of the watchers in the wings. I am still impressed
> by the company for this one! [personal interview, June 15, 2007].

Audience members frequently commented how they felt that energy and
enthusiasm, and, in fact, it was that energy which drew them to the performance. It was also that energy which drew so many of us in the Balkan dance
scene to the artistic, rather than recreational, aspect of performing these dances
that we regarded as magical.

Thus, through the various images of the Balkans, many young mainstream Americans sought through Balkan music and dance a means of acquiring, if only temporarily, new and exotic identities. And yet, this phenomenon remains hidden from view in contemporary society. Stephanie Cowans
notes:

> In spite of unrelenting teasing by my family (who were somewhat embarrassed
> at my interest in ethnic dance, since this was not exactly "mainstream" like bal-
> let or tap or modern), I finally felt like I was *good* at something and that I was
> appreciated. None of my family ever came to see me perform while I was in
> AVAZ ... never. They never wanted to hear me sing and dance "that weird
> stuff" and they probably still don't know/acknowledge that I can sing [personal
> interview, July 6, 2007].

Katina Shields notes that her major friendships were formed during the years
in which she performed in AVAZ and the Intersections dancers: "Folks who

never need to ask why I dance" (personal interview, July 11, 2007). Lauševic remarked in beginning her study of American participation in Balkan music:

> Locating and situating these scenes is often more complex that is usually the case in traditional studies of local music, due to the often ephemeral nature of scene "membership" and the multiple geographic and virtual locations in which scenes develop and live. The places and faces of most importance to insiders are largely irrelevant and unknown even to people living right next door. Even participants' friends, coworkers, and family members are often oblivious to their involvement in such a scene. Yet, by many, this private identity is held more dearly than their more public identities [2007, 17].

Participation in Balkan musical and dance performing ensembles heightened this awareness of acquiring a new identity because the individual "embodied" the Balkans and became, if only for a short moment, a Balkan dancer. "I don't recall ever having 'stage fright,' because, being in costume, I felt like I wasn't presenting me; I was presenting the persona of a Bulgarian/Croatian/Macedonian/Hungarian villager and I was letting the audience into my world" (Stephanie Cowans, personal interview, July 6, 2007). This ability of inscribing new identities, as Rice points out, was often, at least in the beginning, facilitated by the very lack of knowledge that most Americans had of Balkan peoples and their history.

Popular folk dance instructor Yves Moreau undertook a study of Balkan dance and music and "estimated that in 1990 well over 100,000 people participated in Balkan music and dance in the United States alone. Moreau's longstanding experience throughout North America makes his claim quite believable" (Lauševic 2007, 19). Such figures tally with my own observations as well.

Most of the large dance ensembles are now gone, or greatly diminished, although the musical ensembles continue. But for those of us who lived through that time, dances and music of the Balkans created a passport to one of the most colorful periods of our lives.

# SIX

# Belly Dance:
# Embodied Orientalism[1]

IT HAS BEEN ESTIMATED that at one point in the 1970s over a million women dedicated themselves to learning belly dancing in the United States, a trend that reached its peak during the second wave of feminism. "By 1979, ABC television's news program *20/20* reported that more than one million women in the United States were taking belly dance classes" (Sellers-Young 1992, 143). Thus, over the period this study focuses on (1950s to the present), hundreds of thousands of individuals took up belly dancing as an activity. Like Balkan dancing, belly dancing reached its peak numbers in the decades of the 1970s and 1980s and has slowly faded from those peak figures. Nevertheless, there still remain very large numbers of women who still participate in this dance genre.[2]

Such numbers of individuals certainly place belly dance as one of the most popular genres of exotic dance forms through which Americans seek alternate identities that I analyze in this volume. Unlike most of the other genres of exotic dance, the search for new, exotic identities is heightened by the way in which women select Middle Eastern names, or at least romantic names that sound as if they might be Middle Eastern, in order to heighten their exotic new identity.[3] Such an impulse was not characteristic of the vast majority of those who participated in Balkan dancing or classical Asian dance forms. Belly dance journals appealed to, and continue to appeal to, this exotic and orientalist gesture:

> Terms such as "allure," "mystique," and "fantasy" abound in advertisements and articles in belly dance publications. Most of the American and European practitioners of Oriental dance take on romantic Arab-esque names: Zoheret, Chandra, Samisha, Chantel, and Mahala are a few appearing in the advertisements in *Arabesque* (May–June 1986, 31–33), where you are invited to purchase "The Cleopatra Headdress for the Egyptian Goddess in You" [Shay and Sellers-Young 2003, 27].

There were several sociological factors that surfaced in American life in the late 1960s and early 1970s that contributed to the popularity of belly dance, or oriental dance and *raqs sharqi* (Arabic for oriental or eastern dance), as many practitioners prefer to call it in order to give the genre more respectability and diminish its overt sexual references and emphasize what they perceive as its artistic and aesthetic aspects.

First, the sexual revolution made it "all right," even desirable, for women to explore the sensual aspects of their bodies and to proudly display them in public venues. Many writers like Daniella Gioseffi (*Earth Dancing: Mother Nature's Oldest Dance*, 1980) lectured and wrote widely of the appeal of belly dance for women who wanted to "get in touch" with the sexual side of their personality; it was "natural" for women to enhance their sexuality and get in touch with their "female power" through the vehicle of belly dancing. In short, belly dance was viewed as empowering for women, and in a manner that they viewed as "feminine" (see Osweiler 2001; Sellers-Young 1992).

This attitude, an aspect of the sexual revolution, stood in stark contrast to the beginning of the twentieth century. In the early part of the twentieth century, film studies scholar Gaylyn Studlar noted:

> Dance as a "classic" art stood as an ideal symbolic merger between traditional middle-class female gentility and contemporary ideals of feminine freedom from bodily and imaginative restraints. In similar fashion as dance, fan magazines, like other "women's" magazines, attempted to chart a course between affirming the need to embrace the modern while simultaneously upholding traditional sexual and familial values. It followed that fan magazine's strategies for depicting actresses rarely made use of costumes and sexually suggestive poses evoking the harem dance girl and her presumed function for the male gaze [1997, 113].

By the latter part of the twentieth century, feminism challenged the male gaze by the use of those very same images. One aspect of belly dance that appealed to many women was the perception that its performance gave them control over the male gaze, rather than the feeling that they were subjected to it, a perception that many belly dance enthusiasts have expressed. For example, this perception of empowerment constituted the manner in which the American Tribal Dance company Fat Chance, as documented by Barbara Sellers-Young, became an outgrowth of cabaret dancing. In her description and analysis of the Fat Chance belly dance group, Sellers-Young notes: "As one might assume, the name of the company, Fat Chance, is Carolena's [Neroccio] challenge to the male voyeur" (2005, 286).

Second, other writers like Iris Stewart (*Sacred Dance, Sacred Woman: Awakening Spirituality Through Dance and Ritual*, 2000), linked belly dance to the New Age movement that was a feature of the counterculture of the period through the valorization of belly dance as an ancient and timeless vehicle, a

Noted oriental dancer Shareen El Safy performs at the El Leil Nightclub, Cairo, Egypt, 1989. Courtesy of Shareen El Safy.

form of spirituality for women to worship the earth goddesses through dance and ritual. In this manner, the performance of belly dance became almost a sacred and spiritual duty for many feminist women to attune themselves to the divine feminine.

Third, the sudden proliferation of classes in colleges, community centers, churches, YWCA centers, and dance studios advertised belly dance as both healthful and easy to learn, not only in large urban centers but also in small towns and cities throughout America. In many large American cities, the proliferation of ethnic Arab, Armenian, Greek, and Iranian restaurants in the 1960s and 1970s provided venues for experiencing belly dancing, attracting many new dancers, and providing employment for others. Teachers and writers of belly dance also produced a number of popular videos and how-to books that aided in popularizing this dance activity.[4] Today, also contributing to its continuing popularity, YouTube is awash in belly dance performances of all stripes, professional and amateur.

Unlike the Balkans, which constituted an empty space upon which Americans could inscribe new imaginary fantasy identities and visions for themselves, the Middle East formed a geographic, historical, and fantasy space that was over-determined and filled to brimming with orientalist images of harem girls, oversexed sheiks à la Rudolf Valentino, mosques and minarets provided by paintings, novels, Broadway musicals, Hollywood films, advertisements and other genres of popular culture that date back more than a century.[5] These were augmented in the 1950s by new popular domesticated images of *Kismet* and *I Dream of Jeannie*, which made the harem girl and her quintessential belly dance safe for the hordes of middle class white women escaping the humdrum life of suburbia who largely filled belly dance classes while seeking exciting exotic experiences and a fun method of physical fitness.

Unlike Balkan dancers, who tend to cluster locally in cities like Boston, Washington, San Francisco, and Los Angeles, belly dancers constituted a close-knit national community through an intensive network of conventions, retreats, and classes, idolized instructors, international and national journals like *Habibi* and *Arabesque*, as well as several regional newsletters, and more recently, the Internet, which currently hosts over 300 sites. Large conventions and fairs like Southern California's Cairo Carnivale and the Ahlan wa Sahlan Dance Festival held annually in Cairo, featuring classes, workshops, lavish concerts and a veritable bazaar of vendors of baubles, bangles, and beads, dvds that feature performances by famous belly dancers and teaching videos, cds of Arab music, costumes, and other items, convene regularly and attracting both regional and national visitors. Superior dancers are awarded prizes during these events and receive accolades in the oriental dance journals, which report extensively on these events.

# American Belly Dance: The New Dance Genre

In this chapter I am going to propose a radical, or at least alternative, argument that the style of belly dancing which attracted millions of Americans, overwhelmingly female, in the 1970s is not an ancient, or even a very old choreographic genre, but rather a modern choreographic development. This idea did not originate with me. Paul Monty (1986) suggested such a link because, in his view, Serena, one of the dancers he profiles in his dissertation, studied with Ruth St. Denis and utilized some of St. Denis' impressionistic choreographic strategies in her concert work and in teaching classes.

However, I am going to suggest that, while Monty's link may have some relevance, even more important reasons exist for the widespread acceptance of "modern" belly dancing by hundreds of thousands of Western women in the 1970s, and the rejection of authentic belly dancing at the turn of the century. Those reasons are: (1) The nineteenth-century version of the dance seen in the West had no aesthetic resonance with Western audiences; they preferred instead orientalist adaptations and interpretations by Western dancers like Ruth St. Denis, Maud Allan, and Loïe Fuller; (2) The virulent racism that existed in America categorized Arabs as an unacceptable class of non-whites, and thus their dance was regarded with suspicion as lascivious and, more importantly, as a cultural production of the lower "Other." (3) Women dancing in public in the early part of the twentieth century was equated with prostitution in the early period, as I detailed in the chapter on the early pioneers of oriental dance. Middle class and elite women rarely appeared on public stages or other performing venues at that time. By the 1950s and later that had changed, mostly through appearances by the early pioneer dancers like Ruth St. Denis and popular culture figures like Irene Castle and Adele Astaire, Fred Astaire's sister and early dance partner, which created a respectable aura for the professional dancer.

I argue that modern belly dance as we know it today constitutes a parallel tradition with dance practices of the nineteenth century, and perhaps earlier, and constitutes a new dance genre. By parallel tradition, I refer to a practice that references past practices but, in fact, constitutes an almost new genre of dance which retains only a small portion of elements from past dance performances (see Shay 2002, 17–21; 2005, 9–14). A recent example of this phenomenon is the way in which the Broadway blockbuster *Riverdance* references Irish jigging and step dancing from the past but, in fact, constitutes an almost entirely new dance genre.

Dance scholar Joan L. Erdman was one of the first to note: "'Oriental dance' was an occidental invention" (1996, 288). Erdman characterizes the Western oriental dance:

By the 1920s, oriental dance conjured up expectations of exotic movements, glittering costumes, flowing lines, sublime dedication, and minor mode or strangely tuned music. Certain features were perceived as essential: fluid boneless arm and shoulder motion, rhapsodic spirituality, rare and wondrously vibrant jewelry, and hand movements intended to signal more than graceful posturing. Dancing feet were often bare, women's midriffs were usually uncovered, and men danced bare chested in draped or bloused pantaloons [1996, 288].

Erdman's description certainly captures many of the main features of contemporary belly dancing as seen in both Egypt and the West. However, it is of great interest that her article addresses the origin of the modern movement of reinventing classical dance traditions in India. But those early westernized orientalist visions of "authentic" Indian dance were soon abandoned in favor of seeking and developing native dance traditions that characterized the development of classical dance in India. Erdman notes that "In India, however, oriental dance meant dance from Europe.... These oriental dances were never mistaken by Indians for their own dance forms; rather they were appreciated as attempts by artistes to stage dance with Indian themes and costumes" [1996, 289].

Thus, soon after the exposure to oriental dance à la Ruth St. Denis, Maud Allan, and Sergei Diaghilev's Ballets Russes that occurred in the period 1900-1925, Indians imbued with a search for native-based dance traditions quickly rejected these quaint western-inspired artistic productions: "In India by 1934 Uday Shankar and his Company of Hindu Dancers and Musicians were perceived as presenting oriental dance from Europe, not quite Indian, and certainly not authentic" (Erdman 1996, 295).

I suggest that Erdman's astute observations actually better and more accurately characterize current belly dance practices, which developed in Egypt around the same period as the development of contemporary bharata natyam. As I mentioned earlier, the orientalist productions of the early pioneer oriental dancers, in the manner of orientalism detailed by Said, consisted of movements and elements from Egypt, Persia, India, Java, Bali, and the Far East, indiscriminately combined in a kind of choreographic pastiche. As Amy Koritz noted of Maud Allan's performances in 1908, "Her Salome was not Egyptian, Algerian, or Syrian, but 'Eastern' in a vague homogenizing sense of the word" (1997, 144). From these elements, which Erdman astutely claims came from Western theater dance, as performed by Ruth St. Denis, Maud Allan, and Loie Fuller, as well as movements and choreographic strategies from Hollywood films and classical ballet, belly dancers in Egypt adapted many of the elements of movement and costume as their very own for purposes of performing in the new contexts of formal, Western proscenium stages, westernized night clubs, and the burgeoning Egyptian cinema.

As cinema historian Matthew Bernstein notes, "Modern dance — as evidenced in both the Ballet Russes and the performances of the Denishawn troupe — provided Hollywood with a powerful model for visualizing Orientalism (and gave the movies connotations of high-art respectability)" (1997, 6). He adds: "Most decisively of all for the cinema, Serge Diaghilev's Ballets Russes, with its staging of *Cléopatre*, *Thamar*, and *Schéhérazade*, which toured in the United States in the teens, contributed decisively to the mise-en-scène of Orientalist cinema" (*ibid.*, 4).

I would argue that these were not performances of "modern" dance but impressionistic imaginings of the Orient; a genre that might be better termed as interpretive dance. These choreographies were not only decisive for the way in which the American film industry depicted oriental dancing, since Ruth St. Denis and Ted Shawn and the Denishawn company appeared in several of these orientalist productions, but also for the way in which oriental dancers represented themselves in both Egypt beginning in the 1920s and later in America.

Dancers like Badi'a Masabni, Tahia Carioca, and Samia Gamal, among many others, eagerly embraced these westernized creations of a romantic Orient and created what for all intents and purposes became a new genre of dance, based on the torso articulations for which the dance was originally named and other native elements of solo improvised dance that came naturally to these Egyptian artists, but also heavily embellished by Western staging and choreographic techniques, especially the use of new costuming, lighting, and the use of space introduced into the new Egyptian form through Hollywood films and Western theater and ballet performances.

## The New Egyptian Belly Dance

I will make a two pronged argument for the modern origins of this dance genre. First, I will address the part that developed through events in Egypt that occurred beginning in the decade after World I and continued until the 1960s. This was no longer the Egypt of the 19th century but an Egypt that had been exposed to Hollywood. For far too long, those interested in the belly dance phenomenon have encountered a barrage of romanticized writings that attempt to equate contemporary belly dance with ancient, prehistoric choreographic practices purported to form a part of ancient worship rituals involving goddesses or childbirth rites undertaken by female social solidarities and continuing in an unbroken historical line to our own times. These orientalist writings have only obscured how very modern and recent contemporary belly dance choreographic practice as found in the United States, and indeed in Egypt, is.[6]

What I wish to show in this chapter is that the presence of nineteenth-century dancers at world exhibitions, and their dance practices, had almost nothing to do with the contemporary belly dance practiced throughout the United States or currently in Egypt, and that historical developments in Egypt just before and after World War I contributed to the creation of what is essentially a new dance genre.

The second prong of my argument will address the issue of receptivity of Americans of the turn of the nineteenth century to this dance genre. In many ways, this is the more important of the two aspects, because it has been far less written about and analyzed and is crucial to the way in which American women were repelled by the dance as it was performed in 1893 and enchanted by the new belly dance in the 1970s.

In this chapter I will pursue some of the social and aesthetic reasons that the authentic Egyptian form as seen by millions of visitors to the world exhibitions, such as the Columbia Exhibition in Chicago in 1893, did not appeal to those women in that period, for therein lay the reasons why only the modern, twentieth-century version of belly dancing seen in Egyptian films and cabaret performances became popular.

## Belly Dance in Egypt

Serious scholars have looked for historical connections with past practices in order to give contemporary belly dancing a historical context. Serious scholars have also, of course, been far more scrupulous and careful in assessing origins and attributing ancient roots than popular writers, but we, too, have looked back to the nineteenth century, during which considerable attention was paid to this activity. Belly dancing was described in careful, sometimes breathless, detail by foreign visitors to Egypt, visitors like Gustave Flaubert and George William Curtis (See Karayanni 2004, 39–44; Monty 1986 Chapter IV) and Edward W. Lane's famous accounts in the 1830s (1966). In consequence, much of the important development in the cultural production of dance in the first half of the twentieth century has been scanted as modern or unimportant.

I suggest that this lack of attention to the developments of belly dancing in Egypt in the period 1920–1940 has resulted in the widespread and erroneous concept of a dance tradition with an unbroken line with the past. Modern American belly dancers not infrequently indulge in the fantasy that they are embodying Cleopatra, Salome, or some other historical femme fatale or participating in some prehistoric ritual to an unnamed mother goddess (see for example *Habibi* Fall/Winter 2006/2007, volume 21, number 2, 56).

Some of the confusion and attraction of past practices comes from the poorly understood Arabic nomenclature referring to public entertainers. In the nineteenth century, certain female performers were referred to as *'awalim* (singular *'alimah*), which has been translated all too frequently as "learned" or "scholarly" women. Even Karin van Nieuwkerk, a very fine dance scholar, characterized the 'awalim as "learned women or female scholars" (1996, 26). Most readers of this term, unfamiliar with Middle Eastern societies, envision a highly educated woman who is steeped in literature, philosophy, and other intellectual pursuits which they discussed with learned men in colloquia. In fact, ethnomusicologist Jihad Racy agrees that such a translation is unfortunate, and that a better rendition would be "master of her trade, referring to their ability to perform a large repertoire of music" (personal interview, March 19, 2004). How much they composed their own music and poetry, and how

**Ethnic Dance Theatre performs a ghawazi dance in 19th century Egyptian clothing, 1982. Director Donald La Course. Photography by Marc Norberg. Courtesy of Donald La Course.**

much they memorized from the contemporary and classical repertoire, is unknown. These performers were not educated in the way familiar in the West. The majority of them came from the lowest echelons of society; elite women, the only upper class and privileged women who might have been schooled in private with their brothers, would never have performed publicly.

The *'awalim* were primarily singers, although they frequently danced as well. The most esteemed of them performed only in the women's quarters, but their performances were audible from the main courtyard so that male listeners could enjoy the performances, too. Occasionally they performed for male audiences, which were seated behind a screen. In this way, they did not appear before male audience members and preserved their reputations. Clearly, in this segregated Islamic context, they did not sit and discuss philosophy and literature with their male audience members in the manner of the hetaera in Ancient Greek symposia. Although all public performers in the Middle East held low social status to some degree, until the twentieth century the 'awalim escaped the general opprobrium reserved for public entertainers precisely because they did not contravene Islamic custom and law by performing before males who did not stand in proper kinship to them. The reason they became known as "learned" (I adopt the quotation marks from ethnomusicologist Virginia Danielson 1991, 304) is because the finest of these performers memorized copious amounts of poetry, an esteemed practice in the Arab world:

> Women were associated with a genre of song called the *taqtuqa*, a strophic piece in colloquial Arabic dealing with coquetry or other amorous themes. By contrast, the classical qasidah was considered to be a male genre.... In fact, a number of female singers were credited, however grudgingly, with having mastered the repertory of sophisticated song ordinarily associated with their male counterparts [Danielson 1991, 304].

Thus, even the finest of them never achieved the esteem of the finest male vocalists. Nevertheless, some of the 'awalim, like their counterparts, the female *motreb* (public performers of Iran), attained fame, fortune, and sometimes prosperous marriages through their connections (see Fatemi 2005, 51–55). In Egypt:

> The most accomplished singers were in great demand, held in high esteem, and able to profit handsomely from the money given them by audience members. The gifted few attracted the patronage of elite families, including the royal family, who supported a number of 'awalim, actually taking the women into the household [Danielson 1991, 294].

Dancers, who were more frequently termed as *ghawazi* (singular *ghaziah*), did, however, perform unveiled in front of males and consequently held a much lower social status that was equated with prostitution. Both dancers and singers were affected by the dramatic changes that were occurring in the entertainment world of Cairo at the turn of the century. New public venues such as music halls and Western-style theaters opened. The Egyptian cinema, which opened in the early part of the twentieth century, provided conceptual space for choreographic innovation and invention. Exposure to Hollywood films inspired dancers to create new kinds of choreographies and new costumes.

Whereas nineteenth-century performers learned their trade largely through imitation, performing like their mentors beginning especially in the 1920s with the opening of Badi'a Masabni's music hall in 1926, performers began searching for the new and novel. "By the beginning of World War I, few old-style 'awalim remained. Some of the older singers made the transition from one milieu to the other, and newcomers launched themselves immediately into the commercial enterprise" (Danielson 1991, 245).

"Badi'a Masabni's music hall was a model of its genre. Established in 1926 with cash accumulated from her career as an actress and dancer and with gifts from her male admirers, Salat Badi'a, as it was called, featured a variety program centered on a female singer. Badi'a hired performers, trained her own dancers, and would argue, it was said, with anyone over a single piaster" (Danielson 1997, 48). Monty, following Barbara Sellers-Young, notes that Badi'a Masabni "formed a school, eventually graduating such students as Tahia Carioca and Samia Gamal, popular Egyptian dancers in the 1940s and 1950s" (1986, 168). Masabni is also credited by Monty with the creation of the modern costume (*ibid*).

I suggest that in the 1920s and beyond, dance artists like Badi'a Masabni, Tahia Carioca, and Samia Gamal made a conceptual break with past practices and created the new genre that we today call belly dance, and even more specifically cabaret belly dance, which we associate with its iconic bikini-like costume that was also adopted at this time. This break with past dance and aesthetic practices of cultural production occurred not only in Egypt but also in other areas of the Middle East and Central Asia such as Iran, Turkey, and Uzbekistan as documented by scholars such as Doi (2002), Fatemi (2005), and Shay (2008). Dance scholar Karin van Nieuwkerk notes that "In the first decades of the twentieth century, nightclubs and variety shows sprang up to meet the demands of the colonial rulers and Western tourists. The 'Oriental' shows, featuring a *danse du ventre*, belly dance, contained many show elements imported from the West" (1995, 41).

More importantly, the patronage of the native Egyptian upper classes shifted with changing social practices. Weddings and other social gatherings among the newly westernized elite became mixed events. They wanted entertainment that was "modern" and chic. This required a corresponding change for the professional performers; the 'awalim no longer performed only for

Katya Faris performs a cabaret belly dance, circa 2000. Photography by Tom Stio. Courtesy of Katya Faris.

women in segregated spaces and their songs and dances began to appear dated to the elite. The presence of the "new" belly dancers like Tahia Carioca and Samia Gamal rendered the performances of the traditional *'awalim* quaint for the fickle public. The difference between *ghawazi* and *'awalim* became blurred in this period and in the new performing contexts in which they found themselves they were equally held in scorn, except for the top rank of performers:

> The heyday of the common 'awalim was at the beginning of this century. They performed on festive occasions, particularly for other women, as they had done in the nineteenth century. In contrast to that period, however, at the turn of the twentieth century they increasingly sang and danced for the lower and middle classes. The Westernized elite mostly invited well-known nightclub entertainers to perform at their weddings [Nieuwkerk 1998, 24].

The mythology of an unbroken line of dance practices dating from pharaonic times, and earlier, remains so strong that even serious scholars have a difficult time breaking its spellbinding hold. A study of nineteenth century dance practices and the contemporary dance practices of the *ghawazi* dancers of Egypt filmed in the 1970s (Araf records n.d.) and Saleh's filming of a traditional belly dancer in the 1950s demonstrate the movement practices of that period.[7] I suggest that these earlier practices, spatially very restricted, constitute an almost separate genre of dance from contemporary practices. It is difficult for today's dancer and even dance scholars to imagine how different today's cabaret dance form is from the earlier performances. Like their Iranian counterparts, Egyptian public performers included singing, dancing, acting, and acrobatic feats in their repertoire. They were not only dancers, but also singers and acrobats; most of them had specialty virtuosic feats that they performed in order to secure audiences in a highly competitive market.

Further, Egyptian dance historian Magda Saleh details in her study of Egyptian dance how Nazla El Adl, an old style dancer who "is presumed one of the last of her kind," performs in the old style (1979, 119). El Adl had as her specialty the dance with the *shame'dan* (chandelier) in which she actually balanced a fifty pound chandelier on her head, unlike the modern dancers who, according to Saleh, "replaced the heavy chandelier by a sketchy, almost weightless plastic version" (1979, 119). El Adl performs the splits and other virtuosic feats while balancing the chandelier. Saleh documents other highly skilled and athletic specialties of the former public entertainers: balancing hot tea cups, wine glasses, water jars, and other objects such as a live fowl as they danced (119–123).

The modern belly dancers, beginning with performers like Samia Gamal and Tahia Carioca, were simply dancers, which constitutes a conceptual break with the past in which performers generally sang and performed acrobatic feats, and sometimes exhibited other talents. Dancers like Carioca and Gamal created a new genre to respond to new performing conditions, the growth of an elite and prosperous middle class, and changing aesthetic values and tastes created by the rapid spread of cinema and both Hollywood and Egyptian films impelled them to innovation in their performances. Egyptian cinema historian Viola Shafik underscores the role of music and modern belly dance in the Egyptian film and the ways in which Western elements were deployed in the new modern belly dance:

> Most musical films contain at least one dance, most often a belly dance. As early as 1935/36, a film introduced the dancer Badi'a Masabni, who owned a well-known variety theater where several prominent belly dancers were trained. Some of the dancers who subsequently appeared, such as Samya Gamal and Tahiya Carioca, borrowed their music from the cabaret or nightclub, and folklore. Samya Gamal developed a sort of expressive dance as an individual characteristic in her performances.... Na'ima 'Akif, on the other hand, presented a colorful mixture of belly dancing, flamenco, and tap dancing.... The historical films tried to reconstruct the dance of the *djawari* (singing girls) of former times, combining elements from the ballet and the oriental dance as in *Dananir* (1940/41) and *Sallama* (1945) [1998, 103–104].

The older class of dancers did not disappear all at once, but, as Nieuwkerk documents, they were relegated to performing for the lower classes, and "the older generation claims that presently the women's success is mainly based on fraternizing with customers and wearing scanty costumes, not on their artistry" (1998, 25).

I suggest that the only connection and link between the nineteenth-century dance style and the post–World War I cabaret style consists of the rolling articulations of the abdomen and gyrating movements of the hips. In 1836, Edward Lane remarked, "The Ghawazee perform, unveiled in the public streets, even to amuse the rabble. Their dancing has little of elegance; its chief peculiarity being a very rapid vibrating motion of the hips from side to side" (Lane 1966, 384). It is for this reason that I argue that this element, the "rapid vibrating motion of the hips," like Irish step dancing in relation to River-dance, constitutes a parallel tradition, because this movement described by Lane is one of the few elements remaining from the nineteenth century version of the dance. Today's cabaret belly dance constitutes a much richer, more sophisticated (from a Western point of view) movement vocabulary and choreography in its professional performances.

# Belly Dance In the United States

While the first performances of the ghawazi dancers on the Chicago Midway

and other venues in North America and Europe provided Victorian age viewers with a delightful *frisson* for viewing the forbidden erotic dance, in fact,
other than the sexual thrill their performances seemed to provide for a portion of the male audiences, their dances were generally received rather coldly
overall. Nieuwkerk notes: "Little Egypt, a Syrian dancer, was the sensation
of the Midway and attracted more visitors than the seventy-ton telescope. The
audience received the dancers in an atmosphere of expectancy, created by the
descriptions and images of travelers and painters. Yet their appearance was
disappointing and their *danse du ventre* was not appreciated by all on account
of the 'boldness of its pelvic movements'" (1995, 42). Not all of the contemporary observations were as specific in their descriptions of specific movements
that caused the sense of revulsion by many observers. (See Monty 1986, 14–90
for a wide sampling of the contemporary responses to the first appearances of
oriental dance in America.)

     Sol Bloom, the entrepreneur who raked in a fortune by displaying the
Egyptian performers, and who coined the term "belly dance," cashed in on
the reputation of the "hootchy-kootchy," which was "already well entrenched
in the American vocabulary. Its meaning was a sexy kind of erotic dance, with
implications of being suggestive and indecent" (Monty 1986, 24). Indeed,
Bloom commented, "When the public learned that the literal translation [of
*danse du ventre*] was 'belly dance' they delightedly concluded that it must be
salacious and immoral." He adds, "The crowds poured in. I had a gold mine"
(quoted in Monty 1986, 29). And yet belly dance researcher Paul Monty, in
his voluminous collection of responses to these early performances, demonstrates that the Americans generally found the dances "ugly" and "lascivious"
in a general way rather than in any specific movements. As one author wrote,
"It is not dancing as we understand dancing" (quoted in Monty 1986, 52):

> The artist looking only for what is beautiful finds beauty here without any alloy
> of that suggestiveness which probably commends the posturing to the Orientals
> themselves, and which certainly pleases men of simply carnal minds, whether
> they come from Boston, Oshkosh, or Kalamazoo. Those who visit the theatre in
> the Cairo street as merely a part of the ethnological section of the exhibition
> will look upon this posturing in its true aspect and see in it only a difference in
> customs of the East and West [Monty 1986, 53].

What is clear from these observations is that the aesthetic elements of the dance
were foreign and alien in an unattractive way to most American audiences,
while they found the interpretive orientalist performances of St. Denis and
Allan exotic in an exciting and attractive way. American audiences wanted
the performances translated and interpreted by Western artists, not from the
authentic sources that later generations of American practitioners avidly
sought. Thus, I posit the westernized performances of "oriental" dance by St.

Denis and Allan, and the later performances of Egyptian dancers like Masabni, Gamal, and Carioca, were much more influential in the development of the highly popular form of belly dance that was introduced on a grand scale in the 1970s than the authentic nineteenth-century form of belly dancing that was seen at the Chicago World's Columbian Exhibition in 1893.

Viewing the late twentieth-century ghawazi performing in the older style, one is struck by the static and repetitious nature of the dance (Araf 1977). This style of dance did not aesthetically appeal to women at the turn of the century in the United States, who were, through the prevalent taste in orientalism, much more attuned to the performances of Ruth St. Denis, Loïe Fuller, and Isadora Duncan. As Barbara Sellers-Young notes, "The typical woman of the early part of the century, however often she may have pursued her fantasies via the silver screen (Rudolph Valentine as the Sheik) or stage production (Ruth St. Denis), never became an active participant" (1992, 142).

It is significant that many of the first nonnative belly dancers like Jamila Salimpour, who taught thousands of students, mention that one of the methods by which they learned to dance was watching old Egyptian films with dancers like Carioca and Gamal, a method followed by young girls, and even some boys, in the Middle East (Adra 2005; Saleem, personal interview, June 14, 2007). Thus the earliest exposure to the dance for nonnative American dancers like Salimpour and Morocco (Carolina Varga Dinicu) came from the Egyptian cinema, and a generation of native dancers who were featured in the first Arab and Greek nightclubs in New York and San Francisco came from the milieu of nightclubs in Cairo and Beirut in which the modern version known as cabaret belly dance was performed.

A colonial and racist subtext also operated in the Americans and the Europeans viewing these "authentic" performances, in contrast to those of the "Oriental" dances of St. Denis, Allan, and Fuller. It became an important strategy for these women to distance themselves from the actual practices of Middle Eastern and Asian natives: "Eastern dance would have been offensive to respectable British sensibilities. Particularly belly-dancing, it explained, Eastern dancing was 'something lascivious and repulsively ugly.' If Allan had been 'authentic' she would have been dismissed as vulgar" (Koritz 1997, 140).

It is often difficult in the dawn of the twenty-first century to imagine the degree of racism that characterized American life until the 1960s. Arabs were frequently, and often officially, regarded as nonwhite, so dances performed by them would have been regarded with suspicion by the vast majority of white Americans. "It was not until 1914, however, that George Dow was denied a petition to become a U.S. citizen because, as a 'Syrian of Asiatic birth,' he was not a free white person within the meaning of the 1790 U.S. statue" (Suleiman 1999, 7). Dance scholar Jane Desmond states:

In the United States, the dominant structuring trope of racialized difference remains white/nonwhite.... In cases where a cultural form migrates from a subordinate to a dominant group, the meanings attached to that adoption (and remodeling) are generated within the parameters of the current and historical relations between the two groups, and their constitution of each as "other" and as different in particular ways. For example, the linkage in North American white culture of blacks with sexuality, sensuality, and an alternately celebrated or denigrated presumedly "natural" propensity for physical ability, expressivity, or bodily excess tinges the adoption of black dances. On one level, it allows middle- and upper-class whites to move in what are deemed slightly risqué ways, to perform, in a sense, a measure of "blackness" without paying the social penalty of "being" black [1997, 37].

Desmond's description characterizes belly dance in America. In the early part of the twentieth century, as a result of extreme racism, Arabs were widely perceived as nonwhite (see Shay 2006, 126–131). This perception prevented the crossing of that racial and cultural barrier to learn a nonwhite dance, whereas by the 1970s, with the civil rights movement, that barrier had largely dissolved. American women were able to dance the Middle Eastern dance as an exotic lark without paying the social cost that Arab and Turkish women who perform publicly pay, that is, the loss of reputation that is the lot of professional dancers in the Middle East. Turkish anthropologist Öykü Potuoğlu-Cook observes of a professional Turkish belly dancer: "She is unmarriageable because of the 'stain' of her status as a belly dancer" (2006, 633). In America, some belly dancers have earned advanced degrees and hold esteemed positions as well as dancing professionally with no loss of reputation.

A third factor that would have militated against performing the authentic dances from Egypt was the act of performing itself. Women who performed in public, as I remarked in the chapter on the pioneer performers, were considered to be prostitutes. This choreophobic attitude was widespread, so the only women who would undertake this activity, such as the several who performed the hootchy-kootchy on Coney Island and elsewhere under the name "Little Egypt," came from the lowest rungs of American society and needed the money. The studies of Ruth St. Denis and Isadora Duncan, like Kendall (1979) and Koritz (1997) frequently cite this factor of desperately needing money as an important one in the ways in which these women pursued their choreographic strategies, they wanted to earn money and at the same time achieve a respectability that was not possible before they appeared in a way that they claimed was spiritual and artistic, and consequently through their performances and programmatic rhetoric perceived as such by their audiences. I suggest that through their choreographic strategies these early dancers provided the space for later generations of women pursuing belly dance to consider their activity as respectable.

Thus, the only women who pursued the performance of oriental dance at the turn of the century: the hootchy-kootchy, Salome's dance, or acting, as Little Egypt did it, for money. As Sellers-Young notes, "The dance introduced at the turn of the century as part of a cultural exhibit was quickly transformed to a burlesque performance catering to male fantasies" (1992, 148). This stands in stark contrast to the hundreds of thousands of women in the 1970s who pursued this dance form for love, spirituality, seeking a feminist road to sexual and sensual empowerment, losing weight, feeling attractive, and joining other women in an affirming activity. Instead of receiving money, the vast majority eagerly spent money in their new found hobby.

## The Spread of Belly Dance in America

Dance and theater scholar Barbara Sellers-Young astutely addresses the reception of belly dance in the 1970s and 1980s:

> As it has developed and become popular in the United States, Raks el Sharki has not been a relocation of the form in the Middle East. Instead it has been a combination of two phenomena. The first is a romanticization of the Near East and the second is a general movement of increased awareness and acceptance of the female body. Belly dancing in the United States in the 1980s is a method for primarily women to explore their sensuality and the power that some believe is inherent in being female.... The popularity of the movies Zorba the Greek and Never on Sunday and a large influx of post-war Middle Eastern immigrants with their native restaurants and performers from the Middle East made what had been far away and inaccessible, close and easily accessible [1992, 142–143].

The first native American-born belly dancers, like Morocco (Carolina Varga Dinicu) and Jamila Salimpour, now famed and revered teachers and famous throughout the belly dance milieu through appearances at workshops and classes, learned their craft in the 1950s and 1960s through learning on the job. That job was dancing professionally in Middle Eastern nightclubs and restaurants. Morocco (2001) describes the explosion of Greek nightclubs in New York's Greektown, and they needed oriental dancers — desperately:

> The 1960s were a special time in New York: 8th Avenue, from 27th to 29th streets, had 10 restaurant/nightclubs with continual live, nightly Mideastern [sic] music, 3 dancers 6 nights a week, and a 4th on the 3 days the others were off. That's 40 dancers needed in a city that had maybe 10, who knew what they were doing.... In proportion to the economy, dancers' pay was much better then than today and there were so many job openings that if Godzilla had a costume she could have gotten a well-paying and steady gig [2001].

Morocco goes on to describe how she learned on the job by watching the few native dancers from the Middle East who worked in the clubs at that period. In many ways this is how children in the Middle East learn this dance — by watching their elders (Adra 2005).

The other important method of learning was watching old Egyptian films. Jamila Salimpour recounts her learning experiences:

> It was only after I went to dance in San Francisco, where dancers were hired from different countries of the Middle East, that I saw a variety of styles. We worked in the same club and imitated each other's specialties, of course not in the same show, and usually only after they'd left town. Turkish Ayşa wowed the audience with her full-body vibrations. During her show I would run to the dressing room to analyze her pivots. Soraya from Morocco danced almost always in Belledi dress, balancing a pot on her head. Fatima Akef danced on water glasses with "Laura" her parrot, perched on her shoulder. Nartis did the most incredible belly rolls and her entire finale consisted of continuous choo-choos. Fatima Ali did a 4/4 shimmy on the balls of her feet. I was told by Mohammed El Scali that she was a Ouled Nail. And so it went, show after show, night after night, year after year [Quoted from Sellers-Young 2005, 281].

As had happened in the case of Balkan dance, in the 1970s the demand for belly dance classes became widespread throughout America. "Although the transmission of Oriental dance in this country involves a complex web which includes many individuals, media, and performance events, the studio class has developed since the early 1970s as the primary site for conveying the movement knowledge and technique of this dance form" (Forner 1994, 9). Both Morocco and Jamila Salimpour were sought after as teachers by many of the women who came to see them dance. They both opened classes in the 1960s, and by the 1970s Paul Monty introduced the concept of the large-scale convention workshops:

> Credit goes to Dr. Paul Monty for coming up with the wonderful concept in the early '70s — one that I firmly believe set us on the path that brought this Art to its current status and international popularity: he was the first to envision and take the professional and financial risks involved in producing large-scale Mideastern [sic] dance seminars/conventions with evening concerts all over the U.S., presenting and making master teachers of Ibrahim Farrah, Dahlena, Serena, Jamila, myself and several others [2001].

In order to cater to this huge influx of learners, these new instructors had to invent and develop teaching methods different from the watch-and-imitate through the trial-and-error manner that these early performers used to learn the dance. (See Forner 1994; Morocco 2001; Sellers-Young 2005 for descriptions of some of the teaching methods.) These classes, seminars, and retreats became important vehicles for many individuals to immerse themselves in this activity. "One dancer called his [Ibrahim Farrah] week long seminar 'a

Saleem performs an oriental dance, 2003. Photography by Timothy Fielding. Courtesy of Saleem.

transformational experience,' another stressed that taking his classes 'can make a difference in your life'" (Forner 1994, 14).

Belly dance classes became almost a cottage industry in the 1970s and after. Instructors appeared everywhere, and since no type of certification was required, the levels of instruction varied widely. "A few teachers actually taught specific dances from specific countries, but most tended to teach a step from Egypt followed by another from Morocco, or Turkey, or Iran" (Sellers-Young 1992, 143).

Unlike the classical dances from Asia or flamenco, which require years of devoted and focused learning, generally in a master-guru/student-disciple relationship and a formalized special setting for its mastery, many of the movements of belly dance could be acquired in a relatively short time, sometimes within a few weeks:

> When the instructor felt she was ready, the student was encouraged to make a costume and perform before an audience either at a student night in a local restaurant or at a party arranged by the instructor. This teaching method created a situation in which movement styles from different areas of the Middle East were combined into a form that more and more became a medium of its own commonly referred to as belly dancing [Sellers-Young 1992, 143–144].

Thus, if a young woman was relatively attractive and had some type of stage persona, this method of teaching permitted and even encouraged her to take up belly dancing as a profession. Many dancers appearing in Middle Eastern nightclubs began their careers this way.

## Belly Dance as Popular Culture

Today in the United States many of the practitioners of belly dance negotiate the many tensions that constitute the gaps found in this globalized and transnational practice. The first is that the dance has been linked to sex from its first appearance in the United States in 1893, when it was advertised and displayed to appeal to the male gaze.[8] The many impressionistic American dancers of this form, frequently appearing under the name "Little Egypt" in burlesque reviews, quickly established in the popular mind the link between striptease, the hootchy-kootchy, and belly dance.

A century later, with the fad of the bellygram, the same linkage obtained and the perception continued to highlight sex through the appearance of the scantily clad female body and the male voyeur. Usually the bellygram dancer appears in the context of a male's birthday party or a stag party. "The bellygram's obvious sexism has created a certain amount of ambivalence among dancers who perform them. Although dancers may dislike them, they are clearly the most profitable and consistent employment for a dancer" (Sellers-Young 1992, 145). Thus, in the United States, the bellygram fad continues to place belly dance alongside the striptease in the minds of many Americans. This aspect of the dance as sexual makes it difficult for its many devoted followers to convince either Americans or individuals from the Middle East that belly dance is an art form or a spiritual practice.

Related to the issue of the sexual content of the dance, many dancers know that in the Arab world, Turkey, and Iran professional dancing, and even nonprofessional dancing in public contexts can be disreputable, and the professional dancer constitutes the popular trope of a fallen woman in Middle Eastern societies. But very few American dancers fully understand the differences in the Middle Eastern attitudes and those that they confront in the United States. While some American dancers dismiss these negative attitudes as something that happens only in a supercharged Islamist context, this knowledge of the disreputability of the dance in the Middle East forms a disquieting background for others. This issue can come very much alive when a Middle Eastern man, misconstruing the American context in a Middle Eastern nightclub or private party in an American city, importunes the American-born dancer with a lewd suggestion or an outright sexual proposition.

A second area of tension for many dancers is the struggle to have belly dance recognized as an art form. Clearly, in the Middle East belly dancing is regarded as a form of entertainment and one that is widely regarded as a low and disreputable form of entertainment despite its popularity as an indispensable element of weddings and other celebrations in Egypt and other parts of the Arab world.

A third aspect of tension that is specific to the United States involves the position of belly dance in popular culture. Unlike the other forms of dance that I profile in this study, such as classical Asian dances and Balkan dance, which remain almost hidden and underground from most Americans, belly dance is widely known by the general public through its widespread use in popular culture genres such as film and television as a vaguely sexy, exotic dance. The appearance of popular culture figures like Jeannie of *I Dream of Jeannie* and Lalume in the musical film *Kismet* (Dolores Gray) in the 1950s, which featured domesticated, blonde, sanitized harem girls, added a comic, slightly ridiculous aspect to the character of the sexy harem girl that had not previously existed. This aspect is frequently iterated in the many newspaper stories and features that focus on belly dance that invariably take on a tongue-in-cheek approach to the topic. These journalistic attitudes irritate some dancers who seek to place belly dance in the category of high or ethnic art.

A final element, related to the discourse surrounding belly dance and reflecting the transnational and globalized movement of this phenomenon revolves around (mis)appropriation and authenticity. As Sellers-Young noted, the way in which the dance is taught militates against its authenticity. Further, American created forms, such as American Tribal Dance (ATS), described and analyzed by Sellers-Young (2005), have widened the perception of what constitutes belly dance and the degree of authenticity that adheres to its variegated performances.

Arab Americans frequently react negatively to the public performance of belly dance as a representation of Arab culture, and they feel that American dancers misrepresent their culture through orientalist images of sexuality. Thus, when American dancers perform the Arab "other" through belly dance, they face possible charges of appropriation:

> American dancers are ambivalent about both the Americanization of the style and our relationship to the dance's ethnic origins. On the one hand, we distance ourselves through appeals to high art notions in which individual creativity is the ultimate demonstration of talent. We assert that we have as much right as people from the Middle East to alter, perform, and speak for the dance. On the other hand, in our costuming, stage names, advertising, and performance venues, we highlight its Middle Eastern origins [Gould 2006/07, 33].

Many of the articles in journals like *Habibi* address these issues, which have increasingly become an important aspect of the discourse surrounding the performance of belly dance. There is an increasing awareness among many dancers that these tensions and issues exist and must be confronted. As anthropologist Miriam Robinson Gould enquires, "Dance in the West: Striptease, Ethnic Art, or High Art?":

> Even dancers who want to move beyond fantasy, who believe that their dance is an ethnic art form, and who do research on what bellydance [*sic*] means to its Middle Eastern practitioners often end up seeing attitudes that appear to match the Salome discourse. American dancers training with other American dancers often don't have the background in either cross-cultural forms of communication or Middle Eastern studies to distinguish the ways in which the Salome discourse of sexuality in the dance differs from the Egyptian discourse of inappropriate performance, which leaves us continuing to dance in Salome's shadow [1996/07, 36].

Like Balkan dancers, those engaged in the pursuit of belly dance as an art, as a form of fitness, or as a spiritual practice are passionate about the promotion of their chosen form of cultural production. In many ways participation in belly dance constitutes a central and core part of their lives.

Many of the women involved in belly dancing and who identify with Arab, Iranian, and Turkish culture frequently marry Arab, Iranian, and Turkish men as dancers Aisha Ali and Jamila Salimpour have done. When Morocco (Carolina Varga Dinicu) goes to Egypt, she wears the middle class dress and headscarf associated with what one sees the more traditional women wearing, and she speaks fluent Arabic. She clearly identifies with being an Egyptian when she is there and Egyptians admire her for it. Hundreds of other women make the trek, led by well-known instructors like Morocco, to the Middle East to absorb the culture of their choreographically spiritual home.

On the Internet, in workshops, and in the pages of the journals devoted to oriental dance they struggle to resolve the tensions of sexuality and sensuality, authenticity, appropriation, and orientalism that exist in the transnational interstices of their now largely Americanized dance tradition.

SEVEN

# Classical Asian Dance:
# The Arduous Journey

THE PURSUIT OF MASTERY in any of the classical Asian dance genres differs in several important ways from the two genres that I have described and analyzed in the previous two chapters— Balkan dance forms and belly dance. Crucially, this means that those who attempt to learn Asian classical dance traditions on a serious level are far fewer in number than the massive numbers of participants found in the Balkan, belly dance, and Latin American dance worlds. And, yet, there are a surprisingly substantial number of mainstream American individuals who have set out on the difficult but rewarding journey of immersion into Balinese, Japanese, Indonesian or Indian classical dance genres. After long years of hard work, many of these individuals pursue professional performing careers or enter the world of academia where their dance skills provide them with unique perspectives on dance, anthropology, folklore, ethnomusicology, theater, critical theory, and other scholarly disciplines.

In my own experience of learning Iranian solo improvised dance, and as a dancer attuned to acquiring movement, I found that I also experienced embodying "Iranian-ness" to some degree. As I learned the Persian language and learned the dance tradition, I acquired an "Iranian" personality and Iranian movement practices that were contingent on the social contexts in which I found myself. Upon reflection, I found that I was unconsciously using shifting cultural codes such as *ta'ārof*, an elaborate form of Iranian politesse that involves embodied behavior, when I entered an Iranian social or cultural environment. Many years later I realized that whenever I entered an Iranian social environment, I moved and gestured differently, adopting, in effect, another identity.[1]

Tomie Hahn, in learning *nihon buyo*, a Japanese classical dance tradition, was advised by her master teacher to allow other identities to take shape and

148

emerge during the learning process: "I recall her saying — 'When you're dancing you can be anyone.' In context she meant that I needed to focus on embodying a particular character for the dance I was learning, but also hinted that would enable me to experience a variety of identities.... Shifting between identities was an activity I learned both in and outside the dance space" (2007, 12).

Learning the dance of the Other enables many individuals to become the Other on several levels and enables those individuals to shift cultural and social codes through the process of learning and performing choreographic embodiment.

## Gateways

While it might seem surprising that classes in Balinese dancing, nihon buyo, or bharata natyam, for example, can be found even in small colleges all over America, this can be readily explained when one looks at the widespread availability of ethnomusicology classes throughout the United States. I identify two primary gateways through which individuals enter the world of Asian classical dance: performances and ethnomusicology and dance ethnology programs.

The first encounter is often through seeing a performance. Performances of classical Asian dance traditions are more frequent than one might imagine in the United States. I remember in the 1970s two Balinese dance companies in the same concert season that were presented by the Los Angeles County Music Center in performances that featured large gamelan ensembles and several highly trained dancers. In the same period, the Cambodian Court Dancers appeared at UCLA, their first public appearance outside of the Cambodian court, and gave multiple performances of Kabuki. These events took place at the height of the popularity of world dance company performances, frequently produced by Sol Hurok's organization, as well as by other large New York–based firms. On a more frequent level, UCLA, Pepperdine University, Cal Arts, the University of California Irvine and Berkeley held annual concert seasons, as they continue to do, which featured a wide variety of world music traditions. This Southern California pattern is repeated throughout the United States.

Several of these dance traditions, such as bharata natyam, have gained a global reputation, and, like Balinese and Javanese dance and music made popular in Europe during the nineteenth century in the world exhibitions, have recently increasingly gained in popularity with Western audiences (see Décoret-Ahiha 2004; O'Shea 2007). Also, the large recent influx of immigrants from Asian countries, which include a number of well-known classical dance artists,

has increased the visibility of Asian dance traditions wherever large populations of East Indians, Koreans, Cambodians, and other groups are found.
Thus, the availability of performances of these genres over the past decades
has been such that many people throughout the United States have the opportunity to experience these art forms.

**Anne Von Bibra Wharton performs "Gambyong," a classical Javanese court dance,
2003. Photograph by Petronella Ytsma. Courtesy of Anne Von Bibra Wharton.**

However, the serious American student of these traditions soon under-
stands that these choreographic forms, in the context of transnationalism and
global circulation, can change in meaning and impact among the various sites
and communities in which it is performed. These contexts can consist of performances in the home country for cognoscenti, performances in diaspora
communities, and formal concerts and workshops in community and university concert halls for foreign viewers. As O'Shea observes: "No longer relegated to the so-called world-dance margins of a global performance milieu,
bharata natyam appears alongside European and North American forms in
mainstream venues" (2007, 3).

In addition, especially in large urban areas, it is possible to sample a
wide variety of classical Asian dance performances in other contexts. One
important context is in the numerous international folk dance festivals, such
as those held in Minneapolis, San Francisco, Washington, New York City, San

Diego, San Antonio, or Los Angeles, in which various Asian ethnic communities frequently send classical dance performances for representation of their community (Shay 2006).

Citywide arts festivals provide another context for seeing performances of Asian classical dance traditions. In 1994, during the Los Angeles Arts Festival, Peter Sellars and Judy Mitoma, the artistic directors, brought a fabulous assemblage of Asian ensembles, including a large-scale group from Java that performed at the Los Angeles County Arboretum. The Indonesian Government sent a similar ensemble to the Rose Bowl in Pasadena along with a float for the Rose Parade, and both events took place before capacity audiences.

University and college concerts presenting programs for the general public frequently bring Asian classical dance programs within their seasonal offerings. And virtually all of the ethnomusicology programs throughout the United States give end-of-the-semester concerts. The UCLA ethnomusicology program, founded by Mantle Hood in the 1950s and generally acknowledged as the first of these departments, has been offering such annual programs for over fifty years. Their annual spring concert series sometimes features as many as twenty different types of world music; the series is well known, widely advertised, and very popular with the general public in the Los Angeles area (see Tindall 2007). Foremost among the styles of dance and music that are presented throughout the United States are the court musics of Asia and Africa, especially those of Bali, Japan, India, and West Africa:

> A list of typical academic world music ensemble types is certainly shorter than one would imagine, given the great range of interests reflected in general ethnomusicological scholarship. Clearly, certain ensembles are emerging as canonic. These ensemble choices partly reflect historical trends in ethnomusicological investigation since the early 1950s. Befitting Mantle Hood's profound influence, gamelans abound as glittering sonic and visual symbols of "the Other." Perhaps second to these in number have been West African percussion ensembles [Solís 2004, 7].

Sumarsam, a master teacher/artist of the gamelan adds: "It has been more than four decades since gamelan performance was first incorporated into the ethnomusicology program at UCLA. Today, interest in studying gamelan performance remains strong in American colleges and universities: discussion of various gamelan topics and announcements of gamelan events appear almost daily on gamelan@listserve" (2004, 69). A typical student's reaction to experiencing and playing Balinese gamelan music was expressed by Evan Phillips: "'Sometimes I feel the music late at night, long after class is over,' said Evan Phillips, a UCLA ethnomusicology major.... 'Once you've heard it, it's in your blood'" (Tindall 2007, 1).

Pomona College, a relatively small college where I teach, has a gamelan ensemble of which it is inordinately proud, and, of course, knowledgeable viewers expect at least some dancing during a gamelan performance. Those dancers who participate in the Balinese dance class as part of their class and learning experience demonstrate the usually short dance that they have spent twenty weeks learning in order to add color to the concert. The college has a set of Balinese costumes, a rarity for the world dance classes at Pomona, which the students wear for the performance. Students in my own classes at Pomona, like Evan Phillips, were similarly entranced by the music and dance practices of Bali that they experienced in their class.

Another source of world music concerts comes from within the diasporic communities that live in large numbers in specific cities. For example, in Southern California the large Indian community sponsors frequent concerts throughout the year, a pattern that is replicated in communities in the San Francisco Bay area and Minneapolis. The Japanese American community has a major theater in Los Angeles that features concerts of Kabuki, Gagaku, Bunraku, and other forms that are open and advertised to the general public. The Japanese communities in Hawaii, Oregon and Washington similarly hold community celebrations featuring classical and folk dance traditions, along with other Japanese arts like taiko drumming, tea ceremonies, and visual and martial arts. In addition, community theater producers who are frequently aware of large ethnic concentrations in their neighborhood, such as the large Cambodian community in Long Beach, California, will provide special concerts of Asian classical dance and music traditions aimed at those communities and also open to interested members of the general public.

Thus, two of the major gateways for individuals entering the exotic world of Balinese and other forms of classical Asian dance are classes in world dance and ethnomusicology and seeing performances of these dances, either by professional dancers from the countries of origin, or by the master teachers who now live in the United States as part of the diasporic communities, and their students, like the many kathak and bharata natyam master artists that one finds in areas like California with its large Indian, Japanese, Korean, Thai, and Cambodian communities.

## Instructors and Teaching Methods

The master teachers, unlike the Balkan and belly dance worlds in which mainstream Americans often teach, almost always come from the country of origin of the particular dance form. These instructors frequently welcome the opportunity to teach in college and university settings as well as providing private lessons for both members of their own communities and for a few mainstream

American students who are often more devoted, focused, and appreciative of the artistry of their master teachers than young American-born teenagers whose immigrant parents require them to attend classes in much the same way as a finishing school.

Almost every mainstream American person who undertakes one of the classical Asian dance genres in a serious pursuit of mastery — kathak, bharata natyam, or one of the other Indian forms, nihon buyo, classical Japanese dance, Balinese or Javanese classical dance traditions, Cambodian or Thai court dances, to mention a few of them — soon realizes that learning these dances requires many years of focused learning and that the method of teaching is different from any other most of them have ever encountered. And while there exist classes with several students that are offered in one or more of these classical Asian genres in several colleges and universities throughout the United States, in which the students can receive a small taste of an Asian classical dance tradition, what I call a sampler class, the serious student seeking a degree of proficiency must ideally enter the traditional method of learning.

Anne von Bibra Wharton said:

> My first experience with learning Javanese dance was in a dance ethnology class taught by Judy Mitoma with eight or ten students. She attempted to teach the way she had learned in Java and Bali, that is, to have the students follow her movements. It was very challenging because I had performed mostly European or Mexican folk dances, which are concentrated on the feet. In Javanese dance, you must move many body parts all at the same time. I remember I made a conscious choice to learn Javanese rather than Balinese dance because there was one less body part. I didn't think I could add the eyes to all the other body parts I was attempting to coordinate [personal interview, June 11, 2007].

Lynette Whiting, a student in the Balinese dance class at Pomona College, analyzed the first impact of discovering how difficult the learning process in the sampler type of class can be:

> In the dance portion of the class, I had the same "simple enough" attitude: all we had to do was follow the movements of the instructor. I was so proud of myself: how much easier could this be? Nanik [Wenten] nearly never corrected me; I was sure that I was doing very well. At the end of the semester, though, I found that I was wrong. Near performance time, Nanik brought two of her Cal Arts students into our dance class.[2] The reason that she brought these students was for them to dance in front of us at the performance. As we saw the dance unwatered-down for the first time, I realized that I wasn't doing very well at all. As opposed to the way that the dance should actually look, we were all awkward, limp-armed, flat-footed, unexpressive shufflers. The Cal Arts students moved rather gracefully and used movements that Nanik had never attempted to teach us. There was quite clearly a disparity between the way that Nanik taught us and the way that she taught the Cal Arts students. Similarly, seeing

the Cal arts students as compared to Nanik, there was a definite difference in the ways that they danced. The differences that I noted were not in experience or expertise as I thought initially: when Nanik corrected the Cal Arts students and showed them her corrections, she did different movements than when she corrected us [Emphasis in the original, Whiting 2007, 1–2].

In addition, native instructors like Nanik Wenten frequently perform movements so "natural" to them that they are unaware that American students cannot grasp them, in much the same way a student attempts to acquire the subtleties of a foreign language. "When asked for help, Nanik stops and explains the dance as best she can.... Many of the basic movements become unconscious and second nature to native Balinese and Javanese dancers.... Many times, we have asked her about things that she did not realize that she was doing and doesn't know how to explain it" (*ibid.*, 5).

The traditional method in almost all of these choreographic forms is generally a one-on-one, intense, long-term learning process between a master artist and a student. These guru-like systems frequently have formal structures that Americans find alien to the way in which most dance classes in America are taught (see Sellers-Young 1993; Hahn 2007; O'Shea 2007).[3]

Whiting pursued the issue of how differently students are taught in Bali and in America:

> As taught at Pomona, Legong is never learned, nor is any other preparation for that matter; we jumped right into dances which native Balinese dancers do not perform until after learning the basics. The basics deemed necessary for dancers in Bali to move on to higher dances are not only far advanced to the basics that we obtain in our four months of class, they are also different basics. This is partly because, as non–Bali natives, we do not have the same familiarity with Balinese rhythm and movement that Balinese children do. This, I'm sure, is not a decision that an instructor likes to make; under the time constraints of a single semester, what we are taught is all we have time for. Unfortunately, without the natives' basics, the dance cannot look authentic [2007, 3].

The method of master-student teaching that characterizes most Asian classical forms stands in stark contrast to the ways in which belly dancing and Balkan dancing is generally taught. In those latter genres, particularly in large workshop or folk dance camp settings, it is possible to have in excess of one hundred or more students who exhibit various degrees of experience and competence in the same class.[4] The instructor has to gauge the median learning level in order to satisfy and accommodate the majority of participants in such a disparate crowd. In contrast to the Asian tradition of absorption through doing, the often American-born Balkan and belly dance teachers frequently give a great deal of time to verbal explanation. When confronted with a class of nonnative dancers, some teachers are forced to verbalize. Anne von Bibra Wharton notes that

Barbara Sellers-Young performs *Ayame Yukata*, a classical Japanese nihon buyo dance in Kyoto, Japan, 1985. Courtesy Barbara Sellers-Young.

"When my current instructor, Tri Sutrisno, teaches our class in St. Paul, she is forced by circumstances to teach verbally. Some of the students work by counts, because the music is elusive and difficult to master, even though I learned some of the basics of the gamelan" (personal interview, June 11, 2007).

In the American college system, native instructors must sometimes resort to these American methods in order to teach anything of value in the short time they are allotted in the American university system. Cal Arts, which operates as a type of conservatory system, is an exception. Another of Nanik Wenten's students, Jabarri Reynolds, found this out in his experience of learning Balinese dance:

> Next I learned that her style of teaching at Pomona College was different from the way she learned when she was younger and from how she instructs those that she had been working with for years. When beginning to teach, she realized that teaching the way she had learned would be very hard for her students since it would have required them to learn by imitation and by familiarizing themselves with the music. Instead she breaks down the choreography into steps and shorter pieces [2007, 7].

Once an individual, caught up in the magic of a particular tradition, decides to learn that tradition, they soon realize that this is an artistic journey that will require many years. It will also frequently require a sizeable financial outlay. Most of these individuals also find that they wish to spend several months in the country of origin of their chosen choreographic and/or musical tradition. Barbara Sellers-Young, who undertook the study of nihon buyo for many years in both Oregon and Japan, noted that for those who wished to pass the formal examinations to achieve a master's status (*natori*) required both time in the home country and a considerable financial outlay:

> The process of becoming a *natori* represents a commitment by the women not only to study diligently with Kanriye Fujima in the United States, but also to travel to Japan for two months of the year in which they take the performance examination to study with Kansho Fujima, her teacher in Hiroshima. After this two-month period, they perform their two dances, a *matsu* (male) and a *fuji* (female) piece, just as Kanriye Fujima did for her examination, and receive their certification from the head of the school in Tokyo. The cost for each performer's certification is $10,000.00 [1993, 56].

Dance historian Janet O'Shea notes that in the world of bharata natyam, "The foreign dancers who traveled to Chennai [formerly Madras, India] for dance study included not only those trained through the dance networks established by Balasaraswati and Rukmini Devi, but also performers such as Ragini Devi [née Esther Sherman], Nala Najan, and Bruce Murray Turner. Turner's practice of Indian dance led him to relocate to Delhi to facilitate his opportunities for performing in India" (2007, 154).

For the mainstream American entering an Asian classical tradition, almost everything is unfamiliar: the teaching method, the instructor's expectations, and especially a new body language that must be acquired. "The initial obstacle is the basic body stance, which is the opposite of the movement style associated with their school physical education programs and other dance classes" (Sellers-Young 1993, 72). I remember my first (and last) encounter with a class in which traditional hula was being taught. My legs turned to quivering jelly from the effort of maintaining a constant plié position for over an hour.

Also, the formality between the student and master is frequently unfamiliar to the American student:

> There was the consistency of the same teacher and a lesson that always followed the same format. The lesson always began with a bow and the Japanese phrase *onegai shimasu*, a formal request to study the dance. Each dance was always learned. It always ended with a bow and thank-you in Japanese. Beyond this, I was beginning to learn new modes of somatic awareness through the series and sequencing Kanriye Fujima taught [Sellers-Young, 2006, 6].

Although the degree of warmth and contrasting formality differs from teacher to teacher, within each tradition there exists a certain consistency. Within the nihon buyo world, and indeed throughout the Japanese arts as a whole, the master-student relationship is established in the *iemoto* system:

> The *iemoto* system operates like an extended family with members of a school calling themselves *uchi no mono*, or members of the same household. Teachers often refer to their students as their children. Hence a highly personal relationship evolves between student and teacher based on a system of *on* (reciprocal obligations). The teacher is responsible for providing a model for the traditional form, acting as a transmitter of the philosophical and cultural aspects of the form, and providing educational experiences for the learner's self-discovery. The student's responsibility is to exhibit *nyunanshin* (pliant-heartedness) and apply herself as a student with diligence, respect, and perseverance. The attitude of the student toward the teacher and the form is *kansha* (gratefulness) [Sellers-Young 1993, 23].

Tomie Hahn adds: "The sense of family is clearly embodied in the tradition of bestowing the family name, or natori, on qualified students" (2007, 35).

The iemoto system of master-student learning pervades most Asian dance traditions, but also is a general feature of learning. "Strikingly, the iemoto system is prevalent throughout such diverse practices as nihon buyo, musical genres, *noh*, horsemanship, flower arrangements, and martial arts. For a culture that values the continuity of its traditions, the iemoto structure provides a strict and reliable system to cautiously regulate the definitive practice of a tradition. Discipline is vital on several levels" (Hahn 2007, 31).

This attitude is a far cry from the typical dance class in the West in which the student-teacher relationship is dissolved once the student exits through the class door. The relationship between the master and student in the Asian context is a long-term one usually lasting over a period of several years. Prior to and following class, the student in the Asian classical tradition often sits and greets or takes leave of the instructor in a formal, ritualized fashion. Unlike the native student, the master-student relationship can change for the American dancer and their master teacher, since most of them can ill afford to move abroad for long periods of time. Learning bharata natyam in India, Janet O'Shea notes:

> Although the gursishya [master-student or guru] system of continued study with one mentor remained an ideal, instructional relationships established in Chennai reach across geographical boundaries. Student dancers, especially those based abroad, supplement their training by studying with several mentors in the same instructional lineage but in different locations. Because Chennai plays such an important role in the bharata natyam milieu, dancers often desire immersion in that city's life as they seek intensive dance training. Physical distance creates a situation in which the imperatives of uninterrupted tutelage with on mentor and absorption into the Chennai milieu vie with one another [2007, 154].

Leonard Pronko, who learned kabuki and nihon buyo, said, "I was advised not to follow the *natori* practice of adopting a new name (October 13, 2005) because of the difficulties of distance and the expense of training in Japan, as well as following the native custom of training in only one school of dance."

The outstanding characteristic of teaching in Asian classical dance traditions is instructing by imitation, as we saw in the Balinese and Japanese traditions. The teacher moves and the student follows until an entire dance is learned. Whiting observed that "In Bali, the instructors perform the dances in front of the students while neither verbalizing nor explaining the movements. The students just copy the instructor's movements over and over until they remember the basic movements of the dance. At this point, the instructor watches and corrects the students' form" (2007, 4). Hahn notes that:

> Nihon buyo dances consist of kata, formalized body movements that aid the memorization and embodiment of pieces. Kata, or precise exercise, are a distinctly Japanese formal device found in nearly every artistic practice.... In nihon buyo, kata function as the fundamental building blocks for the foundation of dance expression. Rather than learning the discrete forms individually first, as is the case in ballet training, katta are learned gradually and contextually within dance pieces.... Kata operate as artistic motifs that are standard and repeatable [2007, 61].

Interestingly, Persian classical music is taught in the same manner: "From the first lesson, the master shows the student how to hold the instrument, or the manner of singing. Then he improvises some short phrases which the student must reproduce and learn by heart. Then, there are simple melodies, without ornamentation, which the master teaches and fragments of the *radif* [classical musical system], equally simplified" (Caron and Safvate 1997, 191, translation by the author). Thus, we can see that the master-student process and teaching through the demonstration of short musical or dance phrases is common. Moreover, it is a preferred and highly valued manner of learning. It does not derive from the lack of notation or other western teaching aids, but it forms a commitment to the master-student system:

> So, the apprentice must be in constant communication with his master. He must see him every day; to the sounds of his instrument; and try to learn, each day, some delicate little point about the fine structure of this music, so that in the course of many years he may eventually master the subtleties that he has been taking in day after day, and succeed in playing the music properly.... Furthermore, an apprentice must become familiar with the mental and spiritual qualities of his master. In order to become a good musician, he should be able to appreciate these qualities and adapt them as his own [Hormozi 1991, 210].

O'Shea notes of this teaching method in bharata natyam: "Despite these fluid qualities, gurusishya teaching methods are both tightly organized and authoritative" (2007, 41). Hahn notes of this manner of teaching: "In this way nihon buyo students are dependent on teachers for new dance information" (2007, 87).

Thus, we can see that this very different method of instruction, most similar to that of the classical music student and his mentor in the West, is a cherished institution throughout most of Asia. It is so cherished that Western methods, such as the use of notation, are frequently discouraged by many master teachers because they rely on aids to memory that the teachers feel impede the progress and growth of the student.

## Schools of Dance

One of the aspects that American students of Asian classical dance discover in their quest is that different schools of teaching with master-student systems of learning exist. These different schools often reflect different philosophies of dance that may appear superficial to the outsider but constitute deeply held differences of opinion in how the art form is perceived. Masakatsu Gunji, a Kabuki theater historian states:

> We can trace the ancestry of today's numerous [nihon buyo] schools and branch schools of dance; we find that some of them derive from a lineage of Kabuki actor-dancers, some from a lineage of choreographers, and some from a lineage of actor-dancers and choreographers who performed privately in the residences of the shogun and the daimyo. We can count more than 150 present-day schools of dance that derive from these several sources [1970, 182–183].

Upon entering the schools, it is frequently expected that the student will not study with masters and individuals from other schools. Hahn notes that in certain Japanese schools "Notations were (and currently still are in many cases) meant for individuals within the school only.... This 'secrecy' of schools' artistry and transmission is present in virtually every art tradition in Japan. It is one of the factors that strengthens the schools' transmission and social bonding, and shapes the distinct styles of individual schools" (2007, 137).

Through the master-student training system, generations of teachers follow in their masters' footsteps, and some of them eventually become masters, too. Janet O'Shea gives an example: "I entered the field in 1988 as a student of the Thanjavur court style of bharata natyam associated with the legendary dancer T. Balasaraswati. I began studying bharata natyam as an undergraduate at Wesleyan University with Balasaraswati's student Kay Poursine and traveled to India in 1989 to study with Balasaraswati's senior disciple, Nandini Ramani. My connection to Balasaraswati was indirect: she died in 1984, four years before I began studying bharata natyam. My tutelage occurred under her students" (2007, 14).

Barbara Sellers-Young, in her fine study of nihon buyo, devotes the entire chapter two of the study to the career of her instructor, Kanriye Fujima, giving us a genealogy of instructors in her life. Gunji notes: "The line of succession from Shigayama Manasaku through Nakazo down to the present fifteenth-generation headmaster makes this the oldest existing school of dance" (1970, 183). He notes that several of the schools of nihon buyo, like that of Fujima and Hanayagi, which have branches in the United States, can trace their genealogies back for generations. Some of these schools have been highly prolific: "The Hanayagi school alone has produced as many as ten thousand holders of professional names" (1970, 185).

For the professional dancer or musician, the genealogy positions the artist for the knowledgeable audience member and brings a cachet of excellence. Therefore, artists make a point of honoring this artistic heritage. "Another excellent model presented by Djamshid Shemirani was the sense of humble gratitude he expressed for older masters, especially the late Hoseyn Tehrani, who had been his own master. He never failed to put in a few grateful words whenever he referred to Tehrani. The sincerity of his remarks touched the hearts of his students" (During et al. 1991, 214). It is not unheard of, especially in Japan where fathers pass their traditions to sons or close relatives, for masters to be identified and traced back for generations.

In addition to learning the movements of the dance, the devoted student of Asian classical dance must learn many other elements of the context in which the dance is taught: music, language, and frequently the philosophical systems in which the dance tradition is embedded. Besides these important aspects of the dance tradition itself, the new student discovers that the dance, for them, which originally appealed through its aesthetic base, contains different meanings both in the country of origin and within the diasporic communities in which the new student has her or his first encounters. Also, it is not unusual for tension to exist between individual teachers, or the schools of dance to which they belong, all of which the new student must negotiate. The issue of appearance can also create difficulties. If the student appears to be very un–Japanese or un–Indian, repercussions may occur, such as not being taken seriously as a performing artist.

## Music

It is not unusual, for example, for a dancer interested in Balinese classical dance to learn at least the rudiments of playing in a gamelan ensemble, or for an individual involved in nihon buyo to learn the *shamisen*, the Japanese stringed instrument that is paramount in the musical accompaniment of that tradition. An individual wishing to be a true master of Japanese dance, like the sensei, or master teacher, learns the *shamisen*, as part of their training.

The music that accompanies the dance must be mastered, because it frequently forms an alien element to the new student. "A second obstacle is the music which accompanies the dances. Classical Japanese music does not follow conventional western time signatures, but rather the flow of the singer's voice. The student is faced with the two-fold dilemma of remembering movements that accompany lyrics she does not understand, and following unfamiliar rhythms" (Sellers-Young 1993, 72).

"Learning the music was the most difficult aspect of my studying the dance. Last year, for the first time, I performed a solo to a live Javanese gamelan. For the first time I could hear the drumming cues and I did not rely on other dancers. I was forced to understand the music; I wish that I had tried that earlier. Our usual practice is to dance even solo dances as a group, with one or two advanced students in front" (von Bibra Wharton, personal interview, June 11, 2007).

## Language

One of the most important aspect of teaching some of the dance forms, in addition to imitation and following the teacher's example, is the issue of language. Frequently the instructor feels the need to use the native language to teach because there are often concepts that are not easy, even impossible, to translate into English, and in classical traditions, such as ballet where French is still the language of instruction, the various movements, musical scales, and other terminology must be learned by the student. Anne von Bibra Wharton said, "Tri uses Javanese terms and vocabulary, and it actually facilitates the learning process" (personal interview, June 11, 2007).

Instructors also realize that in teaching the dance or music tradition in the native language they are also passing on the culture in general. "Sensei [instructor] creates this environment of warmth and understanding even though she rarely speaks to the students in English. Although she can speak English quite well when necessary, all conversation within the studio before and during lessons between herself and the *natori*, or other students who can speak Japanese, is always in Japanese" (Sellers-Young 1993, 71). Sellers-Young adds an important point about Kanriye Fujima's position in the Japanese-American community: "Kanriye's native fluency in the Japanese language validates her role as an exponent of Japanese culture in general" (*ibid.* 73).

Thus, for the serious American student of Asian classical dance, learning the language of the chosen choreographic or musical tradition is an imperative element in undertaking the learning process.

## *Philosophical and Spiritual Underpinnings*

Many Asian classical dance traditions embody philosophical systems and have a sense of spirituality that is learned as part of the dance training. Many Americans are attracted to Asian forms in the first place due to their perceived or actual connections with spirituality. Many Asians are aware of the connection that Americans make between spirituality and Asians. Bharata natyam artist Ramaa Bharadvaj comments:

> I am dancer — that's what I have been all my life. When you are a dancer from India, actually when you are anybody from India, people attribute all kinds of images to you — you are a meditating divinity, a snake charmer, a fiery curry-eating dragon, a floating vision of beauty, and of course a yogic contortionist. Having mastered all the other aspects of the image (except the snake thing!) it was only this Yoga that stood in the way of my becoming the "perfect" Indian. So you can understand my determination to attempt this as well. Of course, I had no concept of what Yoga postures were all about, but then how difficult could they be? [March 2, 2002].

But Indians also attempted to give bharata natyam a spiritual aspect because, in the revival of the form that occurred in the 1930s and 1940s, spirituality gave bharata natyam a greater respectability. Janet O'Shea describes how E. Krishna Iyer, one of the leading figures in the revival movement, infused the dance tradition, taken from the devadasis, professional dancers who were perceived by many to have debased a formerly devotional tradition to a secular performance style given over to erotic display, with spirituality: "He modified elements associated with the devadasi legacy, such as humorous interludes and spectacular display. His revivalist agenda positioned indigenous tradition within women's practices, while his reforms privileged spirituality over humor and devotion over eroticism" [2007, 116].

Sometimes individual dancers read into or find that the dance genre they have chosen brings a spiritual or meditative quality to them. Tomie Hahn notes: "Nihon buyo lessons often seem spiritual in nature, extending beyond the rudiments of dance steps or music. It is not uncommon for Soke and Iemoto to speak about learning dance as a process for understanding and spirit. They often stress the value of learning through the body and of *kokoro* (literally — heart, soul, spirit), an expressive essence projecting from one's inner self within the body" (Hahn 2007, 41).

Sellers-Young also emphasized the spiritual aspects of nihon buyo: "Despite the secularization of popular performance forms such as kabuki, Japanese theatre purports an emphasis on the spiritual dimension that is not necessarily found in western theatre. This influences the movement style of the forms as they become representations of the continuity of tradition and by extension ancestors and age..." (1993, 37).

The master teachers also implicitly inculcate spiritual values through their teaching methods:

> Their ability to pay attention to detail, concentrate on large amounts of nonverbal information, and develop a sense of stillness is encouraged by the method which Kanriye Fujima uses to teach the dance pieces.... This increased sensitivity is developed from paying attention to the details of your surrounding environment and extending your conscious awareness into the feeling state of those around you. The Japanese phrase for it is omoiyari, or empathetic understanding [Sellers-Young 1993, 154].

Anne von Bibra Wharton said, "I find Javanese dance meditative. It suits my personality because when I perform it I am inwardly focused. I do not look at the audience. I brought that meditative quality from UCLA, Tri does not stress that too often. And when I perform people sometimes ask, 'Where has Anne gone?'" (personal interview, June 11, 2007).

Many of those who undertake the arduous path of learning an Asian classical music or dance tradition most value the spiritual aspect of the learning process, which they are able to use in other areas of their daily existence.

## Appearance

When a mainstream American appears in the context of the Other may experience a variety of responses. In the United States, mainstream American producers, curators, and presenters frequently want, and even demand, Indian-appearing dancers in their productions. Chitresh Das, the master kathak dancer and teacher in the San Francisco Bay area, said, "I had to adamantly resist the requests of promoters to 'darken' the skin of my non–Indian dancers in order to pander to someone's idea of the exotic" (personal interview, June 12, 2004). Such reactions can occur in both large cities and small towns.

Richard Kennedy, following the rigid guidelines for participation in the Smithsonian Institution's Folklife Festival, established by Ralph Rinzler, the original director, excluded a Caucasian woman from performing in a Korean American dance company from Hawaii several years ago. That woman had founded and was the director and teacher of the company and was an outstanding exponent of Korean dance. Her company members begged the directors to allow her to perform, but by the racially based rules of who could participate in the Smithsonian event they would not relent. Kennedy said, "I would not make the same decision today," showing a more enlightened policy (personal interview, June 27, 2003).

Further:

> Harnish notes the double bind of (doing rural Ohio the service of) "creating Bali" where none exists, while experiencing discrimination in being denied participation in an Asian festival. He writes, "The booking agent explained that the Asian Chamber of Commerce, which sponsors the festival, did not think that a gamelan consisting almost exclusively of Caucasians and directed by one could properly represent an Asian culture. We did not appear "authentic" and could therefore not truly "speak for Bali or Indonesia or Asia" [Solís 2004, 13].

Reactions among Japanese viewers and the public toward American and un–Japanese performers vary widely. Barbara Sellers-Young had positive experiences with her sensei [master], Kanriye Fujima, when preparing for a public concert or appearance, "In requesting students to perform, Kanriye Fujima seems to make no distinction between those who are Japanese Americans and those who are either from interethnic families or represent other groups. Her choice seems to be guided by the ability of the dancer to fulfill the needs of a particular event" (1993, 125).

Leonard Pronko experienced mostly positive responses to his extraordinary ability to emulate Japanese movement practices of the Kabuki theater in spite of his obviously un–Japanese appearance. He appeared in Japanese television and received high Japanese government recognition for his artistic accomplishments.

Tomie Hahn observes:

> Within the Tachibana group my Eurasian appearance has never been an issue, and I have always felt a strong sense of belonging and acceptance. This attitude may be particular to my school, however. Unfortunately there are many cases of rejection of foreigners practicing Japanese traditional arts. A genre termed "Japanese dance," while it embraces and embodies Japanese culture, can simultaneously reject outsiders. It is an art expressed by the human form, but must one be Japanese to perform it? ... A culture's philosophies of the body and how philosophical/spiritual practices inform the aesthetic style embodied by the performer are also important factors to consider. Outsiders remain outsiders when such differences are crucial to a performing tradition [2007, 168].

Thus, the American attempting to negotiate another culture must take into consideration how welcoming the response to them will be. Sometimes it is a mixed reception, and there will always be individuals, both American and from other societies, who feel that only a person of the requisite ethnicity can properly perform an art form, an attitude that the folklorists at the Smithsonian Institution Folklife Festival maintained for decades:

> Several non–Japanese colleagues practicing traditional Japanese arts have confided to me that they receive strong reactions from Japanese audiences, particularly to aspects of their physical appearance, which represent Japanese nationalism. I find it interesting that many gaijin [foreigners] visual artists, tea ceremony practitioners, and monks have been more readily accepted within Japanese communities, yet performers whose bodies are displayed in public as instruments of their art are often discouraged, ignored, or merely included as a novelty.... These considerations can be quite painful for performers involved in traditions outside their (physical) heritage.... But if dance is seen as a system of representations that are culturally coded, then "outsiders" practicing the tradition can be included on some level [Hahn 2007, 169].

There are also occasions when nonnative practitioners are regarded as appropriating cultural products from native artists in a neocolonial gesture. These issues of appropriation and colonialism often haunt those of us who have entered the world of Asian dance and music for years:

> Ultimately, it is our personally conflicted relationship to tradition itself that provides our greatest anxieties and profoundest self-examinations. As Westerners, or even as Western-employed non–Westerners, we are vulnerable to accusations of cultural appropriation and misrepresentation. We fall between Scylla and Charybdis in that the more self-consciously we embraced "authenticity," and the more earnestly we attempt to present what we perceive to be "accurate" cultural context and practices to our audiences, the more likely we are to fall into a sort of benevolent, essentializing, and (in the words of Harnish) "domesticating orientalism." In the end, whether we adhere fiercely to what we perceive as orthodoxy, or shed all pretexts to "accurate" reproduction, we know we may be charged with either neocolonialism or irresponsible cultural squandering [Solís 2004, 17].

On the other hand, I have found that many individuals welcome the interest of outsiders in their culture. They find it flattering that foreigners find their cultural production worthy of learning by nonnatives. My own experiences have been overwhelmingly positive in my work with Iranians. That community has honored me with many awards for my creative work in the field of Iranian dance, and, through the many decades that I have researched, choreographed, and performed, many Iranian individuals have reached out and unstintingly taught me everything they could.

## Contingent Meanings of Asian Classical Dances

An important aspect of learning the dance is understanding that performances of these traditions change in different environments. First, in the land of origin, dancers who perform for cognoscenti and native audiences create a meaning for their most knowledgeable audience members. The native individual who studies to achieve professional artistic and perhaps, ultimately, master status study all of their lives. Sellers-Young notes: "The average Japanese student continues to study for a lifetime" (1993, 10). These students of Asian forms generally intend to follow a life of performing.

Others in the country of origin frequently learn these forms not to gain professional status but for social reasons. Sellers-Young notes that for Japan:

> The increased number of schools of dance in the 1920s coincided with Kanriye Fujima's study of buyo. It also coincided with the development of a middle class who could afford to have their daughters study one of the classical art forms. The parents' goal was to prepare their daughters through the study of the arts for their responsibilities as adults. They also believed education in the arts would help them to find more attractive marriage partners. Therefore young women were encouraged by their families to study what was at that time called odori, along with flower arranging, classical music, and the tea ceremony. As a student, the daughter would develop qualities such as seshin or spiritual strength [1993, 20].

This use of the dance resembles the way in which middle class and elite families in England and America arranged for dancing masters to teach their children social dancing to enable them to appear well in debutante balls and the marriage mart. Young girls of these classes, as Jane Austen readers are aware, were generally taught water color drawing, the playing of harp or piano, and other accomplishments to make them more marriageable.

In the diasporic communities of India, Japan, and other Asian groups, dance and music also became vehicles to express ethnicity. When one lives in the country of origin, ethnicity is implicit in one's existence; it is not necessary to express ethnicity through specific art forms. Most individuals take their native cultural traditions and genres for granted. In the native environment, an individual generally undertakes the learning or performing of an art form for aesthetic reasons. "Growing up in Japan you take for granted art forms like nihon buyo and want to learn about western things, but when you get to the United States and look at Japanese arts from the perspective of living here you begin to see how beautiful they really are and what important values they can teach you" (Sellers-Young 1993, 68).

On the other hand, those living in the diaspora communities frequently find a need to explicitly express their ethnicity for the continuity of that ethnicity through the younger generations in an alien environment. Also, one finds that immigrant communities utilize dance and music traditions as a means of representing their ethnicity and as a means of burnishing the image of the community in performing arenas like international folk dance festivals (see Shay 2006). Barbara Sellers-Young notes that, for the Japanese American community, "The kimono clad Japanese female performer seems to represent for Japanese American communities in the Pacific Northwest both the country from which they came and the life their families have created in America ... what Sherry Ortner refers to as a 'summarizing symbol'" (1993, 164).

These summarizing symbols, through constant visual reinforcement in the contexts of festivals, restaurants, films and other popular media, provide an instant, essentialist image of the community for both insiders, as noted by Sellers-Young, and outsiders. The kimono clad female figure symbolizes Japan for most people. The sari-clad figure and bharata natyam hold a similar place in Indian society:

> The dance form, and especially its amateur practice, also provides a means for immigrants to maintain their social identity in diaspora.... Parents encourage their daughters to study bharata natyam in the hopes of their performing an arangetram, or solo debut. The arangetram, for many young women, marks their entry into a middle-class diasporic Indian community rather than into the performance milieu, often terminating a period of dance study instead of inaugurating a dance career [O'Shea 2007, 3].

Such performances also show the daughter in a favorable light, and helps to present her as a desirable and culturally accomplished marriage partner.

Yet, a third major performance arena generates meaning for Asian classical forms and that is within the concert halls and festivals of the west, in which for over a century since the first appearances of Asian dances in world exhibitions, in true orientalist style, audiences search for meaning and truth in "ancient" and "timeless" in traditional dance and music performances that they feel are lacking in their own lives:

Critics, dancers, and scholars who have queried the recontextualization of bharata natyam in the early twentieth century have seen it as a transformation as well as a restoration. Yet some performers, promoters, and viewers, both within and outside the form, still label bharata natyam as unproblematically, consistently traditional, classical, and ancient, fixed and untroubled by modern concerns [O'Shea 2007, 14].

And yet recent studies have revealed that many of these "timeless" and "ancient," practices like those of bharata natyam, described by Janet O'Shea, and Javanese court dance, as described by Felicia Hughes-Freeland, have been considerably reinvented and recontextualized, and even to a large degree nationalized, that is, seized upon by some nationalists to embody an essentialized Indonesia or (Mother) India:

> During the New Order period (1966–68), President Suharto began to emphasize the development of a national culture based on regional traditions. Despite this emphasis on regional diversity, it was the history and values of the Javanese, the largest ethnic group, that were used to promote Indonesian nationhood.... Javanese court dance was transformed into the Indonesian classical tradition. Continuity and longevity are emphasized in written histories of classical court dance in Java and in stories about origins of the dances. Local historians play down processes of change and construct the dances as genres that are defined by essential and unchanging qualities. My anthropological research into contemporary performances, on the other hand, revealed that in practice, rather than being fixed as discrete genres, dances varied over time according to the context [2006, 54].

In the new world of transnationalism and hybridity, and the continued circulation of exoticism suggested by Savigliano's magisterial study of the marketability of passion and exoticism, Indian, Japanese, and other teachers of Asian classical dances offer courses through their Websites.[5]

Thus American dancers seriously devoted to the study of these Asian genres must negotiate the often muddy shoals of meaning they must traverse in their quest for learning and mastering a specific tradition that is fraught with conflicting meanings — national, aesthetic, gendered, personal. And yet, even if they are individuals who have spent many years in training in a specific style, they find that the learning of an Asian classical dance tradition has bequeathed them the gift of new ways of learning that sustain them in other ways of moving if they enter new or different movement traditions. Conversely, the spiritual lessons learned in acquiring the Asian tradition gives the gift of "stillness" and other methods of confronting the difficulties of quotidian life. As Barbara Sellers-Young observes through learning nihon buyo, "I realized I had become comfortable with suggestion, irregularity, and simplicity" (2006, 8).

# EIGHT

# Latin American Dances: Sex and Sin Made Safe

STANDING IN STARK CONTRAST to the perceived spirituality and timeless high art that characterizes the way in which mainstream Americans generally view Asian classical dance traditions, Americans for over a century have regarded, and continue to regard, Latin dance genres such as tango, salsa, mambo, and samba as sexy, deliciously dangerous forms of choreographic expression, reflecting the dangerous and exotic types of Latinos who dance them. Asian classical dances are generally regarded as elite high art, and indeed the most visible connections of Cambodian, Javanese, Thai, Northern Indian kathak, and Japanese classical dance forms like *Noh* and *Bugaku* are associated with the palace, and other forms such as Balinese dance and Southern Indian *bharata natyam* are, in the popular imagination, connected to temples. Sometimes these forms carry both the royal and spiritual connection since the palace and temple in many Asian societies are intimately connected, thus these forms can carry a double cachet of prestige: royalty and spirituality.

Too, for Americans, the Asian classical music forms are accompanied by musical forms that are either ethereal like the gamelan or Indian ragas, or very foreign and incomprehensible like Japanese classical music for Bunraku. The rhythms, melodies, and lyrics which guide the choreographic forms are difficult to discern — all is alien. Latin American music, with its frequently African base, is driven, above all, by compelling rhythms, which mainstream Americans perceive as hot and fiery. And even though those rhythms are frequently extremely complex and dense, Americans feel that they are able and compelled to move to them. "I've Got Rhythm" became an anthem for many middle-class Americans from the advent of the popularity of Latin American rhythms and dance forms in the 1930s and 1940s.

Thus millions of Americans who have seen exciting performances of

169

these dances in films or stage performances have been drawn to perform some form of these exotic and exciting dances. That trend continues today with the salsa craze. At a recent conference on Latin American dance at the University of North Carolina the conference organizers issued notices of classes and dances to accompany the conference: "While the promise of dance instruction at 8:00 P. M. had lured several hundred curious North Americans for whom the lambada had served as the most recent illusion in the U.S. media phantasmagoria of 'hot!' 'sexy!' Latin dances, the cosmopolitan Latin American students and professionals living in the Triangle came expecting 'authentic sounds.'" (Delgado 1997, 5–6).

Thus, we can see that the meanings of these dances' cultures circulating transnationally throughout the northern and southern hemispheres are contingent and complex. The ballroom versions of these dances danced in social environments may provide a moment of excitement and thrill to move in a new and exotic way for many North Americans, but they hold nothing central to his or her identity. For Latin Americans they constitute an integral part of identity, politics and history: "The body dancing to Latin rhythms analyzes and articulates that conflicts that have crossed Latino/American identity and history from the conquest of the continent to California's passage of the racist Proposition 187" (Delgado and Muñoz 1997, 9).[1] Such divergence of meaning between mainstream Americans and Latin Americans leads to observations like "Ernest Sábato echoes widespread feeling in Argentina when he says, 'Only a gringo would make a clown of himself by taking advantage of a tango for chat or amusement'" (Taylor 1998, 11). Sábato, in his comment, touches on the notion of the issue of patrimony, ownership and appropriation by foreigners who do not, in his eyes, fully understand a dance tradition that stands as an icon of Argentinean identity.

Thousands of mainstream Americans, beginning in the 1980s, give their lives to the tango, Cuban dance forms, samba, and other dance forms. Like their earlier Balkan counterparts, the Americans pursuing Latin American dance forms learn the languages and travel to Brazil, Cuba, and Argentina to make a pilgrimage, often defying American governmental orders, to Havana, or to Buenos Aires to inhabit the *milongas* to experience real Argentineans performing the tango or to Bahia and Rio de Janeiro to see candomblé rituals, *capoeria* events, and perform the samba.[2] They search for a real and authentic dance experience and colorful if poor native existence, perceived by many to be absent in suburban American life since World War II:

> I had wondered why my seeking out tango practices in Buenos Aires had taken
> on a dimension so compelling that sometimes I found myself abandoning all
> other activities to sleepwalk to another shabby dance hall. It seemed at first that
> in a culture physically expressive of affection, I, as a member of a culture that is

Linda Yudin teaches Brazilian dances at the Pierre Verger Foundation, Salvador, Bahia, Brazil, 2006. Photograph by Mauro Rossi. Courtesy of Linda Yudin.

not, was simply pulled to a moving statement of that affection among companionable, *tiernos*, serious dancers who accept me as one of them [Taylor 1998, 69].

There sometimes exists a kind of reciprocity between the country of origin and the Americans seeking new identities through dance: "The late 1980s tango boom in the Northern Hemisphere continues to reverberate in Argentina — not only are there more Argentines who dance for the love of it, but also there are more foreigners who come to learn to teach" (Taylor 1998, 33). Loreen Arbus called Buenos Aires "the Mecca of tango" (personal interview, June 28, 2007). In this way we see a major difference between the earlier generations of tango lovers at the turn of the century and those at the end of the twentieth century. The earlier generations took up the dance as a fad, learning the tamed, safe version taught by the Castles and others in elite tango teas. Those early generations did not seek new identities in the countries of origin, nor did they wish to encounter any actual Latinos but confined their fantasies to Hollywood films and safe studio dance classes, none of which featured Latino persons.

But the newer generation, like the followers of Balkan dance, Middle Eastern belly dance, and Asian classical dance forms, seeks the authentic and makes the pilgrimage to Argentina to experience the "real" tango, rumba, or samba. They live it in local *milongas* in Buenos Aires and dance studios in Havana as well as Argentinean, Cuban, or Brazilian night clubs in Los Angeles, New York, and Chicago and sometimes make the pursuit and performance of tango, samba, or rumba the center of their life.

Many of the Americans who pursue these dance traditions sense a kind of ecstasy. "By this time I had observed four days of fabulous dancing in Havana and wildly exciting, contrasting forms, and I had already fallen in love with Cuban folkloric dance. But rumba was profoundly different from the other Caribbean dances I had come to know, perform, and love. Rumba was Cuban, not African or Spanish" (Daniel 1995, 7). I heard this theme of entrancement with dance forms echoed throughout my own experience and research with passionate fans of each genre.

Latin American dance genres more often constitute a part of popular culture with both Hispanic and African roots; they are, more often than not, the people's cultural production — dances of the streets and fields, the favelas and slums, of the down-trodden and enslaved. "For a sense of order and dignity they [the Blacks in Brazil] turned again to the two things slavery had not confiscated and used against them: samba and *candomblé*— music and religion, the end products of centuries of clandestine worship of the African gods" (Guillermoprieto 1990, 8). Many of the Latin American dances have folk dance or social dance roots, some of the dances of African origins have spiritual and religious roots, and local as well as Spanish, European, and African origins.

Above all, Latin American dances were, and still are, ambivalently regarded by many mainstream Americans as sexual: curved rather than square, rotating pelvises and flexible torsos rather than upright and uptight spines:

> The ascription of sexuality (or dangerous, potentially overwhelming sexuality) to subordinate classes and "races" or to groups of specific national origins (blacks, "Latins," and other such groups lumped together terms to denote non–Anglo-European ancestry) yields such descriptions as "fiery," "hot," "sultry," "passionate." All of these terms have been used to describe the tango, for instance, or the lambada, or in marketing recent movies using those dances, such as *The Gypsy Kings*.... But in almost every case the spread of the dance craze to the non–Latin population is represented and promoted in terms of the dance's sexual allure [Desmond 1997, 40–41].

Some of these dance traditions have been popular in the United States for over a century. A few, like the tango, have retained popularity in American ballrooms throughout the century, especially popularized as they were by Rudolph Valentino and other dance stars of the cinema and the ballroom from 1910, in which the dance stars created the image of Latin "hotness," and later by a series of theatrical productions like *Tango Argentino,* which established a new wave of Anglo American tango aficionados for the younger dancers and a revival for the older generation in the 1980s. Other dances, like the *lambada,* constitute fad dances and have a shorter shelf life.

Like the dances of the Balkans, Latin American dances can often become generic in the sense that many Americans perceive the different dances as vaguely "Latin" rather than Cuban, Brazilian, Mexican, Puerto Rican, or Argentine. I will examine this essentialist Anglo-American approach to Latin American dances later.

## Historical Roots and the Development of Latin American Dances in the Countries of Origin

Latin American dances also stand in contrast with Asian classical forms, which are regarded as timeless, unchanging and traditional, because many of the Latin forms last for a single generation and then, through constant changes created by the Latino participants who constantly reinscribe the dances with inventive improvisations, they become new dances: "The tango is a dance with a non-rigid structure that developed through trial and error; it is continually transformed through improvisation and is passed on from generation to generation" (Azzi 1998, 93).

In addition, these dances often become new dances, the same way in which the mambo morphed into cha-cha-cha, *candombe* and other dances into tango, etc. For example, dance historian Morton Marks notes that today's popular Latin dance floor hit, the salsa, comes from such a choreographic genealogy:

> Perhaps the best musical example of such an interplay is the *son-montuno.* The son began as a couple dance in Cuba's Oriente Province, accompanied by a mix of Spanish-based folk guitars and Afro-Cuban percussion; moving west to Havana, it expanded in percussive elements, especially in the final *montuno* section. This dance became internationally popular in the 1930s, sometimes mistakenly called "rumba." The *son-montuno's* synthesis of Spanish and African musical elements forms the basis of contemporary New York City salsa, whose dance elements have been derived from the mambo [1998, Volume II, 274].

Marks illustrates through several examples of this type of choreographic development that resonate in American ballrooms. For example, instead of originating as a folk dance of African origin like the rumba or samba, the French *contredanse,* introduced into Cuba by white Haitian landowners fleeing the revolution, evolved into the *habanera,* and then the *danzón,* which is "considered the national dance of Cuba … and remained an upper-class genre for private clubs and literary societies" (*ibid.* 275). Then in the 1930s some musicians "created what was called the 'new rhythm' danzón, which came to be the mambo.... The cha-cha, one of the most popular of all Cuban dances, is an extension of the *danzón-mambo*; through a long series of steps it too may be traced back to the French *contredanse*" (*ibid.*).

One can trace many of these popular dances to other dances, as the African *umbiguado* to the samba, and those with the most compelling rhythms and sexy movements ultimately are, through time and the process I call "taming," and in a somewhat altered, sometimes almost unrecognizable, form are introduced into middle class ballrooms:

> Rumba was and is associated with African communities in the Americas; however, in its most commercial form it has also been associated with whites and a style of ballroom dancing called rhumba rhythms; the popularized ballroom style does not resemble the original Cuban dance, sometimes contrasted as *rumba del campo*, or rumba from the countryside [Daniel 1995, 18].

Ultimately, there are multiple tangos, rumbas, and sambas, named for context, historical period, musical characteristics and tempi, and the class of people who dance them. They form parallel traditions to one another (see Azzi 1998; Marks 1998; Savigliano 1995).

These dance traditions are sometimes deeply implicated in the construction of national identity. Following the example of the founding of Ballet Folklorico de Mexico, and in the case of Cuba the example of the state supported folk dance ensembles in the former Soviet Union, dance became a vehicle for displaying specific national identities:

> Rumba has been selected by Cuban authorities (either the Ministry of Culture, the directors of the national dance companies, or the organic educational process of the Cuban Revolution — no one is quite sure which entity is fully responsible) as important dance material. Since the Revolution of 1959, rumba has emerged as a symbol of what Cuba stands for among its own people and what Cubans want the world to understand when the international community envisions Cuba and Cubans [Daniel 1995, 7].

Linda Yudin, a devotee of African-Brazilian dance and director of the Vivir Brazil! Ensemble of Los Angeles, had her first experience of that tradition through a dance company sponsored by the Bahia tourist organization. Such companies produce iconic images that, sponsored by tourist bureaus, are designed to draw tourists through colorful and exciting performances that feature stereotyped images (see Shay 2002). Since Carmen Miranda's iconic appearance in a highly theatricalized version of the African-Brazilian Baiana costume, samba has become the iconic image of Brazil that has drawn thousands of American tourists to Carnival in Rio de Janeiro. Jane C. Desmond astutely observes:

To the Brazilian audience that first saw the stylization of the black baiana woman, often seen selling food on the streets of the northern city of Bahia and associated with the practice of the candomblé religion, would have been immediately apparent ... but the origins and meanings attached to such recreations were lost on the middle-class United States populations who flocked to her movies and sambaed the night away. For most North Americans, Miranda came to symbolize "Latin" music and dance. Within Brazil, a different type of genericization took place. The samba, which developed in the African-Brazilian community and which Miranda helped popularize in the United States, soon spread to all sectors of the Brazilian population and came to be a marker of "Brazilian" culture [1997, 42].

In the same way that the samba, after its popularity spread to North America, became popular in its land of origin, Brazil, the tango has come to represent Argentina, both within Argentine society and throughout the world. In the latter case, rather than simply crossing racial lines, class and sexuality constituted barriers within Argentine society:

Like other Latin Americans, but perhaps even more accurately and constantly, Argentines remember that tradition had phrased their dilemma in cruel terms: Civilized or barbarian? Respected nation or banana republic? Independent agent or pawn? The tango reflects this Argentine ambivalence. Although a major symbol of national identity, the tango's themes emphasize a painful uncertainty as to the precise nature of that identity. For Argentines, this dance is profound, although at the same time profoundly enjoyable [Taylor 1998, 3].

But, reflecting Savigliano's themes of exoticism in her masterly portrait of the emblematic dance, *Tango, and the Political Economy of Passion* (1995), the tango, and the spectacle of Argentine identity has been packaged for a series of popular and highly profitable tours, beginning with *Tango Argentino*, that have reinvigorated interest in the tango throughout the world and added to the economy as well.

## Images of Latin American Dance in the American Imagination

In the decade of 1910–1920, a dance craze swept the United States that reflected an increasing economic and social independence for American middle-class and elite women. The media, especially the exploding Hollywood film industry and women's magazines, produced the first images of the tango. "In the popular image of the tango, Valentino or a counterpart, dressed dashingly in bolero, frilled shirt, and cummerbund, flings a partner backward over the ruffled train of her flamenco costume. One or the other holds a rose" (Taylor 1998, 1).

This fantasy image, which owed as much to Andalusia as to Argentina, was not uniformly welcomed by all Americans; it was looked at askance by much of the homophobic male population. Males who participated in dance, especially on a professional level, were frequently regarded as gay. American men still react to the potent gay image: "Several teachers reported that Argentine, Japanese, and European men readily learn dancing with their male teachers, but that it is necessary to provide a female partner when teaching a North American male student" (Tobin 1998, 92). Had American men known that Argentine men danced together in Buenos Aires at the turn of the century, they would have been stunned. Their negative reactions toward the tango would have been more violent and they would never have undertaken learning it. Ignorance of geography again permitted American men and women to learn exotic dances and inscribe themselves within the fantasy images depicted in Hollywood films rather than the realities of the port district of Buenos Aires.

This view of dancers as gay was especially true of Rudolph Valentino, who epitomized the "tango gigolo," those males who were paid by wealthy women in New York City and other locales to escort them to tango teas, a popular social activity of the period. "The paid dance partners at tango teas were often immigrant, lower-class Italians and Jews who had acquired a sufficient veneer of clothes and manners to allow them to cater to American women's new preoccupation with the pleasure of dance" (Studlar 1993, 26).

While Valentino's appearances popularized the tango with women, at the same time, his foreign appearance and graceful mien drew censure and suspicion from men. "By offering up an eroticized and androgynous male body, dance appeared to be threatening to an athletic, physically based American masculinity" (Studlar 1993, 34). She adds:

> Valentino's first appearance in the film [*The Four Horsemen of the Apocalypse* 1921] occurs in a "stunning designed" dance scene that crystallizes the era's fascination with (and fear of) dance as a stimulus on the sexual imaginations of American women.... Women's pleasure, dance, and the future of American male identity were united in popular discourse even as Rudolph Valentino, film star, would be grafted on to this same controversy [1993, 29, 27].

Studlar notes that "Even Vernon Castle, the darling of café society until he went off to World War I to train pilots, could not escape slurs.... Vernon's masculinity could be redeemed by [a heroic] death; Valentino would not be so lucky" (*ibid.* 40). Musicologist Susan C. Cook adds: "As the quotations from his obituaries make all too clear, Vernon Castle's dancerly manhood was not entirely recuperated until his death" (1998, 148).

This attitude changed dramatically in the decades of the 1930s, when dancing stars like Fred Astaire, who established himself as "a regular guy"— heterosexual, white, middle class in spite of being a dancer — within the first

Loreen Arbus and Alberto Toledano perform a classic Argentine tango, 1995. Photograph by Mike Hishimoto. Courtesy of Loreen Arbus.

few minutes of all of his films, made it safe for American men to dance. Through Astaire's unassailably masculine, but not handsome, persona, men could more safely dance, provided that the dances were properly tamed — no roses, no hips, no pelvises. Literary and cinema historian Steve Cohan notes: "Fred Astaire is a highly theatricalized representation of maleness on screen which oscillates between, on the one hand, a fictional character grounded in the static and reductive binarism of traditional gender roles and, on the other, a musical persona whose energy choreographs a libidinal force that revises conventional masculinity and linear desire" (1993, 63–64). Through this astute packaging, Fred Astaire was able to successfully negotiate the shoals of masculinity in ways that permitted him to evade the censure that Rudolph Valentino and Vernon Castle endured throughout their careers. And American men could venture more safely onto the dance floor.

In the pursuit of new and exotic identities, after the 1920s, Anglo-Americans were, and continue to be, attracted in mass numbers to sensual dance genres that they perceived as sexy, hip, and hot. A few of the more daring ones went slumming to experience the dangerous sexuality of the other because the one could experience the exotic natives and "the pleasures and passions that they enjoy [which] are closely related to their 'natural' as opposed to 'civilized' geographical and cultural environments" (Savigliano 1995, 86). In the Latin American dances they could, for a brief time through temporarily crossing class and racial barriers, assume the identity of the sexual lower "other," and then, after the dance, they could safely reassume their comfortable and safe middle class persona as they exited the dance space.

Anthropologist Jeff Tobin remarks that Americans like "playing whorehouse": In December 1995, Marta [Savigliano] and I attended a dance in San Francisco for which 'tango attire' was requested. Most of the men and women were dressed according to their ideas of how early tango pimps and prostitutes dressed. To me, the dancers looked like the cast of *Guys and Dolls*—gangsters and chorus girls — tangoized by the addition of a silk scarf here or a slitted skirt there [1998, 97].

Loreen Arbus describes the Sunday tango teas held at the Hollywood Roosevelt Hotel in the late 1980s and early 1990s harking back to the turn of the century, in which everyone "dressed up in everything we had ever fantasized, skirts with deep slits and stiletto heels. We all dressed in black because someone from Argentina said that tango dancers wore black, and in our ignorance, anyone from Argentina, whether or not they knew the tango, who said anything was like Holy Scripture, and we all believed. I later found out that it wasn't true" (personal interview, June 28, 2007). These events were the most popular for the tango community in Los Angeles in this period. In New York City the annual Tango Black and White ball is popular. The "tango" dress continues.

In contrast to the behavior and lifestyles that most mainstream middleclass Americans follow in their daily lives, these seekers of the Latin exotic flock to a night at a local club where they can dance salsa or tango Walter Mitty style. "In sum, all of these dramatic personae — the throw-back Guys and Dolls (and Carmens) of San Francisco and the updated pimps and prostitutes of Buenos Aires — evoke transgression, but it is a transgression that is kept safely straight — and white" (Tobin 1998, 98). In this environment Americans can don clothes they would never be caught dead in during the day and reappear after dark as Rudolph Valentino, a hip mobster, or a tango slut. As dance historian Jane C. Desmond observes:

> So what does it mean for an upper-middle-class Anglo suburban couple in Indiana to dance the tango, or samba, or lambada? On one level, by dancing "Latin" or "black" dance styles, the dominant class and/or racial group can experience a frisson of "illicit" sexuality in a safe, socially protected and proscribed way, one that is clearly delimited in time and space. Once the dance is over, the act of sexualizing oneself through a performance of a "hot" Latin style, or temporarily becoming or playing at being a "hot Latin" oneself, ceases.... But in doing so the meaning of the dance and the act of dancing undergoes a change. It is no longer "Latin" but now "Anglo-Latin" [1997, 41].

Many Americans receive a number of their impressions of these genres, and the Latino populations with which they originated, through the lens of films and television. As I remarked in my earlier study of Ballet Folklorico de Mexico:

> White America has generally regarded Mexico and Mexicans with a guarded ambiguity in which segregation and division derived through racism and linguistic distance has played a role. Images of street gangs, run-down East Los Angeles housing, and zoot-suiters jostle against those of docile, simple, polite domestics, oppressed farm workers, and dusty villages in Mexico. Hollywood films have dramatically portrayed mustachioed cruel and lethal Mexican revolutionary bandits, such as Pancho Villa, Emiliano Zapata, and Santa Ana, fighting and murdering the beleaguered good (American) guys in the Alamo. These melodramatic images vie with other Hollywood-created images of the Cisco Kid, Zorro, romantic Old California, festive holidays in the sun in Acapulco, and Betty Grable falling in love with a series of dashing (and rich) Latin lovers that dominated musical comedy films from the 1930s to the 1950s [2002, 86].

One only needs to recall that television in the 1950s, through the whitewashing of Ricky Ricardo (Desi Arnaz) in *I Love Lucy,* the series writers and producers turned the Ricky character into a Disneyesque, middle class, (almost) white man by making him cute and cuddly, and, therefore, safe to love Lucy, whose mangling and mimicking of Ricky's Spanish formed part of the plot. His appearances as the leader of a Cuban dance band also made his Latin music safe. In the 1950s, appearances by bands like those of Xavier Cugat and Desi Arnaz at ritzy nightspots in New York City and Hollywood announced that it was safe for the white folks to (safely) attend the dances and gingerly move their pelvises, a part of the anatomy that many of them did not know they possessed. "North American promoters and producers ultimately diluted Cuban social and popular dance forms for commercial purposes. Authenticity in terms of regional variation was disregarded; often any Latin-looking dance was called a rumba or a conga" (Daniel 1995, 43).

Linda Yudin performing the Brazilian samba de roda, 1998. Photograph by Steven Miller. Courtesy of Linda Yudin.

Through these iconic appearances, the frenetic and febrile renditions of Carmen Miranda's (the Brazilian "bombshell") samba are outstanding, but also in cartoon features like Walt Disney's *Three Caballeros*, essentialist fantasy images of "*the* Latin American" were constructed and reduced to stereotypes of "Latin Americans as overly emotional, inefficient, unorganized, and pleasure-seeking" (Desmond 1997, 43), and consumed by delighted middle class American audiences.[3]

## The Essential Latin American

"African-inspired rhythms ranging from tango to danzón to rumba and mambo have traveled across the continent, embodying static and interchangeable 'Latin' or even 'Spanish' identities in first-world music and film while paradoxically setting motion processes of Pan-Latino identification" (Delgado and Muñoz 1997, 12). In the same manner that I have described for Balkan and Middle Eastern belly dancers, many, if not most, of those mainstream Americans who dance Latin American dances have little idea of the specific countries and societies in which a dance originated. Jeffrey Tobin noted in a recent tango evening he attended: "A few geographically-challenged women were dressed as 'Carmens': Spanish señoritas, complete with peinetas in their pulled-back hair and mantillas draped over their shoulders. These women were examples of what Savigliano. calls 'Hispanolism': a stereotypical, colonizing representation in which the near-Other Spanish female stands in for extended Latin American hordes" (1998, 97). Thus stereotypical clothes, rhythms, and other elements of Latin American dances can be interchanged one for the other by those for whom Latin America, as does Edward Said's Orient, constitutes one large undifferentiated place:

> Rhythms have been an integral part of the complicated process of establishing and maintaining Latin American nations ... but Latin American music and dance have also been used by "others" to collapse such markers of national difference. Thus "Latin music" in the United States has often existed in a colonialist vacuum as a catchall category that collapses all the carefully nurtured (though often imagined) nationalistic origins of specific rhythms [López 1997, 311].

Much of this confusion comes through the media, such as television shows and Hollywood films in which the actors and dancers are quintessentially Latin rather than Cuban, Brazilian, Argentinean, or Mexican. As Jane C. Desmond observes:

> The Carmen Miranda figure, perhaps the most enduring and potent stereotype of the Latin bombshell ... [a] singer and a dancer, her bodily display was significant

in her rise to stardom in North America where her flirtatious charm ... and style of florid excess made her the premier symbol of Latinness during her heyday.... Miranda was by 1945 the ninth-highest-paid person in the United States. Her Brazilianness was soon turned into a generic "Latin" stereotype [1997, 42].

## Slumming

In this chapter I will show how twin processes allowed Desi Arnaz, tango, and samba to become chic, safe, and desirable. The first of these processes was "slumming" and the second was "taming."

Slumming is a phrase that is used to describe the process by which upper- and middle-class individuals escape from their daily lives, which they perceive to be gray and hum-drum although privileged, to have an excellent adventure among the lower orders. This concept is not new. The *Thousand and One Nights* contains stories in which the Sultan or Shah dresses like a commoner and goes among his people in Baghdad to hear what they think of him and to experience their lives.

In this instance, I use the term to describe upper-class white individuals in New York City going to Harlem to experience hot jazz, or Brazilian white men stealing off for an evening of dancing the samba. It can also apply to rich men going to watch the can-can in Paris or to tango in the brothels of Buenos Aires, Russian noblemen spending an evening among Gypsies, samurai viewing the kabuki in its earliest days, Spanish dons stealing away to hear flamenco, Iranian aristocrats visiting coffee houses, or wealthy Athenian Greeks going to the *taverna* to listen to the music of the down-and-out refugees from Turkey. It was definitely a process by which individuals, society's rich and dominant, usually male, patronized the poor; and a special frisson of excitement was provided if the performing lower class danced and played "in the societal margins" and, best of all, if the performers were also sexual outlaws whose services were available:

> Until this point [1910], the tango was considered to be a marginal, immoral, and indecent dance and as such was rejected by the *porteño*—the Buenos Aires high society. Nevertheless, the *niños bien* (sons of well-to-do families) frequented the brothels, where they danced and often fought with the *compadritos* [young men from the outskirts of Buenos Aires who imitated the attitudes of the *compadres*, gauchos who had moved to the city] [Azzi 1998, 92].

These men (and in the beginning it was largely men, but women too could participate in the process) were searching for that moment that Marta Savigliano calls "tango high": "That moment at which a particular, stabilized, experience of it is achieved. That moment, that event, is what I have improperly termed the tango 'high.' Improperly, because it is not euphoric, bubbly or happy, supernaturally transcendent or otherworldly. It is calm and fluid, comforting, as when things finally fall into place, difficulties are left behind and the reward is pure serenity, fully in control without effort, a fix of 'naturalness'" (1998, 104). Other American aficionados, however, do describe the sensation of the perfect night of tango dancing as euphoric and transcendent. They want to be part of the "naturalness" that Savigliano describes, to be as one with the natives.

Slumming constitutes an important part of the process of recognizing and then taming a particular dance or form of music. First, upper class individuals come to recognize a form of music and dance as "hot" and then they want to possess it. And in order to posses it they must tame it. In Brazil the slumming process for samba began at the turn of the century and accelerated by the 1930s:

> By the turn of the century carnival had become the staging ground for a new battle fought between the proponents of a "civilized" celebration and the recalcitrantly "African" blacks.... In Aunt Ciata's spacious residence on the outskirts of the Old City there may have been formal dances in the parlor, but there were African drum sessions in the backyard, and when the party got hot, there was samba. Her house soon became a meeting ground for sambistas.... Sinhô, the earliest master of the samba form was a regular. So was Donga, one of the first samba composers to tour in Europe. The samba chronicler Cold-Feet Turkey never missed a session. It could be argued that it was from Aunt Ciata's house that samba itself made the final leap to respectability.... The whites' official loathing of black culture always masked a secret attraction.... There were samba radio programs and samba recording stars, and the kind of fashionable slumming to samba parties that Harlem blacks of the same period would have recognized. Indeed, white love of samba emerged from the closet thanks to gramophone records [Guillermoprieto 1990, 24–31].

The slumming process, and contact with lower class individuals, creates a need to touch something that is "authentic" and "real." "For the middle-class listener, attending to this heartache is to live in fullness. So it happens that flamencas sing, and aficionados come away convinced that they have been involved in a truly and authentically HUMAN activity" (Washabaugh 1998, 35, capital letters in the original).

Slumming is not dead. Loreen Arbus remembers in the late 1980s that many middle class Americans, in their craving for the tango, braved going into dangerous areas of Los Angeles to satisfy their quest:

> There was a place near Wilshire Boulevard that was very unsafe and run down, where people lay in the streets with needles in their arms and you were lucky to find your car when you returned. It was the most amazing place; similar to the turn-of-the-century space in Buenos Aires where tango was born. You had to pass money through a barred window, the huge bouncer, who stood at the door

and never spoke, motioned you down a long flight of stairs. Once you entered, you found yourself in a smoke-filled bar that was filled with pimps and prostitutes wearing wigs, fake leopard skin, leather, heavy make-up and some cross dressers — a Latin version of Toulouse-Lautrec. Then you passed into yet another very long room with chairs on either side and there was a nineteen-piece *tropicál* orchestra. During the break a three-piece orchestra played tangos, the dancing featured Orlando Paiva. This occurred only on Wednesdays. I lived for these most miraculous nights of my life. Thursday morning inevitably brought depression [personal interview, June 28, 2007].

## Taming

The second part of the process, "taming," requires that the lower class dances and music had to be "tamed," that is, made safe for middle class white people. "The Latin couple, on the other hand, is enacting an entirely different narrative of courtship. This is one in which sex is the main attraction, their gyrating hip actions not merely referencing but reenacting movements from sexual intercourse" (McMains 2006, 142). Dance historian Yvonne Daniel describes her first encounter with the Cuban rumba: "Several other couples took turns looking for the possibilities of the pelvic thrust, or *vacunao*. I later learned that this word came from the Spanish verb *vacunar*, meaning primarily 'to vaccinate.' Cubans coined it to signify this erotic pelvic gesture, the object of male pursuit and female flight that is the aim of the dance" (1995, 4).

Thus taming means, first and foremost, that the dance must be transformed, cleansed of sexual references in order to be made safe for mainstream Americans. It is important to note that when the tango was introduced into Paris in 1905 it was eagerly "acquired by the upper classes, and then quickly spread to artistic milieus" (Décoret-Ahiha 2006, 86). "This bored and rigid society was suddenly passionately thrown into the possibility of living out their dancing nights to live in a naughty fashion, while safeguarding the appearance of respectability in an exotic style" (*ibid.*). The upper classes of Paris, unlike their American counterparts, appeared not to need the frankly sexual dances they learned to be made safe. Rather, they embraced the danger and open sexuality of them, at least in the beginning. But taming became inevitable as the dance spread to the French middle classes. Lewis Segal notes that the Castles, those popularizers and tamers of naughty Latin American dance genres, got their start in Paris.

In terms of Latin American dances in the United States, and for use in the media, taming required placing an unquestionably "American," and thus sexually pure, figure in the action of the film or television program in which Latin American actors and dancers performed. One way to achieve this was to have Lucille Ball as the star or to pair Betty Grable with a handsome Latino, sometimes the equally blond Argentine-born Dick Haymes, in a Hollywood version of an off-the-rack Latin American costume of vague origin, where they danced an American version of a Latin American dance in a ritzy hotel in Buenos Aires or Rio de Janeiro.

The second process, related to the first, was to make the dances safe, marketable and profitable, through simplifying them and "Anglo size-ing" them by watering them down and standardizing them. This process requires cleansing the dances, as far as possible, of improvisation, one of the hallmarks of most of the Latin American dance traditions.

Deleting the improvisation from the dance makes them easy to teach, and therefore more easy to market. Marta Savigliano notes: "The capitalist production and consumption of the Exotic (exotic Passion) does not affect only those directly involved in hierarchical exchanges of cultural and emotional capital. Exoticism is an industry that requires distribution and marketing" (1995, 3). Then it becomes easy to teach the passionate dances in dance studios like Arthur Murray's and send them down the ultimate road to popularization, featuring them on *Dancing with the Stars.* Many individuals, with their eyes fixed firmly on the main chance, can then make a fortune from teaching, making musical recordings, designing sexy costumes, and staging mega television programs, Hollywood movies, and Broadway shows. "Hollywood musicals' attention to Latin America also paralleled the rise of the Latin music boom in the United States in the 1930s and 1940s. The cinematic musical genre and the popularity of Latin rhythms developed simultaneously, each feeding off the other to maximize their market potential" (Lopez 1997, 315).

The ultimate means of creating a market was to tame the dances for wide public consumption, to teach the dances all over the country to match the popularity of the films featuring Carmen Miranda and Betty Grable. "The ballroom version of Latin dance are Western appropriations with only limited similarity to forms practiced in Latin America and that rely extensively on Western stereotypes of Latinness for their emotional and aesthetic appeal" (McMains 2006, 112).

> The method devised aimed not at keeping pace with a changing form, but with bringing the unruliness of improvisation under control: "the technique I then offered has come to be accepted as standard almost in its entirety, and Latin-American dancing now has a recognized standard technique, as static as may possibly be expected for a living and still developing form." Through a relentless process of Anglicization, [dance master Frank] Borrows sets out to standardize Latin American dance to the point of stasis.... The static standard of Anglo-American "Latin dance" must expel what Fernando Ortiz has described as "the rapid and extremely complex movements of the African dance, in which

feet, legs, hips, torso, arms, hands, head, face, eyes, tongue, and finally all human organs take part" [Delgado and Muñoz 1997, 12].

The most popular and beloved of these popularizers and dance tamers were Vernon and Irene Castle, who wrote books, set styles, appeared in Hollywood movies, ran a sensationally successful dance school, and became nationally prominent through their teaching of dances, including the tango, to high society. "Public discourse usually cited moral concerns behind the demand that suggestive and barbaric dances be cleaned up. In any case, the era's most popular dancing team, British-born Vernon Castle and his fashion-setting American wife, happily obliged" (Studlar 1993, 26). Susan C. Cook adds: "Thus, the public discourse surrounding the Castle's career and the dances they promoted relied on a set of historically specific dichotomies of primitivism and modernism, passion and control, that reflected contemporaneous concerns about racial appropriations, class and changing constructions of white masculinity and femininity" (1998, 133).

Central to the Castles' campaign of sanitizing dance was changing the discourse surrounding dance from a dangerous entertaining, sexually stimulating activity to dance as good, clean, healthy physical exercise and fun. Among the many suggestions in their "Castle House Suggestions for Correct Dancing" they wrote, "Do not wriggle the shoulders, do not shake the hips, and avoid low, fantastic, and acrobatic dips" (Quoted in Cook 1998, 143). These suggestions would hardly make it possible to authentically perform the rumba, samba, or any other Latin American dance.

Through this watering down process, what was in essence a new Euro-American form of the dance barely related to the original was created. This new version of the dance that was created became a parallel tradition. The Castles

> "Toned down," "tamed," and "whitened" such popular social dances as the Turkey Trot and the Charleston. Such revisions tended to make the dances more upright, taking the bend out of the legs and bringing the buttocks and chest into vertical alignment. Such "brokering" of black [and Latin] cultural products increased the circulation of money in the white community which paid white teachers to learn white versions of black dances.... On one level, it allows middle- and upper-class whites to move in what are deemed slightly risqué ways, to perform in a sense, a measure of "blackness" [or Latinness] without paying the social penalty of "being" black [Desmond 1997, 34–35, 37].

## Ambiguous Masculinity

Of course, in Latin America a similar process of taming occurred, since dances like the tango originated in the brothel district and, as historian Jorge Salessi convincingly argues, within the homosocial and homoerotic milieux of the port of Buenos Aires:

> Danced in the brothels or on the city street corners by pairs of men, "uranists" or the "like-inclined," cutting "lascivious figures" or making an overall representation of an erotic simulation, in the so-called age of forbidden music, the tango has significant homosexual and homoerotic connotations. This sexuality and this (homo)eroticism are characteristic of the worlds of prostitution and immigration of the Buenos Aires of the age [1997, 158–159].

Thus, when the tango was "discovered" by the *haute monde* of Paris, London, and New York, the elite classes of Argentina contested the ownership of this suddenly precious national treasure and attempted to wrest it away from the unworthy lower classes consisting of "longshoremen and pimps, of masons and electoral committee bullies, of criollo and foreign musicians, of butchers and procurers" (Salessi 1997, 158). It became imperative that the newly contested dance, with its sensually insistent music and salacious and suggestive lyrics, be made safe for the upper classes of Buenos Aires. This was done by cleaning up the lyrics and slowing the music "through the influence of music schools ... [so that] the tango began to lose the old cutting edge, transforming it into the sentimental dance we know now" (Catulo Castillo, composer of tangos, quoted in Salessi 1997, 168). It also required heterosexualization.

The ever-present specter of homosexuality lurked in the practices of the tango and created panic among Argentines almost as much as among their North American brethren. Unlike the Brazilians, the Argentines have a phobia about moving their torsos and pelvises. Anthropologist Julie Taylor heard her tango teacher warn his male students: "'Neither in the entire inventory of folk dances in Argentina nor in the tango do dancers move their hips.... For the Argentine man, in contrast with men of the rest of the continent,' the minilecture continued, 'to move the hips is effeminate'" (1998, 110). However, as anthropologist Jeffrey Tobin notes:

> Fieldwork in the contemporary Buenos Aires tango scene reveals that many men continue to spend much of their time on the dance floor in the arms of other men despite the availability of female partners.... Thus, contemporary tango-dance continues to be marked by forbidden homosocial desire. The contemporary tango couple dances its way back and forth, over the fortified and leaky border separating the straight and gay. After decades of traveling across marital, class, and national boundaries, it is possibly tango's nightly trip across this sexual boundary that continues to be its dangerous and forbidden passion [1998, 91, 84].

Homosexuality also appears as a theme in the United States in the world of professional ballroom Latin American dancing. Dance historian Juliet McMains notes:

Perhaps this dual macho/effeminate image of the Latin male in general, and Latin dancers in particular, is what leads so many gay men to participate in the Latin division of DanceSport. It offers them an opportunity to negotiate their own complicated relationship to the masculine/feminine binary. Although few Standard [Euro-American dance] male dancers identify themselves as homosexual, nearly half the professional male Latin competitors in the United States are openly gay [2006, 143].

## The Latin American Dance Scene Today

Television programs like *Dancing with the Stars*, hit stage shows like *Tango Fusion*, which appeared in April 2007 (Segal, April 26, 2007), street and community fairs, and local Argentinean, Cuban, Brazilian, and other nightclubs catering to Latin American clientele constitute the most prominent spaces for viewing and participating in the performance of Latin American social dances. In this variety of locations one can see the disparity between variations of the dance as performed by those native to the tradition and mainstream Americans who perform Latin American dances as social dance forms such as those found in ballroom dance competitions. "DanceSport Latin is a stylization of social ballroom dances that, although inspired by Afro-Caribbean and Latin social dance practices, were popularized in the West. After five to seven decades of revision at the hands of English, European, and American dancers, the DanceSport versions of the Latin dances bear little in common with contemporary or historical practices of Latin America" (McMains 2006, 110).

Cities like Los Angeles and New York, with their large Spanish-speaking populations, have always had many nightclubs and street fairs for the devotees of Latin American dance. And while it is popular to perform ballroom, or, in McMains' terms, DanceSport versions of Latin American dances in close to authentic forms because of the many clubs that cater not only to generic Spanish-speaking or Portuguese-speaking populations, but to specifically Argentinean and Brazilian ones. With the growth of Spanish-speaking populations generally throughout the United States, even in areas like North Carolina, which I indicated in the opening of this chapter, where thirty years ago it would have been nearly impossible to experience Latin American dances performed by native dancers, now one is able to find dance locales in many areas of the United States.

But, now a change has occurred in some contexts, like performing or DanceSport, and that change is a sort of reverse racism — "donning a mask of Latin-ness," as dance scholar Juliet McMains phrases it (June 24, 2006). Performers attempt to look like the natives, a phenomenon that did not occur in the earlier part of the century when individuals went slumming or danced

Loreen Arbus and Alberto Toledano perform the Argentine tango, 1995. Photograph by Mike Hishimoto. Courtesy of Loreen Arbus.

the tamed dances in tango tea dances at fashionable hotels. Through this process people acquired new identities. In DanceSport, dance historian Juliet McMains notes that:

> Every fair-skinned dancer has tested a dozen self-tanning products before settling on one that stains her skin dark enough to "pass" as a professional Latin DanceSport competitor.... After three generous coats of the bronze elixir have been absorbed into the skin, her "brownface" is complete, and this dancer is ready to withstand an entire evening of competition cha chas.... In America's racially fraught sociopolitical climate, there is no way to read the practice of brownface, particularly that of the Latin DanceSport competitors, that does not in some way have to do with race and the ethnic and national groups invoked by its visual marking [2006, 109–110].

She adds: "Brownface hides the history of actual racial discrimination out of which these dances were born and substitutes for that real-world inequality the illusion that racial and ethnic difference can be slipped on and off like a fashion accessory" (2006, 111).

This desire by many Americans to become the native through visual, linguistic, and other means, to adopt a new identity through the dances of the Other, constitutes a choreographic motif throughout this study. In many ways, those who pursue the tango with an intense passion are reminiscent of those in the other genres I described and analyzed. They go to Buenos Aires, study with the most famous teachers, and strive for authenticity. They even have their own ethnic police. Susan Lambreth, in her study of the large tango community in Chicago, found that among the overwhelmingly Anglo American participants that fill five venues every night "Argentine, as opposed to show or ballroom, tango is fraught with aggression and conflict" (unpublished paper, 2007).

The tango scene, like the Balkan and belly dance scene, is filled with devoted and passionate participants. Loreen Arbus notes:

> The tango is a dance that is about feelings, emotions, and individualism. Of course, it requires a basic tango vocabulary, but that can be simple. What one feels as opposed to the steps is important; if they just listen to the music and interpret it, then one can perform the real tango. The tango is a metaphor for everything in my life; it is everything I need in life. There is no emotion, feeling, or experience that is not conveyed through the tango. From happiness to the deepest depression, it is all there. What other dance has all of this? [personal interview, June 28, 2007].

With the popularity of lambada and salsa, and the reinvigoration of the tango, and the so-called Latin American dances of the ballroom dance scene, popularized by television shows like *Dancing with the Stars*, Americans look set to pursue Latin American dances in even greater numbers. Some will learn

Spanish or Portuguese and journey to Argentina and Brazil, Cuba and Peru to find and bring to life their choreographic dreams, where the fell hand of the Euro-American craving for standardization and taming has not yet destroyed the life of these choreographic treasures by desexualizing them and making them as bland and unpalatable and American as Mac-tango.

# Conclusion

IN THIS STUDY, I described and analyzed a phenomenon, both historical and contemporary, that occurred throughout the past century and continues today: the pursuit of learning and performing dances and musical traditions of exotic Others by hundreds of thousands of mainstream Americans who were not of the ethnicity or native to the dance and musical traditions they sought to learn and perform. Through the learning of these exotic dance traditions, many of these Americans, if only briefly, created new, more exciting and more romantic identities. This activity peaked in the periods of the 1960s and 1980s, but the movement continues today. Some genres of dance, like the tango and some other Latin American dances, have had a resurgence of interest, while belly dancing and Balkan dancing have somewhat faded in terms of the massive numbers of individuals who pursued learning and performing these dance genres in the period 1960–1990.

This mass interest in the exotic in the latter half of the twentieth century stemmed, in part, from increased travel opportunities for middle class individuals, the expansion of television programming with historical documentaries like *Roots*, the increased popularity of the recreational international folk dance movement, the spread of interest in classes in ethnomusicology, and the appearance of state sponsored folk dance companies. Moreover, many respondents cited a lack of warmth and a feeling of anomie in American life, or a repugnance, especially in the 1950s and 1960s toward racism, religious bigotry, and the violence of war and street crime that they perceived as rampant in American life during that period as a reason for escape into the world of exotic dance genres and as an impulse for seeking new identities through those dance forms. They were in search of the "real" and the "authentic."

Some individuals longed for the simplicity of peasant life (albeit in colorful costumes and without the backbreaking work and lack of plumbing), while others sought the sensual, slightly dangerous swank and glamour of a Middle Eastern harem or a Buenos Aires brothel. The degree to which this attraction for the exotic ranged widely from individual to individual. Some enjoyed surface aspects of exoticism like wearing colorful costumes and clothes, while others went more deeply into their passion for exotic dance genres; they learned the languages, history, and anthropology of the Balkans, Latin America, or Asia in depth, and plunged into exotic new worlds by spending months or years in foreign countries, sometimes changing their names, and occasionally becoming citizens of other nations.

Through their participation in the dances and music of other peoples, these Americans sought, if only briefly, to assume the identity of an exotic other. because many Americans, especially at the peak of the movement of learning and performing exotic dance forms, felt that they were leading dull and colorless lives, and that they possessed no ethnic roots of their own. Today, as three decades ago, "The overwhelming majority of white ethnics of European extraction are third-, fourth-, and later-generation Americans" (Waters 1990, 3). Television programs like *Roots*, which held many people spellbound for many weeks, impelled individuals to explore ethnicity, "but there was an awful lot of flux going on among these later-generation Americans" (*ibid.*, xii). This flux and malleable ethnicity provided an empty space for Americans to inscribe new, more exciting identities through performing the music and dance of exotic others.

Clearly, many Americans perceived life in the United States, particularly in the rapidly expanding suburbs and the economic boom following World War II, to be bland, colorless, and stultifying. Social critics like William J. Lederer described the lifestyle as a *Nation of Sheep* (1961) and David Riesman called Americans *The Lonely Crowd*, critiquing the blind, automaton-like behavior of Americans in a series of popular books in which terms like "rat race" and "gray flannel suits" became iconic expressions that described the blind consumerism, proliferation of fast food and quick gratification, and anomie that gripped many suburban Americans and characterizes the lives of many, even today.

Many of the younger generation reacted not only to the consumerism and blandness, but to the violent face of American culture such as the war in Vietnam, rampant racism, the ugliness of the Red Scare with its attack on civil liberties and a string of ruined lives, and religious intolerance that characterized American life, especially in the period following World War II. Many young people of the generation of the 1950s and 1960s turned their backs on their parents' and grandparents' values.

In the 1950s a number of liberal Americans turned to the folk song movement of Pete Seeger, Sam Hinton, and Theodore Bikel, but in the 1960s millions of the "baby boomer" generation avidly attended rock concerts — which featured rebellious, antiauthoritarian lyrics with antiwar and antiracist messages — such as those held at Woodstock. Moreover, an increasing number of middle-class and working-class youth enrolled in newly affordable universities and colleges. The explosion in higher education available after World War II provided another forum for deep questioning of American values, further driving a wedge between the generations. It was in the settings of the colleges and universities across America that many students discovered classes and clubs in which they could learn a variety of exotic dance genres.

Also, Americans purchased and avidly read the much-reported-upon Kinsey Reports (1949, 1952) and works by Betty Friedan and Simone de Beauvoir, which led many individuals to question the traditional gender roles and standards of rigid sexuality that characterized the middle classes in the United States into the 1960s. These studies and reports caused many Americans not only to question gender roles but also led many to regard their bodies in new ways. Seeking new sources to express a new-found craving for experiencing the sensuality of their bodies led many to experiment with new ways to use their bodies, and that included dance.

Many people, especially women, found the means to express their individuality, sexuality, and sensuality through forms of dance like belly dancing and various forms of Latin American dances. Through the performances of these new, exciting exotic dances they also found new, colorful identities. These individuals frequently found these new identities, and the corporeal senses that they released through dancing were liberating — socially, culturally, and sexually.

This confluence of changes in societal attitudes, the proliferation of venues in which individuals could experience and view exotic dances, and new opportunities in the form of classes in colleges and community centers, the formation of performing folk dance ensembles directed primarily by mainstream Americans, concerts by foreign state-supported dance companies, and the spread of ethnic restaurants and nightclubs provided hundreds of thousands of Americans the opportunity to experience these colorful and exciting choreographic and musical genres.

For many individuals, participation in groups like AMAN, Komenka, and Koleda provided a haven and a release from the confrontational politics and violence of the time. Rehearsals, classes, and nights in coffee houses became sanctuaries where one could live in the identity of a Balkan peasant, harking back to a perceived simpler time, to lives lived in honest labor at the end of which was a festive dance. Most of those who participated in folk dancing lived in happy ignorance of the ethnic horrors that characterized life in the Balkans from the gruesome Balkan wars, World War I, the ethnic strife in the interwar period, and the horrifying massacres of World War II. These horrors were brought home for many people only during the disintegration of the former Yugoslavia in the early 1990s.

Some of us who pursued exotic dance traditions were moved by the aesthetic aspects of the dances and music. Many of us, even though we embraced the performance of Balkan dance or belly dance as a core activity, also maintained an interest in other cultural forms. Several of the musicians in AMAN also played rock music and attended rock concerts. In addition to their heavy commitment to the time-consuming activities of AMAN several individuals participated in playing gamelan music, learning Asian classical dances, Scottish country dancing, flamenco, or other forms. I continued to play classical music and attend the opera and ballet performances. Other individuals threw themselves into the Balkan scene, tango, or belly dance world, to the exclusion of all others.

In no way do I wish to imply that the description and analysis of the phenomenon of acquiring alternative identities was a simple one. The individuals in these various dance activities frequently maintained several personae, and the multilayered meaning of their lives was complex. However, the fact remains that these activities formed a core identity for hundreds of thousands of individuals during the period 1955–1990, and, for many, the process continues today.

During the research I conducted on my most recent book, *Choreographing Identities* (2006), the issue of mainstream Americans participating in dance activities of other ethnic groups cropped up again and again. In many of the performances I attended of ethnic and immigrant groups performing in America in festival contexts, most of the groups included many individual performers who were not of the requisite ethnicity. This passion for the dances of the other had come to the unwelcome attention of folklorists all over the country — especially those involved with the Smithsonian Institution's Folklife Festival and similar events — who attempted to rigorously exclude participation by mainstream Americans in their presentations.

As folklorist Barbara Kirshenblatt-Gimblett states, "The 'performers' at the festival are to be those to whom the arts 'belong' by virtue of their having been acquired in a traditional manner and setting, that is, by insiders from insiders — by descent.... 'Outsiders,' that is, those who have chosen to learn the art even though they were not born into the communities that transmit it, are generally considered revivalists and may be excluded on this count.... Thus those who are licensed to do are distinguished from those who are mandated to watch" (1998, 75). As one of the excluded, following my study of the "insiders" (2006) I decided to undertake the study of the "outsiders" who were not content to simply watch.

The study addresses issues of heritage and ethnicity, gender and sexuality, cultural appropriation, and an analysis of which elements in American life and in these participating individuals impelled them to adopt identities that were frequently orientalist and exotic. Within these elements lie the many factors that contributed to the meaning of these mass movements.

**Ethel Hemsi and Victor Sirelson of the Dancing Crane Georgian Dance Theater of Warwick, New York, perform Kartuli, a Georgian folk dance, 2001. Courtesy of Victor Sirelson.**

What struck me so vividly in my research and life experiences participating in the dances of the Other, was the American-ness of the phenomenon of the numbers participating — hundreds of thousands of Americans. This massive movement contrasts with the relatively small numbers of individuals who participate in such countries as Japan, France, and Germany.

For purposes of better understanding this movement, I identified four gateways through which individuals were exposed to, enabled by, and sought participation in exotic dance genres. The first of these gateways is the enabling performance or other activity, such as a folk dance class that a friend takes one to that enables the individual to learn. This is expressed frequently by "I was hooked" (Anne von Bibra Wharton, June 11, 2007) or "I almost swooned" (Dick Crum, March 11, 2003).

I suggest that the second gateway that enabled many to undertake performances of exotic dance traditions was the performances of pioneer oriental dancers like Ruth St. Denis and La Meri, who through their interpretive dances created a space of respectability for women to perform in public as esteemed artists rather than as entertainers. They created the possibility for later generations of women to perform publicly. At the turn of the century, when those dancers performed, women who danced in public were considered prostitutes. Fifty years later, when I formed the AMAN Folk Ensemble and the AVAZ International Dance Theatre, dancing on stage was considered a privilege and an honor—a far step from previous attitudes. The research for this study enabled me to view the performances of those pioneer dancers in a different light. I suggest that these dancers were the mothers of the performance of various genres of oriental dance, not of modern dance.

The third gateway was provided by the recreational international folk dance movement that became established in the 1940s and peaked in numbers of participants in the 1950s. Many dancers began their careers in folk dance classes that had proliferated in colleges and universities and in community centers all over America. In many ways, the Balkan dance movement has deep roots in the recreational international folk dance movement, but the Balkan movement, as well as the other genres that I address in this study, provided a more profound experience for its participants than the social evenings in recreational international folk dance clubs did.

The fourth gateway was provided by the proliferation of ethnomusicology and dance ethnology classes that were established on many college and university campuses and spread in the 1960s and after. These classes today constitute a major way today for young people to encounter the magic of the gamelan, the excitement of Ghanaian drumming and dancing, or the richness of Bulgarian harmonies and rhythms.

Many Americans who entered one or more of these dance activities learned the steps and movements, the music and other aspects of the genre, but many also often acquired an alternate identity. For the geographically challenged Americans, in the beginning on their first exposure to a new genre of dance, they often entered a confusing generic world. Through the learning process, many learned that "Balkan" or "Latin American" had little meaning.

Rather, Serbian, Croatian, Bulgarian, or Brazilian, Cuban, and Argentinean and other specific ethnic groups carried more salience. Through travel and other encounters with individuals from Argentina, Brazil, or Cuba or Serbia, Croatia, and Macedonia, the generic became the specific.

Such a generic approach to learning the new dances courted the danger of trivializing the various dances and people new learners encountered. As I showed in examples in the study, the individual who thoughtlessly appropriates dances and publicly performs them in stereotypical fashion can deeply hurt members of the culture or society in which the dance originated. On the other hand, I have found that those of us who approach the learning of a dance genre, and the encountering, in a deep fashion, the culture and people who originally created it, can enrich our lives immeasurably.

Almost every individual in this work who participated, even briefly, in these choreographic activities holds them in fond memory. No one felt that they had wasted their lives or wasted their time in learning and performing these dances and musical forms. Almost every single person felt that they had enriched their lives through the contacts they had made, the human connections and friendships they established in the scene, the traveling they had done to the countries of origin. Above all, they learned to treasure the dances and songs and musical pieces they had learned and performed.

For many, the learning and performing of exotic dances and music was the core activity of their lives, and for those who no longer perform it still constitutes their fondest memories. For tango dancer Loreen Arbus and her partner, the late Alberto Toledano, "It was the only thing that we could not live without" (personal interview, June 26, 2007). I will let Mark Morris, who during his youth was absorbed by flamenco and Balkan dance, have the last word: "Then those experiences with different dance forms and different rhythms and different kinds of music just sort of became part of everything else that I know about" (1995, 204).

# Notes

## Introduction

1. I remember in my earliest participation in the folk dance movement in the 1950s and 1960s that the participation of individuals from ethnic minorities — Asian-Americans, African Americans, and Mexican-Americans, the largest minority communities in California at that period — was so rare as to be remarkable. Currently, the scene is only slightly more nonwhite.

2. The Uribe family attended my mother's 75th birthday party. Estella is still chic and beautiful.

3. Slumming refers to members, mostly male, of the elite classes visiting poor areas of the city to experience popular music. See the section on slumming in the chapter on Latin American dances in this volume.

4. I thank Barbara Sellers-Young for pointing out the existence of several institutions and centers in Japan and India that attract foreign students.

5. During the period when I served as choreographer and artistic director of two groups that specialized in dance traditions of the Middle East and Eastern Europe (1958–1995), many of the dancers and musicians under my direction undertook a variety of other genres outside of those included in our repertoire. These included various Asian dance forms like kathak, bharata-natyam, African forms, Scandinavian dances, flamenco, Hungarian dances and music, English Morris dancing, Scottish exhibition dancing, Mexican folklorico, and contra dancing, among others.

6. I will give two examples: (1) After an AVAZ performance in New York City, HRH Farah Pahlavi stated to the assembled audience in New York City that "I never expected to see my homeland again" (May 12, 1997). After a performance of the Podravina Wedding by AMAN, an elderly Croatian woman came up to me and said, "I was married in that village and that's just how it was" (1976). But that is not how it was: her wedding lasted five days, while my staging was 17 minutes.

7. At a recent 30th anniversary celebration for AVAZ International Dance Theatre (June 9, 2007), the old members, many of whom had not seen one another for over 15 or 20 years, and who were in their fifties and sixties, heard the music and began to perform as if it were only yesterday that they had rehearsed the dances. One bystander said wonderingly, "They look like they are in a trance." And, indeed, their faces glowed with wonder and enthusiasm. Averill's "light trance" descended on them during their performances of these choreographies that many had not danced for more than a decade. Mark Angel, one of the dancers, called it "bodily knowledge" (personal interview June 9, 2007). Others refer to the ability to remember old choreographies as "muscle memory."

8. When I speak of a diminishing and fading "scene," I refer to participation by American participants. The immigrant and ethnic communities continue to produce vibrant performance ensembles (see Shay *Choreographing Identities* 2006).

9. I vividly remember being attacked by two zealous graduate students of dance, both

199

Americans, when I delivered a paper on Iranian Women's Theatrical Games. They asked me what right I had to talk about women and Iranians, since I was neither. I replied that the information had been given to me by Iranian friends and respondents who readily agreed to be interviewed. By extension, Leo Tolstoy should never have written *Anna Karenina*, since he was a man.

10. Theresa J. Buckland documents a similar movement in England, but there the enthusiasm, performance, and nostalgia engaged English Morris dancing by English individuals from middle class backgrounds (2006, 199–227). In that case, regional dancers resented the English practitioners who came from other regions of England. On the other hand, a large Armenian performing dance company from France came on a tour to the United States in 1985, and the Armenian community of Glendale, among whom I have several acquaintances, invited the AVAZ International Dance Theatre, the company I directed, to perform an Armenian dance for this group. The director of the Armenian company marveled: "I have not seen dancing like that since my grandmother. How did you learn it? In France, no French person has ever shown the least interest in Armenian dances."

## One. "I Nearly Swooned"

1. The spelling of Sada Yacco's name is also given as Sada Yakko (full name Kawakami Sadayakko). Sada Yacco trained as a geisha in Japan, and with her husband, Kawakami Otojiro, was one of the first Japanese dancers to tour extensively around the world, appearing at the World Fair in Paris in 1901; she toured extensively throughout Europe under Loïe Fuller's aegis. For a fuller description of her life and art see Décoret-Ahiha (2004).

## Two. The Early Exotic Dancers

1. I want to mention that many dancers, besides the ones that I address in this chapter, performed pseudo-oriental dances during this period: Gertrude Hoffman, for example, depicted Salome in the United States with great success, and dance historians Iris Garland (2000) and Anne Décoret-Ahiha (2005) have recuperated the lives and performances of several of these artists.

2. See Rydell 1984 for a thorough description and analysis of the world exhibitions and their racial biases and Hinsley (1991) for the representation of the "ethnic other" at the Chicago World Fair of 1893. Also see Monty 1986 for descriptions of early belly dance performances and public reactions to them.

3. People at that time, as many living today, do not realize that in Ancient Greece, those "pristine" white statues and temples were painted in highly garish colors. The Archeology Museum in the Topkapi complex of Istanbul has an exhibition showing the statues and temples as they appeared in ancient times.

## Three. The Recreational International Folk Dance Movement

1. I follow the usage of the term recreational international folk dance (RIFD), by Ron Houston, the chronicler of the RIFD movement and president of the Society of Folk Dance Historians (see Houston 2006).

2. Folk dancing had become so popular in California since its inception in 1938, when Song Chang taught the first four couples, that the Folk Dance Federation of California formed a northern and southern division from 1946, each with its own publication and set of officers. Annually the two groups would combine to hold a statewide festival alternating between the northern and southern parts of the state, a practice that continues today (see Getchell 1995, 19).

3. A major reason for the difficulty in conducting research on the history of this movement is that no one attempted to write a comprehensive history until the 1980s, after many of the leading figures had passed away, and most of the materials they left behind constitute ephemera in the form of programs, letters, and diaries that lie hidden in archives or have been destroyed. Also, the movement began at nearly the same time in different parts of the country with no apparent connection, as Casey (1981) and Laušević (2007) note.

4. The practice of having spring festivals was still very alive in the Los Angeles public school system when May Day was celebrated

with folk dances and a maypole at my elementary school. The late 1940s ushered in the McCarthy era, and suddenly these celebrations came to a screeching halt when widespread awareness of the meaning of May Day as a communist holiday in the then Soviet Union was realized. I remember putting on crepe paper sashes and ribbons for the dances we performed, with the entire school on the playground and parents in attendance.

5. In addition to Avramenko, two other figures, Louis Chalif (1876–1948) and Anatol Joukowsky (1908–1998), created character dances for the folk dance community, most of which have been forgotten. Joukowsky used florid musical arrangements with large "folk" orchestras and choruses, such as those produced by Radio Televizija Beograd for popular dances like Fatiše Kolo and Ajde Jano.

I learned several of the dances that were taught by Avramenko through Vincent Evanchuk, who learned from Avramenko as a young boy in the large Canadian Ukrainian community. Evanchuk, a fellow member of the Gandy Dancers and an outstanding dancer in Avramenko's styling, taught the dances for performance.

6. Other individuals, such as John Filcich, Kenneth Spears, Paul Erfer, and Rickey Holden, among others, also contributed to producing recordings, many of them field recordings or recordings obtained in the countries of origin.

7. Both Laušević and Houston give 1937 as the date of that first class, but Getchell is the "official" California Folk Dance Federation authority. My late friend and colleague Vilma Matchette danced in Changs International Dancers as a teenager alongside her parents in 1939. She often related to me what the experience was like because the group was in great demand to give performances and I use her recollections as well as the written sources. Her lifelong interest in authentic traditional clothing began with her experiences in Changs.

8. Dick Crum stated, "Vyts taught dance after dance after dance, and would never say where they were coming from, and nobody ever asked him. He would never tell his sources. He enjoyed the impression that everyone had, that he somehow came to the U.S. with all this knowledge.... He was often forced into situations where he was called on for expertise that he did not have" (quoted in Laušević 2007, 145).

9. Of course, the Moiseyev Dance Company, unlike the Yugoslav companies, performed character dance; his dancers, like everyone in the former Soviet Union, were all smiling, all happy, all the time.

## Four. Ethnomusicology and Dance Ethnography

1. This concept parallels the one that I detailed for attitudes held by later choreographers of state-sponsored folk dance ensembles, like Igor Moiseyev and Amalia Hernandez of Ballet Folklorico, of the relative value of authentic dance in the field and the choreographies and interpretations, however loose, that they prepared for stage (Shay 2002).

2. I remember that a friend of mine, a physicist who played in several of the UCLA Institute of Ethnomusicology ensembles, observed that many of the graduate students were writing impenetrably technical papers using Ellis' system of commas and limmas to determine scales and tonalities, dryly commented that "At UCLA the study of ethnomusicology was science gone mad."

## Five. Kolomania

1. This characterization was famously made by Lady Caroline Lamb, who was madly in love with the bisexual Byron. As his biographer Louis Crompton remarked (1985, 197), it actually applied more to Lamb than to Byron because of her relentless pursuit of Byron, which ultimately, through her exposures of his unorthodox sexual activities, forced him to flee England and return to Greece, where he died while attempting to organize the Greeks to fight the Turkish army.

2. For the interested reader, Maria Todorova's outstanding book, *Imagining the Balkans* (1997), analyzes in great detail how the Balkans were imagined and still are, not only in various nations in the West, but also from other points of view, such as those of the Russians, who were searching for their own Slavic origins during the nineteenth century. As Todorova cautions us, both the West and the Balkans are not essentialized places, not a

simple binary, but highly differentiated. Another work of importance to the reader who wishes to understand not only how images of the Balkans and, more generally, Eastern Europe came to be accepted in the West is Larry Wolff's *Inventing Eastern Europe* (1994).

3. These state-supported ensembles were established right after World War II in imitation of the Moiseyev Dance Company, which enjoyed immense popularity in the West. In keeping with the Socialist/Communist principle of exalting "the people," the Moiseyev Dance Company was known in the USSR as the People's Ensemble of Folk Dances of the USSR, while Kolo, Lado, and Tanec traveled outside of the former Yugoslavia as the Yugoslav State Folk Ballet, and the Koutev Ensemble was known in Bulgaria as the Bulgarian State Ensemble of Folk Dances and Songs (see Shay 2002.) Technically speaking, by the time the Yugoslav companies toured America, Yugoslavia was no longer behind the Iron Curtain, but most Americans remained ignorant of that fact and went to see "the Communists" dance.

4. Other early teachers of Balkan dance genres included Michel Cartier, John Filcich and Vilma Matchette.

5. The detailing of the history of folklore studies is beyond the scope of this essay. Those interested in a fine detailed study of the development of folklore studies in Europe may consult Cocchiara 1981 [1952].

6. Americans largely still remain ignorant of geography. A recent survey by the National Geographic Education Foundation and Roper Public Affairs report found that half the population could not locate the state of Mississippi on a map. Further, "Three quarters of young Americans polled could not find Indonesia on a map. And half or fewer could pick out New York or Ohio on a map of the United States" (Stall 2006, B19). Imagine, then, the chances of Americans, even many Balkan enthusiasts, locating Croatia, Serbia, or Montenegro in their atlases. Many of my acquaintances confuse the Balkan states with the Baltic republics.

## Six. Belly Dance

1. In this article, by belly dance I mean "cabaret" belly dancing, the genre of belly dance that is typically performed by a dancer in a beaded bra, with a bare midriff, and low-slung girdle with a (generally) long paneled skirt attached. This version of the genre remains the most popular and it is this version that has entered popular culture. This variant is generally considered to have originated in Egypt. Once this form became popular, a few individuals undertook folk dances from the Arab world and explored other forms of oriental dance such as Iranian, Uzbek, and Afghan choreographic forms. The belly dance scene has many variants, such as Turkish, American Tribal Dance. For a full definition of belly dance and a discussion of its forms, see Shay and Sellers-Young 2005.

2. As an example of the continuing popularity of belly dance, Latifa notes that "Two of the larger Washington [D.C.] studios alone offer over 70 classes a week. SaharaDance offers 40 weekly belly dance classes and is home to 16 faculty members and four resident dance companies; Joy of Motion has 32 belly dance and tribal dance classes on the fall schedule and 9 instructors" (*Habibi* 21, no. 2 (Fall/Winter 2006/2007): 70).

3. For a sampling of these names, one can pick up copies of journals such as *Habibi*.

4. Certainly, every time that I mention belly dance to individuals that I know personally, nearly every one of them knew, or currently knows, a niece, an aunt, a cousin, a sister, a friend, or someone who had a friend or relation that was avidly caught up in this activity. ("Remember when your sister Jane took up belly dancing?" is a recently heard example of frequently mentioned comments at informal dinner parties and other social events.)

5. Other newer, grittier images of the Middle East — of masked terrorists and bloody carnage in Baghdad market places — have much more recently unpleasantly intruded themselves into this formerly pleasant phantasmic vista of oriental images and heady aromas. Via CNN, the lives of Americans — who innocently and happily remained ignorant of such visual images that disturb what political scholar Marta Savigliano calls "a daydream guided by pleasurable self-reassurance and expansionism" (1995, 169) — have been disrupted by the toll of American and Iraqi war victims that have, to a large extent, shattered these orientalist dreams.

6. For example, see Helland who claims that "Far from just a simple entertainment,

belly dancing is believed to have originated in the Paleolithic era" (2001, 128). On pages 134–135 Helland gives a "Chronology of the Belly Dance: History in the Shaking" in which she cites dates such as 2300 BCE, "sacred love-making practiced in the temples in worship of the Mother Goddess," and 1800 BCE, "end of the era of matriarchal dominance in Egypt."

The oft-cited Buonaventura states that belly dance is "one of the oldest dances in creation ... once found throughout the world" (1989, 10).

7. I thank Barbara Sellers-Young for providing me with videos of the early dancers.

8. According to Barbara Sellers-Young the dance was also a feature of the 1876 world's fair held in Philadelphia, but, lacking Sol Bloom, the advertising and popularity of the dance did not approach the appearances of Little Egypt that characterized the Chicago World's Columbian Exhibition, and so I take 1893 as the crucial year for the development of the popular image of belly dance as an exotic, sexualized dance genre.

## Seven. Classical Asian Dance

1. *Ta'arof* includes both linguistic and extralinguistic elements, some of which are bodily practices (see Beeman 1986 and Shay 1999, 121–128).

2. Cal Arts is a university built by the Walt Disney Company to teach a wide array of classes in the performing and visual arts. They have an extensive world dance and music program in addition to Western forms.

3. It is a common practice in many American colleges and universities to provide a one-semester or one-quarter "sampler" class in one of these Asian classical traditions, generally as part of a multicultural imperative that the dance department is required to provide, often reluctantly. The instructors are rarely part of the regular faculty but are, rather, adjunct instructors. Little financial backing is provided for these classical Asian activities in these institutions, where virtually all of the funding goes to modern dance, which has a stranglehold on dance programs throughout the United States. At Pomona College where I teach, bharata natyam and Balinese dance are frequently taught by master artists, in the same way Mexican folklorico and other genres of dance are taught. Un-

like modern dance, which is taught at several levels of difficulty depending on the student's experience and ability, there is no attempt to provide continuity in the "world dance" genres. Thus the instructors must find ways of coping with class situations that vary greatly from their traditional method of teaching.

4. I have taught such classes at the Kolo Festival held each year on the Thanksgiving weekend in the San Francisco Bay region and in the classes that my company, AMAN, arranged over a period of several years during the 1970s. I have witnessed belly dance classes taught by teachers with more than 100 students at the Second International Conference on Middle Eastern Dance, Orange Coast College, May 25–28, 2001. Such workshops are held all over the United States.

5. I thank Barbara Sellers-Young for calling to my attention that interested students can find instruction in these various Asian classical traditions at conferences such as the American Theatre in Higher Education and International Federation of Theatre research, both of which hold workshops in Asian classical forms. Japanese traditions can be found through the Internet: www.nohtrainingproject.org and www.janvier.com/other are links in which students can find nihon buyo training (personal communication, May 23, 2007).

## Eight. Latin American Dances

1. Proposition 187 was one of many successful propositions put in front of voters to deny medical treatment and education to undocumented aliens in California. The promoters, led by conservative governor Pete Wilson, played upon the fears of voters concerning the expanding Latino population figures in California, because the typical undocumented person was equated by Wilson as specifically Mexican.

2. The milonga refers to both a rapid dance related to the tango and the space or event in which the tango is danced.

3. I make a similar point about the way in which the Serbian State Folk Dance Ensemble Kolo, through their choreographic representations, reduce the Roma (Gypsy) population to childlike, over-sexed, irresponsible, pleasure-seeking stereotypes (Shay 2007 forthcoming).

# Bibliography

Acocella, Joan. *Mark Morris*. Middletown, CT: Wesleyan University Press, 1995.

Adra, Najwa. "Belly Dance: an Urban Folk Genre." In *Belly Dance: Orientalism, Transnationalism, and Harem Fantasy*. Edited by Anthony Shay and Barbara Sellers-Young. Costa Mesa, CA: Mazda Publishers, 2005.

Ambler, Eric. *Judgment on Deltchev*. London: Fontana, 1989 [1951].

_____. *Mask of Dimitrios*. London: Fontana, 1966 [1951].

Armbrust, Walter. *Mass Culture and Modernism in Egypt*. Cambridge University Press, 1966.

Ash, Timothy Garton. "There she is, Miss Montenegro." *Los Angeles Times*, June 1, 2006, B11.

Averill, Gage. "'Where's One?'": Musical Encounters of the Ensemble Kind." In *Performing Ethnomusicology: Teaching and Representation in World Music Ensembles*. Edited by Ted Solis. Berkeley and Los Angeles: University of California Press, 2004.

Azzi, Maria Susana. "Tango." *International Encyclopedia of Dance*. Vol. 6. Oxford University Press, 1998.

*Balkan Dancing*. A film by Mario Casetta. Los Angeles: Film Associates, 1964.

Barthes, Roland. *Mythologies*. NY: Noonday Press, 1957, 1992.

Beeman, William O. *Language, Status, and Power in Iran*. Bloomington: University of Indiana Press, 1986.

Benstock, Shari. "Paris Lesbianism and the Politics of Reaction, 1900–1940." In *Hidden from History: Reclaiming the Gay & Lesbian Past*. Edited by Martin Duberman, Martha Vicinus, and George Chauncy, Jr. New York: Meridian, 1989.

Bentley, Toni. *Sisters of Salome*. New Haven: Yale University Press, 2003.

Bernstein, Matthew. "Introduction." In *Visions of the East: Orientalism in Film*. Edited by Matthew Bernstein and Gaylyn Studlar. New Brunswick, NJ: Rutgers University Press, 1997.

Blum, Stephen. "Prologue." In *Ethnomusicology and Modern Music History*. Edited by Stephen Blum, Philip V. Bohlman, and Daniel M. Neuman. Urbana and Chicago: University of Illinois Press, 1991.

Browne, Edward G. *A Year Among the Persians: 1887–1888*. NY: Hippocrene, 1893 [1984 reprint].

Buckland, Theresa J., ed. "Being Traditional: Authentic Selves and Others in Researching Late-Twentieth-Century Northwest English Morris Dancing. In *Dancing from Past to Present: Nation, Culture, Identities*. Madison: University of Wisconsin Press, 2006.

_____. "Dance, History, and Ethnography: Frameworks, Sources, and Identities of Past and Present." In *Dancing from Past to Present: Nation, Culture, Identities*. Madison: University of Wisconsin Press, 2006.

_____. *Dance in the Field: Theory, Methods and Issues in Dance Ethnography*. Macmillan Press Ltd., 1999.

Bunoaventura, Wendy. *Serpent of the Nile: Women and Dance in the Arab World*. New York: Interlink Books, 1989.

Burchenal, Elizabeth. *Dances of the People: A Second Volume of Folk Dances and Singing Games*. New York: G. Schirmer, 1913.

_____. *Rinnce Na Eirann: National Dances of Ireland*. New York: A.S. Barnes, 1924.

Calhoun, Craig. "Introduction: Social Theory and the Politics of Identity." In *Social Theory and the Politics of Identity*. Edited by Craig Calhoun. London: Blackwell, 1994.

Caron, Nelly, and Dariouche Safvate. *Musique d'Iran: Les Traditions Musicales*. Paris: Buchet/Chastel, 1997.

Carpenter, Susan. "Getting Wiggly with It: Belly dancers of all ages, shapes and sizes converge at this year's Cairo Carnivale in celebration of femininity." *Los Angeles Times*, June 11, 2002, E 1.

Casey, Betty. *International Folk Dancing U.S.A.* New York: Doubleday, 1981.

Christie, Agatha. *Murder on the Orient Express*. New York: Bantam Books, 1983 [1934].

_____. *Secret of Chimneys*. New York: Bantam Books, 1987 [1925].

Coccharia, Giussepe. *History of Folklore in Europe*. Translated from the Italian by John N. McDaniel. Philadelphia: Institute for the Study of Human Issues, 1981 [1952].

Cook, Susan C. "Passionless Dancing and Passionate Reform: Respectability, Modernism, and the Social Dancing of Irene and Vernon Castle." In *Passion of Music and Dance: Body, Gender and Sexuality*. Edited by William Washabaugh. New York: Berg, 1998.

Crompton, Louis. *Byron and Greek Love: Homophobia in 19th-century England*. Berkeley and Los Angeles: University of California Press, 1985.

Daniel, Yvonne. *Rumba: Dance and Social Change in Contemporary Cuba*. Bloomington: Indiana University Press, 1995.

Danielson, Virginia. "Artists and Entrepreneurs: Female Singers in Cairo During the 1920s." In *Women in Middle Eastern History*. Edited by Nikki R. Keddie and Beth Baron. New Haven and London: Yale University Press, 1991.

_____. *Voice of Egypt: Umm Kulthum, Arabic Song, and Egyptian Society in the Twentieth Century*. Cairo: American University in Cairok 1997.

Deagon, Andrea. "The Dance of the Seven Veils: The Revision of Revelation in the Oriental Dance Community." In *Belly Dance: Orientalism, Transnationalism, and Harem Fantasy*. Edited by Anthony Shay and Barbara Sellers-Young. Costa Mesa, CA: Mazda Publishers, 2005.

Décoret-Ahiha, Anne. *Les Danses Exotiques en France: 1880–1940*. Pantin, France: Centre national de la danse, 2004.

Delgado, Celeste Fraser. "Preface: Politics in Motion." In *Everynight Life: Culture and Dance in Latin/o America*. Edited by Celeste Fraser Delgado and José Esteban Muñoz. Durham, NC: Duke University Press, 1997.

_____, and José Esteban Muñoz, eds. "Rebellions of Everynight Life." In *Everynight Life: Culture and Dance in Latin/o America*. Durham, NC: Duke University Press, 1997.

Desmond, Jane C. "Dancing Out the Difference: Cultural Imperialism and Ruth St. Denis's Radha of 1906." In *Moving History/Dancing Cultures: A Dance History Reader*. Edited by Ann Dils and Ann Cooper Albright. Middletown: CT: Wesleyan University Press, 2001.

_____, ed. "Embodying Differences: Issues in Dance and Cultural Studies. In *Meaning in Motion: New Cultural Studies of Dance*. Durham, NC: Duke University Press, 1997.

Doi, Mary Masayo. *Gesture, Gender, Nation: Dance and Social Change in Uzbekistan*. Westport, CT, and London: Bergin & Garvey, 2002.

Dox, Donnalee. "Spirit from the Body: Belly Dance as a Spiritual Practice." In *Belly Dance: Orientalism, Transnationalism, and Harem Fantasy.* Edited by Anthony Shay and Barbara Sellers-Young. Costa Mesa, CA: Mazda Publishers, 2005.

Dunne, Bruce William. "Sexuality and the 'Civilizing Process' in Modern Egypt." PhD diss., Georgetown University, 1996.

During, Jean, Zia Mirabdolbaghi, and Dariush Safvat. *Art of Persian Music.* Washington, DC: Mage, 1991.

Erdman, Joan L. "Dance Discourses: Rethinking the History of the 'Oriental Dance.'" In *Moving Words: Re-writing Dance.* Edited by Gay Morris. London and New York: Routledge, 1996.

Evanchuk, Robin J. "Inside, Outside, Upside-down: the Role of Mainstream Society Participants in the Ethnic Dance Movement." In *Balkan Dance: Essays on Characteristics, Performances and Teaching.* Edited by Anthony Shay. Jefferson, NC: McFarland & Co. 2008.

Fatemi, Sasan. "La Musique Legere Urbaine dans la Culture Iranienne: Reflexions sur les notions de classique et populaire." PhD diss., University of Paris X–Nanterre, 2005.

Flandez, Raymund. "Navel Maneuvers: Men Wiggle in on Female Art Form." *Wall Street Journal,* August 11, 2003, p.1.

Forner, Michelle. "Transmission of 'Oriental' Dance in the United States: A Case Study of Ibrahim Farrah as Teacher." *UCLA Journal of Dance Ethnology* 18 (1994).

Frost, Helen. *Oriental and Character Dances.* New York: A.S. Barnes, 1930.

Garland, Iris. "The Eternal Return: Oriental Dance (1900–1914) Versus Multicultural Dance (1990–2000)." In *Conference Proceedings.* Presented at Dancing in the Millennium: An International Conference. Washington DC, July 19–23, 2000.

Geertz, Clifford. *Interpretation of Cultures.* New York: Basic Books, 1973.

_____. *Local Knowledge: Further Essays in Interpretive Anthropology.* New York: Basic Books, 1983.

Georges, Robert A. "Toward an Understanding of Storytelling Events." *Journal of American Folklore* 82, no. 326 (1969): 313–328.

Getchell, Larry. *A History of the Folk Dance Movement in California with Emphasis on the Early Years.* Folk Dance Federation of California, 1995.

Gioseffi, Daniella. *Earth Dancing: Mother Nature's Oldest Rite.* Harrisburg, PA: Stack Pole Books, 1980.

Goldsworthy, Vesna. *Inventing Ruritania: The Imperialism of the Imagination.* New Haven and London: Yale University Press, 1998.

Goodall, Jane R. *Performance and Evolution in the Age of Darwin: Out of the Age of Wonder.* London and NY: Routledge, 2002.

Gould, Miriam Robinson. "In the Shadow of Salome." In *Habibi* 21, no. 2 (Fall/Winter 2006/07): 22–37.

Guillermoprieto, Alma. *Samba.* New York: Vintage Books, 1990.

Gunji, Masakatsu. *Buyo: The Classical Dance.* New York and Tokyo, Walker/Weatherhill, 1970.

Hahn, Tomie. *Sensational Knowledge: Embodying Culture through Japanese Dance.* Middletown, CT: Wesleyan University Press, 2008.

Halberstam, David. *Fifties.* NY: Random House, 1993.

Hallett, Judith P., and Marilyn B. Skinner. *Roman Sexualities.* New Jersey: Princeton University Press, 1997.

Heffner Hayes, Michelle. "Disciplining Passion: Flamenco as a 'World Dance' Form in the Academy." Unpublished paper delivered at the Rethinking Practice and Theory, International Symposium on Dance Research. Centre national de la danse, Pantin, France, June 21–24, 2007.

Helland, Shawna. "Belly Dance: Ancient Ritual to Cabaret Performance." In *Moving History/Dancing Cultures: A Dance History Reader*. Edited by Ann Dils and Ann Cooper Albright. Middletown, CT: Wesleyan University Press, 2001.

Hinsley, Curtis. M. "The World as Marketplace: Commodification of the Exotic at the World's Columbian Exposition, Chicago, 1893." In *Exhibiting Cultures: the Poetics and Politics of Museum Display*. Edited by Ivan Karp and Steven D. Lavine. Washington, DC: Smithsonian Institution Press, 1991.

Hope, Anthony. *The Prisoner of Zenda*. London: J.W. Arrowsmith, 1894.

Hormozi, Sa'id. "Oral Transmission." In *Art of Persian Music*. Edited by Jean During, Zia Mirabdolbaghi, and Dariush Safvat. Washington, DC: Mage, 1991.

Hughes-Freeland, Felicia. "Constructing a Classical Tradition: Javanese Court Dance in Indonesia." In *Dancing from Past to Present: Nation, Culture, Identities*. Edited by Theresa Jill Buckland. Madison: University of Wisconsin Press, 2006.

Hutchinson, John, and Anthony D. Smith, eds. "Introduction." In *Ethnicity*. Oxford University Press, 1996.

Houston, Ron. "How Folk Dancing Grew." In *Folk Dance Problem Solver*. 2–10.

Janković, Danica S., and Ljubica S. Janković. *Narodne Igre* [Folk Dances]. Vols. 1, 2, 3. Beograd: Srpske Kraljevske Adakemije Nauka, 1934, 1937, 1939.

_____. *Narodne Igre* [Folk Dances]. Vols 3–8. Beograd: Prosveta, 1948–1962.

Karayanni, Stavros Stavrou. 2004. *Dancing Fear and Desire: Race, Sexuality, and Imperial Politics in Middle Eastern Dance*. Waterloo, Ont.: Wilfrid Laurier University Press, 2004.

Karp, Ivan, and Steven D. Lavine. *Exhibiting Cultures: The Poetics and Politics of Museum Display*. Washington, DC: Smithsonian Institution Press, 1991.

Kealiinohomoku, Joann. "An Anthropologist Looks at Ballet as a Form of Ethnic Dance." *Impulse* (1970): 24–33.

_____. "Ethnic Historical Study." In *Proceedings of the Second Conference on Research in Dance: "Dance History Research: Perspectives from Related Arts and Disciplines."* Warrenton, VA, July 4–6, 1969.

Kendall, Elizabeth. *Where She Danced*. New York: Knopf, 1979.

King, Desmond. *Making Americans: Immigration, Race, and the Origins of the Diverse Democracy*. Cambridge, MA: Harvard University Press, 2000.

Kiossev, Alexander. "Dark Intimacy: Maps, Identities, Acts of Identification." In *Balkan as Metaphor: Between Globalization and Fragmentation*. Edited by Dušan I. Bjelić and Obrad Savić. Cambridge, MA, and London: MIT Press, 2002.

Kirshenblatt-Gimblett, Barbara. *Destination Culture: Tourism, Museums, and Heritage*. Berkeley and Los Angeles: University of California Press, 1998.

_____. "Objects of Ethnography." In *Exhibiting Cultures: the Poetics and Politics of Museum Display*. Edited by Ivan Karp and Steven D. Lavine. Washington, DC: Smithsonian Institution Press, 1991.

_____. "On Difference." *Journal of American Folklore* 107, no. 424 (1994): 235–238.

Kitwana, Bakari. *Why White Kids Love Hip Hop: Wankstas, Wiggers, Wannabes, and the New Realities of Race in America*. New York: Basic Civitas Books, 2005.

Klíma, Otakar. "Bahram V Gor." *Encylcopaedia Iranica*. Vol. 3 (1989): 518–519.

Koritz, Amy. "Dancing the Orient for England: Mad Allan's *The Vision of Salome*." In *Meaning in Motion: New Cultural Studies in Dance*. Edited by Jane C. Desmond. Durham, NC: Duke University Press, 1997.

Kurath, Gertrude Prokosch. "Panorama of Dance Ethnology." *Current Anthropology* 1, no. 3 (1960): 233–254.

Kurth, Peter. *Isadora: a Sensational Life*. Boston: Little, Brown, and Co., 2001.

Lamberth, Susan. "A Fight as Celebration: Embodied Conflict within the Argentine Tango

Community in Chicago." Unpublished paper delivered at the Rethinking Practice and Theory, International Symposium on Dance Research. Centre national de la danse, Pantin, France, June 21–24, 2007.

Lane, Edward W. *Account of the Manners and Customs of the Modern Egyptians.* London: Everyman's Library, New York: Dutton, 1966 [1836].

Lauševič, Mirjana. *Balkan Fascination: Creating an Alternative Music Culture in America.* Oxford University Press, 2007.

_____. "Different Village: International Folk Dance and Balkan Music and Dance in the United States." PhD diss., Wesleyan University, 1998.

Lee, Dorothy Sarah. "Native American." In *Ethnomusicology: Historical and Regional Studies.* Edited by Helen Myers. New York: W.W. Norton & Company, 1993.

Leibman, Robert Henry. "Richard George 'Dick' Crum." In *Balkan Dance: Essays on Characteristics, Performance and Teaching.* Edited by Anthony Shay. Jefferson, NC: McFarland & Company Publishers, 2008.

Lomax, Alan, Irmgard Barenieff, and Forrestine Paulay. "Choreometrics: A Method for the Study of Cross-Cultural Pattern in Film." *CORD Research Annual VI.* Proceedings of the Third Conference on Research in Dance, 1968. 103–212.

Lopez, Ana M. "Of Rhythms and Borders." In *Everynight Life: Culture and Dance in Latin/o America.* Edited by Celeste Fraser Delgado and José Esteban Muñoz. Durham, NC: Duke University Press, 1997.

MacKenzie, John M. *Orientalism: History, Theory and the Arts.* Manchester and New York: Manchester University Press, 1995.

Malefyt, Timothy deWaal. "Gendering the Authentic in Spanish Flamenco." In *Passion of Music and Dance: Body, Gender and Sexuality.* Edited by William Washabaugh. New York: Berg, 1998.

Maners, Lynn G. "Utopia, Eutopia, and E.U.-topia: Performance and Memory in the Former Yugoslavia." In *Dancing from Past to Present: Nation, Culture, Identities.* Edited by Theresa J. Buckland. Madison: University of Wisconsin Press, 2006.

Manning, Susan. "Duncan, Isadora." *International Encyclopedia of Dance.* Vol. 2. Oxford University Press, 1998.

_____. "The Female Dance and the Male Gaze." In *Meaning in Motion: New Cultural Studies in Dance.* Edited by Jane C. Desmond. Durham, NC: Duke University Press, 1997.

Marcus, Scott. "Creating a Community, Negotiating Among Communities: Performing Middle Eastern Music for a Diverse Middle Eastern and American Public." In *Performing Ethnomusicology: Teaching and Representation in World Music Ensembles.* Edited by Ted Solís. Berkeley and Los Angeles: University of California Press, 2004.

Marks, Morton. "Cuba: Folk, Ritual, and Social Dance." *International Encyclopedia of Dance.* Vol. 2. 1998.

McMains, Juliet. *Glamour Addiction: Inside the American Ballroom Dance Industry.* Middletown, CT: Wesleyan University Press, 2006.

_____. "Reality Television and Off-Camera Dance Realities." Paper delivered at the Rethinking Practice and Theory, International Symposium on Dance Research. Centre national de la danse, Pantin, France, June 21–24, 2007.

Merriam, Alan P. "Anthropology and the Dance." *CORD Research Annual VI.* Proceedings of the Third Conference on Research in Dance, 1972.

_____. *Anthropology of Music.* Chicago: Northwestern University Press, 1964.

Mitchell, Timothy. *Colonizing Egypt.* Berkeley and Los Angeles: University of California Press, 1991.

Monty, Paul Eugene. "Serena, Ruth St. Denis, and the Evolution of Belly Dance in America (1876–1976)." PhD diss., New York University, 1986.

Moreau, Yves. "Observations on the Recent Widespread Adoption and Adaptation of

Bulgarian Folk Music and Dance in North American and Elsewhere." Ethnomusicology in Canada, Proceedings of the First Conference on Ethnomusicology in Canada, held in Toronto 13–15 May, 1988.

Morocco [Carolina Varga Dinicu]. "Loving Remembrance and Requiem: the Best 'School' That Ever Was." Address given at Second Middle Eastern Dance Conference, Orange Coast College, CA, May 25–28, 2001.

Morris, Mark, and Joan Acocella. "Growing Up Multicultural: A Choreographer Soaks Up the World." In *Looking Out: Perspectives on Dance and Criticism in a Multicultural World* (Dance Critics Association). Edited by David Gere. New York: Schirmer Books, 1995.

Myers, Helen. "Introduction." In *Ethnomusicology: Historical and Regional Studies*. Edited by Helen Myers. New York: W.W. Norton, 1993.

Nahachewsky, Andriy. "Ukraine: Traditional Dance." *International Encyclopedia of Dance*. Vol. 6. Oxford University Press, 1998.

Nieuwkirk, Karin van. "Changing Images and Shifting Identities: Female Performers in Egypt." In *Images of Enchantment: Visual and Performing Arts of the Middle East*. Edited by Sherifa Zuhur. Cairo: American University in Cairo, 1998.

_____. "A Trade Like Any Other": Female Singers and Dancers in Egypt. Austin: University of Texas Press, 1995.

Noll, William. "Music Institutions and National Consciousness among Polish and Ukrainian Peasants." In *Ethnomusicology and Modern Music History*. Edited by Stephen Blum, Philip V. Bohlman, and Daniel M. Neuman. Urbana and Chicago: University of Illinois Press, 1991.

O'Shea, Janet. *At Home in the World: Bharata Natyam on the Global Stage*. Middletown, CT: Wesleyan University Press, 2007.

Osweiler, Laura [Amara]. "The Role of Gender in American-Middle Eastern Dance." Paper given in Dance Under Construction, UC Graduate Cultural Dance Studies Conference, University of California, Riverside, 2002.

Patterson, James T. *Grand Expectations: The United States, 1945–1974*. New York and Oxford: Oxford University Press, 1996.

_____. *Restless Giant: The United States from Watergate to Bush v. Gore*. New York and Oxford: Oxford University Press, 2005.

Potuoğlu-Cook, Öykü. "Beyond the Glitter: Belly Dance and Neoliberal Gentrification in Istanbul." *Cultural Anthropology* 21, 4 (2006): 633–660.

Racy, Ali Jihad. "Historical Worldview of Early Ethnomusicologists: An East-West Encounter in Cairo, 1932." In *Ethnomusicology and Modern Music History*. Edited by Stephen Blum, Philip V. Bohlman, and Daniel M. Neuman. Urbana and Chicago: University of Illinois Press, 1991.

Rasmussen, Anne K. "Bilateral Negotiations: Insiders, Outsiders, and the 'Real Version' in Middle Eastern Music." In *Performing Ethnomusicology: Teaching and Representation in World Music Ensembles*. Edited by Ted Solís. Berkeley and Los Angeles: University of California Press, 2004.

Reynolds, Jabarri. "New Ways of Teaching Balinese Dance Culture." Paper given in World Traditions of Dance, Pomona College, April 30, 2007.

Reynolds, Nancy, and Malcolm McCormick. *No Fixed Points: Dance in the Twentieth Century*. New Haven and London: Yale University Press, 2003.

Rice, Timothy. *May It Fill Your Soul: Experiencing Bulgarian Music*. Chicago and London: University of Chicago Press, 1994.

Rodriguez, Gregory. "The Hustler in All of Us." *Los Angeles Times*, June 4, 2007, A15.

Royce, Anya Peterson. "Choreology Today: A Review of the Field." *CORD Research Annual VI*. Proceedings of the Third Conference on Research in Dance, 1972.

Ruyter, Nancy Lee. "La Meri and Middle Eastern Dance." In *Belly Dance: Orientalism,*

*Transnationalism, and Harem Fantasy.* Edited by Anthony Shay and Barbara Sellers-Young. Costa Mesa, CA: Mazda, 2005.
_____. *Reformers and Visionaries: The Americanization of the Art of Dance.* New York: Dance Horizons, 1979.
Rydell, Robert W. *All the World's a Fair: Visions of Empire at American International Expositions, 1876–1916.* Chicago and London: University of Chicago Press, 1984.
Said, Edward. *Orientalism.* New York: Vintage, 1978.
Saleh, Magda Ahmed Abdel Ghaffar. "A Documentation of the Ethnic Dance Traditions of the Arab Republic of Egypt." Ph D diss., New York University, 1979.
Salessi, Jorge. "Medics, Crooks, and Tango Queens: The National Appropriation of a Gay Tango. In *Everynight Life: Culture and Dance in Latin/o America.* Edited by Celeste Fraser Delgado and José Esteban Muñoz. Durham, NC: Duke University Press, 1997.
Savigliano, Marta E. "From Wallflowers to Femmes Fatales: Tango and the Performance of Passionate Femininity." In *Passion of Music and Dance: Body, Gender and Sexuality.* Edited by William Washabaugh. New York: Berg, 1998.
_____. *Tango and the Political Economy of Passion.* Boulder, CO: Westview, 1995.
Segal, Lewis. "'Fusion Tango' is in the tradition." *Los Angeles Times,* E12, April 26, 2007.
Sellers-Young, Barbara. "Body, Image, Identity: American Tribal Belly Dance." In *Belly Dance: Orientalism, Transnationalism, and Harem Fantasy.* Edited by Anthony Shay and Barbara Sellers-Young. Costa Mesa, CA: Mazda Publishers, 2005.
_____. "Identity, Corporeality, and the Ethnographic Perspective." Paper given at CORD conference in Tucson, AZ., November 6, 2006.
_____. "'Nostalgia' or 'Newness': Nihon Buyo in the United States." 1992.
_____. "Raks El Sharki: Transculturation of a Folk Form." *Journal of Popular Culture* 26, no. 2 (Fall 1992): 141–152.
_____. *Teaching Personality with Gracefulness: The Transmission of Japanese Cultural Values through Japanese Dance Theatre.* Lanham, MD, New York, and London: University Press of America, 1993.
Seroff, Victor. *The Real Isadora.* New York: Dial Press, 1971.
Shafik, Viola. *Arab Cinema: History and Cultural Identity.* Cairo: American University in Cairo Press, 1998.
Shambaugh, Mary Effie. *Folk Dances for Boys and Girls.* New York: A.S. Barnes, 1929.
Shay, Anthony. *Choreographic Politics: State Folk Dance Companies Representation and Power.* Middletown, CT: Wesleyan University Press, 2002.
_____. *Choreographing Identities: Folk Dance, Ethnicity and Festival in North America.* Jefferson, NC: McFarland & Company, 2006.
_____. *Choreophobia: Solo Improvised Dance in the Iranian World.* Costa Mesa, CA: Mazda Publishers, 1999.
_____. "Introduction." In *Balkan Dance: Essays on Characteristics, Performance and Teaching.* Jefferson, NC: McFarland & Company, 2008.
_____. "The 6/8 Beat Goes On: Persian Popular Music from *Bazm-e Qajariyyeh* to Beverly Hills Garden Parties." In *Mass Mediations: New Approaches to Popular Culture in the Middle East and Beyond.* Edited by Walter Armburst. Berkeley and Los Angeles: University of California Press, 2002.
_____, ed. "Choreographing the Other: The Serbian State Folk Dance Ensemble, Gypsies, Muslims, and Albanians." In *Balkan Dance: Essays on Characteristics, Performance and Teaching.* Jefferson, NC: McFarland & Company, 2008.
_____, and Barbara Sellers-Young. "Belly Dance: Orientalism — Exoticism — Self-Exoticism." *Dance Research Journal* 35, no. 1 (Summer 2003): 13–37.
_____, and _____, eds. *Belly Dance: Orientalism, Transnationalism, and Harem Fantasy.* Costa Mesa, CA: Mazda, 2005.

Shelton, Suzanne. *Divine Dancer: Biography of Ruth St. Denis.* Garden City, NY: Doubleday and Company, 1981.

Shoberl, Fredric. *Persia.* (In 3 volumes) London: R. Ackermann, 1828.

Siegmann, Johanna. *Tao of Tango.* Victoria, BC: Trafford Publishing, 2000.

Snyder, Allegra Fuller. "The Dance Symbol." *CORD Research Annual VI.* Proceedings of the Third Conference on Research in Dance, 1972.

_____. "Past, Present and Future." *UCLA Journal of Dance Ethnology* 16 (1992): 1–28.

Solís, Ted, ed. "Introduction: Teaching What Cannot Be Taught, an Optimistic Overview." In *Performing Ethnomusicology: Teaching and Representation in World Music Ensembles.* Berkeley and Los Angeles: University of California Press, 2004.

Somers, Margaret R., and Gloria D. Gibson. "Reclaiming the Epistemological 'Other': Narrative and the Social Constitution of Identity." In *Social Theory and the Politics of Identity.* Edited by Craig Calhoun. London: Blackwell, 1994.

Stall, Bill. "Where's Tannu Tuva?" *Los Angeles Times,* May 27, 2006, B19.

Steingress, Gerhard. "Social Theory and the Comparative History of Flamenco, Tango, and Rebetika." In *Passion of Music and Dance: Body, Gender and Sexuality.* Edited by William Washabaugh. New York: Berg, 1998.

Stewart, Iris. *Sacred Woman, Sacred Dance: Awakening Spirituality Through Movement and Ritual.* Rochester, VT: Inner Traditions, 2000.

Stimpson, Catharine R. 1993. "Somagrams of Gertrude Stein." In *Lesbian and Gay Studies Reader.* Edited by Henry Abelove, Michele Aina Barale, and David Halperin. New York: Routledge, 1993.

Studlar, Gaylyn. "'Out-Salomeing Salome': Dance, the New Woman, and Fan Magazine Orientalism." In *Visions of the East: Orientalism in Film.* Edited by Matthew Bernstein and Gaylyn Studlar. New Brunswick, NJ: Rutgers University Press, 1997.

_____. "Valentino, 'Optic Intoxication,' and Dance Madness." In *Screening the Male: Exploring Masculinities in Hollywood Cinema.* Edited by Steven Cohan and Ina Rae Hark. London and New York: Routledge, 1993.

Suleiman, Michael W., ed. "Introduction: The Arab Immigrant Experience." *Arabs in America: Building a New Future.* Philadelphia: Temple University Press, 1999.

Sumarsam. "Opportunity and Interaction: The Gamelan from Java to Wesleyan." In *Performing Ethnomusicology: Teaching and Representation in World Music Ensembles.* Edited by Ted Solis. Berkeley and Los Angeles: University of California Press, 2004.

Taylor, Julie. *Paper Tangos.* Durham, NC: Duke University Press, 1998.

Tenneriello, Susan. "O-Mika: Ruth St. Denis's Image of the East." In Society of Dance History Scholars. 23rd Annual Conference *Proceedings.* University of New Mexico, Albuquerque, June 10–13, 1999.

Tindall, Blair. "Bang a Gong, Strum a Bandurria." *Los Angeles Times,* May 20, 2007, F1, 11.

Tinmberg, Scott. "Fire in His Belly." *Los Angeles Times.* January, 14, 2005, E1.

Titon, Jeff Todd. *Worlds of Music.* New York: Schirmer Books, 1992.

Tobin, Jeffrey. "Tango and the Scandal of Homosocial Desire." In *Passion of Music and Dance: Body, Gender and Sexuality.* Edited by William Washabaugh. New York: Berg, 1998.

Todorova, Maria. *Imagining the Balkans.* New York and Oxford: Oxford University Press, 1997.

Tomko, Linda J. *Dancing Class: Gender, Ethnicity, and Social Divides in American Dance, 1890–1920.* Bloomington: University of Indiana Press, 1999.

Trimillos, Ricardo D. "Subject, Object, and the Ethnomusicology Ensemble: The Ethnomusicological 'We' and 'Them.'" In *Performing Ethnomusicology: Teaching and Representation in World Music Ensembles.* Edited by Ted Solis. Berkeley and Los Angeles: University of California Press, 2004.

Turner, Bryan S. *Orientalism, Postmodernism, and Globalism.* London: Routledge, 1994.

Vail, June Adler. "Balkan Tradition: Dance, Community, and the People of the Pines." In *Balkan Dance: Essays on Characteristics, Performance and Teaching.* Edited by Anthony Shay. Jefferson, NC: McFarland & Company, 2008.

Wagner, Ann. *Adversaries of Dance: From the Puritans to the Present.* Urbana and Chicago: University of Illinois Press, 1997.

Washabaugh, William, ed. "Fashioning Masculinity in Flamenco Dance." In *Passion of Music and Dance: Body, Gender and Sexuality.* New York: Berg, 1998.

_____. "Flamenco Song: Clean and Dirty." In *Passion of Music and Dance: Body, Gender and Sexuality.* New York: Berg, 1998.

_____. "Introduction: Music, Dance, and the Politics of Passion." In *Passion of Music and Dance: Body, Gender and Sexuality.* New York: Berg, 1998.

Waters, Mary C. *Ethnic Options: Choosing Identities in America.* Berkeley and Los Angeles, University of California Press, 1990.

Webster, Jason. *Duende: A Journey into the Heart of Flamenco.* New York: Broadway Books, 2002.

West, Rebecca. *Black Lamb and Grey Falcon: A Journey Through Yugoslavia.* New York: Viking, 1966 [1940, 1941].

Whiting, Lynette. "Differences Learning and Teaching between Balinese Dance in and out of Bali." Paper for Traditions of World Dance Class, Pomona College, April 30, 2007.

Williams, Craig A. *Roman Homosexualities.* Oxford: Oxford University Press, 1999.

Wolff, Larry. *Inventing Eastern Europe: The Map of Civilization on the Mind of the Enlightenment.* Stanford University Press, 1994.

# Index